The Royal Hospital School

Celebrating 300 Years

The Royal Hospital School

Celebrating 300 Years

Written and edited by **Val Horsler**
with **Bernard de Neumann** and **Rob Mann**

III

THIRD MILLENNIUM
PUBLISHING, LONDON

To all pupils and staff of the Royal Hospital School, past, present and future

© **Authors and Third Millennium Publishing Limited**

First published in 2012 by Third Millennium Publishing Limited, a subsidiary of Third Millennium Information Limited.

2–5 Benjamin Street, London, United Kingdom EC1M 5QL
www.tmiltd.com

Paperback   ISBN 978 1 908990 02 0
Hardback   ISBN 978 1 906507 94 7

British Library Cataloguing in Publication Data
A CIP catalogue record for this book is available from the British Library.

Written and edited by Val Horsler
with Bernard de Neumann and Rob Mann

Design	Matthew Wilson
Principal photography	Julian Andrews
Production	Bonnie Murray
Editorial and picture research	Neil Burkey
Proofreading	Matthew Christmas (RHS)
	Pieter van der Merwe (NMM)
Reprographics	Studio Fasoli, Italy
Printing	Gorenjski Tisk, Slovenia

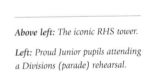

Above left: The iconic RHS tower.

Left: Proud Junior pupils attending a Divisions (parade) rehearsal.

Contents

Preface

It is a great privilege for me to be the Headmaster of the Royal Hospital School in its tercentenary year. The School continues to evolve and move forward without losing its sense of self and the values derived from its unique history.

I believe that there is nothing more important than the education of children and young people and, probably more than any other school of its type, the Royal Hospital School recognises the truth of the great Chartist slogan that 'education is a liberating force'.

It is my aim to unlock the potential of each individual by offering them a whole new world of life-changing opportunities and an environment in which academic excellence is promoted through learning and shared experiences. It is a place that encourages boys and girls to discover themselves; quite simply, to develop a passion that will endure for the rest of their lives. Through passion comes purpose, and from purpose the journey ahead becomes clear.

As a parent, I want to give my children the best possible start in life. School experience should be a happy one founded not on learning alone, but on relationships formed and values shared. I firmly believe that a well-balanced individual needs a sense of spiritual awareness, along with academic and sporting achievements and I place great store by the values of kindness, service, generosity of spirit, and integrity; these are the invisible strands that hold a community such as ours together.

By working together, the staff at the Royal Hospital School ensure that our pupils are able to form strong relationships and make a valuable contribution both here at school and in the adult world, in which many will become leaders in their chosen field.

With a commitment to leadership, service and an international outlook at the heart of the School's values, it is my goal that the Royal Hospital School becomes the first choice for parents seeking an outstanding all-round, balanced, broad and full education for their children.

James Lockwood MA, Headmaster (with his wife Sarah).

To achieve this, my pledge is to ensure academic and pastoral excellence, maintain breadth and challenge, inspire individual and social responsibility and develop the life skills that will prepare our pupils to meet the future with confidence. In short, my intention is to produce happy, rounded, grounded young people who live balanced and full lives.

I hope that you enjoy this book celebrating the School's 300 year history – so rich in heritage and so proud in tradition. The School is indeed fortunate to have inherited such a legacy as it continues to chart its own course towards greater independence. We are proud of the past and can look to the future (beyond our tercentenary year) with confidence, ambition and a real sense of purpose; the primary focus being the provision of a first class education for all our pupils.

James Lockwood MA

Foreword

HRH Prince Andrew, The Duke of York KG GCVO. The School Visitor.

Being your Visitor is an appointment that I am honoured to fulfil, one which is very important to me, especially coming, as I do, from a Naval background. I am delighted to have this unique role and I am well aware of the historical relationship between the Royal Family and The Royal Hospital School. My visits are always inspiring for me and reinforce that special sense of loyalty and service epitomised in the naval service.

Over the past 20 years, I have visited this outstanding School on many occasions; to inspect impressive parades, open new facilities and attend Speech days and other School events. I have enjoyed watching the School grow, redevelop its infrastructure and flourish.

I have always been impressed with the enthusiasm of the student body of young men and women I have met. The commitment of the teachers and other members of staff are second to none. I have clearly seen that there is something extra, giving the sure foundation upon which the students can go forth from the School in the knowledge that they have been well prepared for their future.

It is also very clear to me, perhaps not least as a result of my service in the Royal Navy, that the values taught at the Royal Hospital School have evolved from its unique heritage. The School has not stood still and has developed into a forward-thinking, progressive educational establishment that turns out balanced, well-educated young people with a set of values of which any parent, or future employer would be proud.

This book celebrates the School's rich 300 year history. It is testament to the sound principles that have provided the very firmest of foundations for the School as it grows in confidence and develops a clear vision for the future.

The next 300 years are a blank canvas and I wish the School fair winds and a following sea as it looks forward to the next exciting stage of its development.

Timeline: Greenwich

1694
Royal charter established by William and Mary includes provision for educating children

1712
A school is formed to educate children in writing, arithmetic and navigation

1715
First record of ten sons of Pensioners being educated by Mr Thomas Weston as day pupils at the Weston Academy

The School began in 1712

1758
A new School is built on King Street (now King William Walk) at Greenwich Hospital. Boys continue to sleep in Queen Mary Court

1765
Rev. Thomas Furbor appointed as the first actual GHS Headmaster, going on to become the longest serving Head, in post for 35 years

1700 — **1750**

Greenwich Hospital

Greenwich Hospital School

1703
Queen Anne Commission establishes Greenwich Hospital which will go on to administer the School

1730s and 1740s
A period of steady growth both in numbers of pupils and reputation: 12 pupils in 1715, 60 in 1731 and 100 in 1747

1728
The National Archives in Kew hold a complete record of all charity boys attending the School and destinations upon leaving

1768
Captain James Cook leads three voyages between 1768 and his death in 1779, discovering Australia, circumnavigating New Zealand and charting the Pacific. It is likely that Greenwich boys would have served on the expeditions.

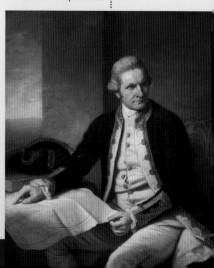

1805
Prime Minister, William Pitt, pledges his support for the School and King George III (**right**) resolves to make the School a Royal Foundation.

1803
Lloyd's Patriotic Fund is created and becomes a major supporter of the School, subsequently donating £61,000

1783
A larger three-storey school is built combining teaching and boarding facilities. It became the infirmary in 1821 and today is the south-west wing of Devonport House

1800
British National Endeavour School is formed by Andrew Thompson in Paddington – but it falters due to claims of fraud; eventually it becomes the Royal Naval Asylum

1816
By this date completion of major extensions to the Greenwich site with colonnades joining flanking wings to the Queen's House. The Asylum grows in size to over 800 boys and girls

1800 ★ 1820

British National Endeavour later becoming the Royal Naval Asylum

1806
Following his death at Trafalgar, Nelson lies in state at the Painted Hall. His body is then transferred by river on its journey to St Paul's Cathedral

1807
A Royal Warrant names the School 'The Royal Naval Asylum' backdated to Trafalgar Day and the School patron, The Duke of Cumberland, gives an inscribed Turkish bronze cannon

The King grants the Queen's House for the education of children at the Asylum

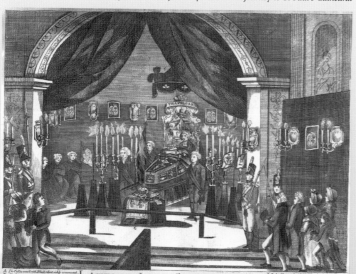

A VIEW OF THE LAYING IN STATE, OF THE REMAINS OF our illustrious Hero LORD NELSON in the Painted Hall at Greenwich Hospital.

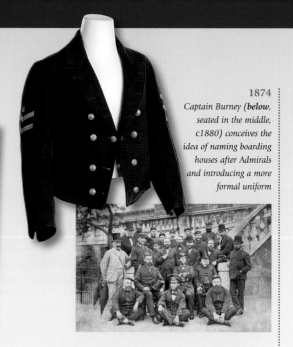

1874

*Captain Burney (**below**, seated in the middle, c1880) conceives the idea of naming boarding houses after Admirals and introducing a more formal uniform*

1821

*Edward Riddle (**above**) appointed as Mathematics Master and goes on to develop the academic curriculum and become Headmaster*

The amalgamation of the Greenwich Hospital School (boys) and the Royal Naval Asylum (mixed)

1843

The first of three block ships is constructed and erected on the parade ground. Pictured above is the third of these, called Fame

1872

School boys march to Trafalgar Square

1820

1850

Greenwich Hospital Schools

1833
Bathing Pool completed, establishing a strong swimming tradition

1841
Co-education ceases with the last girl leaving the School

1831
Introduction of the Greenwich Hospital Silver Medal, with William IV attending prize giving in 1832

1828
Formation of the School Band

1845

Gifford Sherman Reade is born into a Suffolk landowning family in Cape Town, South Africa

School boys attend the distribution of Trafalgar Medals, 40 years on

1873
The gymnasium, Neptune's Hall, is completed followed by the dining hall in 1876

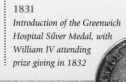

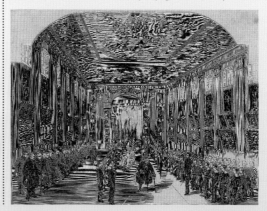

1886

The Sir William
Boreman Foundation
approves sending boys to
the School as day pupils.
George Berry (*above*)
was the last Boreman
Boy to leave, in 1931.
George entered the
Royal Hospital School in
Greenwich in May 1927
and was discharged to
HMS *Fisgard* as an ERA
(Engine Room Artificer)
apprentice in December
1931

1894

Headmaster, George Pulsford (**below**)
attends Windsor Castle with 1,022
pupils, who perform a whole School
parade for Queen Victoria

1909

The whole School (1,040 pupils)
parades for King Edward VII at
Buckingham Palace

1922

Rear-Admiral Laurence Oliphant becomes
School Superintendent and steers the
School through its move from Greenwich
to Holbrook

1925

The Old Boys Association is formed

1900

1930

Royal Hospital School

1892

A series of royal visits culminates
in the official adoption of the title
'The Royal Hospital School'

1907

First School magazine published

1918

King George V presents the School with the King's
Banner in appreciation of its wartime service

1933

On 23 March the School departs Greenwich for its new home in Suffolk

Timeline: Holbrook

The Royal Hospital School, Holbrook, Competition
The Winning Design

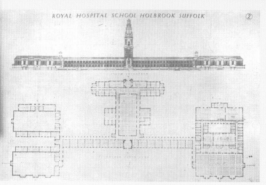

ROYAL HOSPITAL SCHOOL HOLBROOK SUFFOLK

1934
Chapel completed and dedicated by Archbishop Cosmo Lang

1938
Cinema equipment starts functioning in the Assembly Hall

1939
Consideration of evacuation, but instead numbers are reduced to just over 500 pupils

1925
Herbert T Buckland and William Heywood appointed architects

1920 · 1930 · ★ · 1940

1921
Following communications with the Admiralty via Dame Agnes Weston, Reade gifts his Holbrook Estate

1922
Arthur Smallwood, Director of Greenwich Hospital, proposes the Royal Hospital School should move from its cramped Greenwich site

1928
J Gerrard appointed main contractors and on 28 October HRH The Duke of York lays Foundation Stone

Holbrook opening

1933
On 27 April a train from Liverpool Street connects with 16 double decker buses to transfer the School to Holbrook

On 26 July HRH The Prince of Wales lands his plane to officially open the School

1943
On 5 April the Bruntisfield Committee is formed. It agrees to remove the requirement for compulsory entry to the Royal Navy and also agrees that modest fees would be charged for those gainfully employed

ATION STONE CEREMONY — H.R.H. THE DUKE OF YORK
ETING THE GUARD OF HONOUR

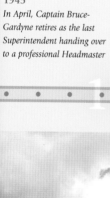

The Royal Hospital School

1956
Norman York becomes Headmaster for the next 18 years and develops a more academic syllabus

1970
End of meals served at the tables and the 'red light' system with introduction of cafeteria

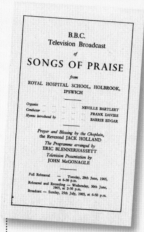

1953
Admiralty approval granted for the School to have its own flag, a blue ensign defaced with the Greenwich coat of arms

The sixth form is launched and the first candidates are prepared for GCE A level

1945
In April, Captain Bruce-Gardyne retires as the last Superintendent handing over to a professional Headmaster

1960
The Combined Cadet Force (CCF) is established and Lord Mountbatten attends

1965
The first televisions arrive so that pupils can view the funeral of Winston Churchill, the Songs of Praise broadcast from the School and the World Cup in 1966

1950 · 1960 · 1970

1953
The rigged mast on the parade ground is dismantled

1958
On 15 June the Remembrance Tablet and Book are unveiled

1962
The first housemasters' flats are built and the School celebrates its 250th anniversary

1968
HM Queen Elizabeth The Queen Mother visits the School and presents the Queen's Banner

The Royal Hospital School: Celebrating 300 Years

1971
Introduction of a new school uniform. The Naval uniform is retained for ceremonial occasions

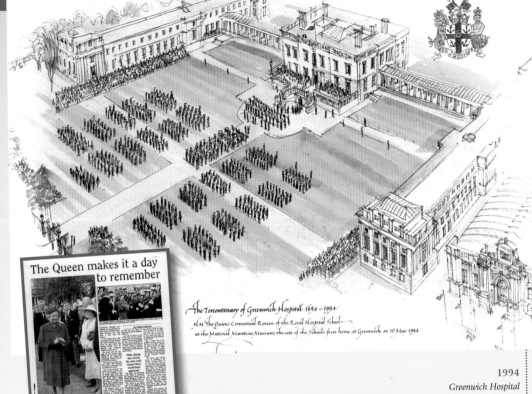

The Tercentenary of Greenwich Hospital 1694–1994
HM The Queen's Ceremonial Review of the Royal Hospital School at the National Maritime Museum, the site of the School's first home at Greenwich, on 10 May 1994

The Queen makes it a day to remember

1994
Greenwich Hospital tercentenary celebrations. A spectacular parade at the National Maritime Museum attended by HM Queen Elizabeth II on 10 May and a banquet in the Painted Hall attended by HRH Prince Andrew, The Duke of York on 4 November

1978
First Inter-House Drama Competition

1983
Fire destroys the School's historic Robson Organ

1991
The opening of the first girls' House: Hood

1970   1980   1990

Co-educational

1976
HMS Ganges closes and the School inherits its figurehead for the next 30 years

1977
The School's first major musical production is the rock opera Tommy

1988
First Inter-House Shout Singing Competition

1989
A bill is passed enabling girls and children of non-seafaring families to attend the School

Opening of Nelson House as a modern university-style boarding residence

WHOSE "TOMMY"?

ROYAL HOSPITAL SCHOOL
NELSON HOUSE

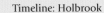

www.royalhospitalschool.org

The Royal Hospital School

RALEIGH

THE READE MUSIC SCHOOL was opened by John Rutter CBE

2008
Opening of the Reade Music School
by John Rutter CBE

2006
The first day pupils join
the School in September,
initially all attached to
boarding houses and
from September 2009
Raleigh becomes a
dedicated day house

1995
The School enters its first team
in the Devizes to Westminster
Canoe Marathon going on to
win Best CCF, Best School and
Best Junior teams in 2012

2004
The School establishes its relationship
with the Arthur Phillip Memorial Trust

2012
RHS pupils salute the Queen's barge during
the Thames Diamond Jubilee Pageant

2000   2010

Tercentenary

1998
Opening by The Duke of York
of the all weather sports pitch
named in his honour

2005
A year after Howard Blackett is appointed Headmaster the
School embarks on an ambitious five-year refurbishment
programme and multi-million-pound investment

2009
The establishment of dedicated Junior
Houses for year 7 and 8 pupils. Drake
for boys and Blake for girls

Multi-Million Investment for RHS

"Welcome to our review of another highly successful year at the Royal Hospital School.

I am delighted to inform you that RHS is about to embark upon a multi-million pound development programme. Over the coming years ten boarding houses will be completely refurbished and a new music school will be built from scratch. RHS is in excellent shape as you will see from the rest of this publication."

Howard Blackett, Headmaster

15

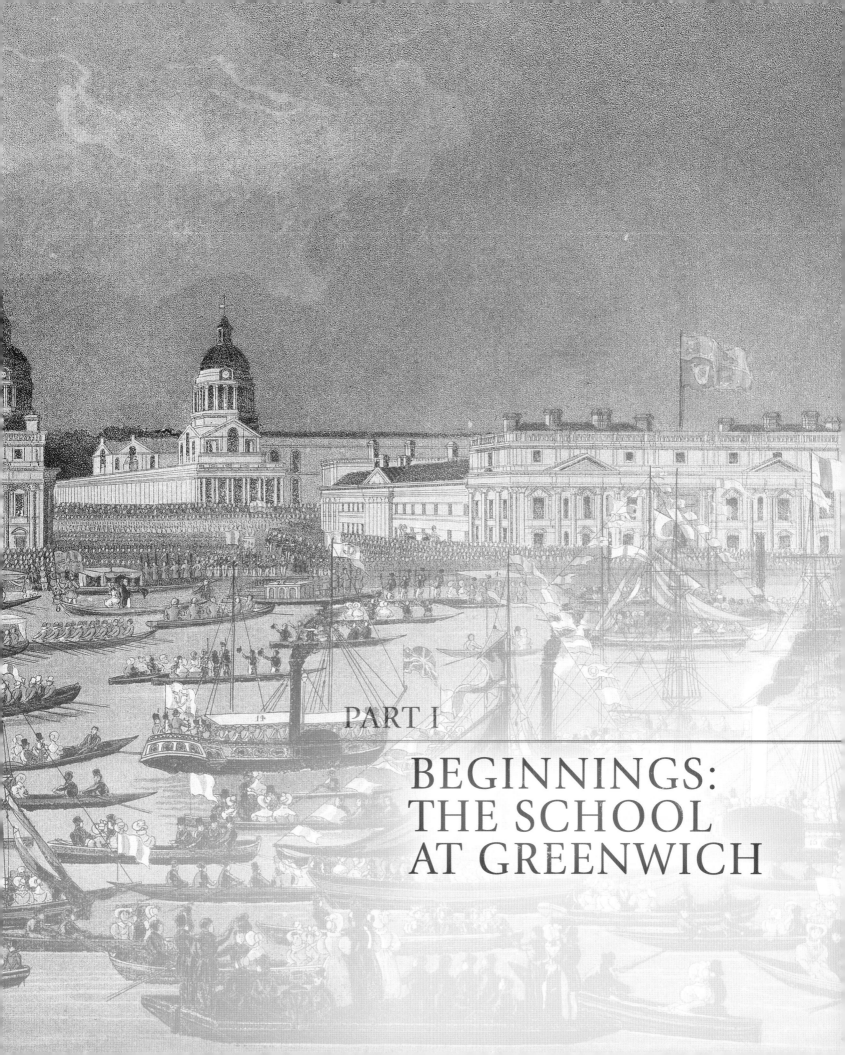

PART I

BEGINNINGS: THE SCHOOL AT GREENWICH

Greenwich Hospital

It was Henry VIII who initiated the expansion of the fleet into what was at first called the 'Navy Royall' in 1803, and built the naval power of his kingdom into a force that could challenge and defeat the fleets of his European enemies. Under his daughter, Elizabeth I, the Armada of Catholic Spain, intent on overthrowing her Protestant regime, was overwhelmed by a combination of English naval power and storms. The Navy had quickly become paramount in the defence of the realm, but the attention shown by the naval authorities to the welfare of the men who served and fought in the small ships of the Elizabethan fleet was a disgrace. Those who were not killed often died from diseases that raged through the fleet, and when not on active service they went unpaid so their families too faced destitution.

In 1590, to help remedy this appalling situation, Sir John Hawkins (supported by Sir Francis Drake) set up the Chatham Chest, a national endowment for the support of injured and disabled sailors funded by contributions taken from the wages of all English seamen. It continued in existence until its control was ceded to Greenwich Hospital in . The principle that soldiers and sailors who were injured or had grown old in the service of their country should expect to receive treatment and help thereafter became established as a necessary concern of the military authorities, along with the obligation to look after their widows, wives and children. It became an issue for royalty as well. After Charles II was restored to the throne, he appointed regional 'commissioners for the sick and wounded and prisoners of war', with power to appoint doctors and officials and the right to use parts of existing hospitals.

The diarist John Evelyn was one such commissioner, who went on to be involved with the establishment of Chelsea Hospital for sick and wounded soldiers. King James II, after he came to the throne in 1685, toyed with the idea of an equivalent for sailors, for which there was a clear need. Long-term care for the sick and disabled and pensions for the elderly were necessary. The Chatham Chest could help, as could

Far left: Thomas Cavendish, Sir Francis Drake and Sir John Hawkins. Drake helped Sir John Hawkins establish the Chatham Chest (1590) and thereby introduced the concept of a benevolent and charitable fund that could be used to support seamen (and eventually their families). It is appropriate that one of the RHS boarding houses is named after Drake and it currently operates as the boys' Junior House.

Left: The Chatham Chest with a large lock in the lid and five hasps for padlocks. Ordered in 1625 to hold the money for the mutual benevolent fund for disabled seamen, it was deposited with Greenwich Hospital by the Lords Commissioners of the Admiralty in 1845.

Queen's House – forever associated with the School at Greenwich

The Royal Hospital School will always be closely associated with the Queen's House, Greenwich. From 1696, the surrounds were given over to the development of Greenwich Hospital (including the School) and in the early 19th century royal patronage enabled the School to occupy this most historic building. The royal palace at Greenwich was the principal royal residence in London for two centuries after its foundation in the middle of the 15th century. In 1616 James I's queen, Anne of Denmark, commissioned Inigo Jones to build a new pavilion for her in its grounds. It was to be a place where she could retreat and entertain guests, and it was also to provide a bridge between the palace gardens and the park behind over the Greenwich to Woolwich Road.

Work stopped in 1618 when the Queen became ill; she died the following year. The building was thatched over at first floor level, and construction did not start again until Charles I gave Greenwich to his queen, Henrietta Maria, in 1629; the house was structurally completed in 1635.

Prior to receiving the commission, Inigo Jones had spent three years in Italy studying architecture, and his design reflected what he had observed and learnt there. The Queen's House was a complete stylistic departure and a major contrast to the architectural norms usually until then expressed in England in Tudor red brick. It was the first truly 'classical' building in England, and reflected the Renaissance ideas of mathematical symmetry and harmony which had been so widely employed in Italy by Andrea Palladio. Its 'tulip stairs' was the first centrally unsupported spiral stair to be built in Britain.

Leading European painters were employed to provide paintings for the ceilings and walls and Charles I's vast art collection provided the classical statuary which adorned the house. But the outbreak of the Civil War in 1642 led to the Queen's exile in France and eventually to the king's execution and the sequestration of all his property. The Queen's House became a government building while around it the remains of the Tudor palace fell into further decay.

After Charles II was restored to the throne he refitted the house for his mother, but she was there for only a short while before moving to Somerset House, dying in 1669. In the early 18th century the road which ran under it was moved to a new position between the river and the rear of the Hospital buildings (where it still runs today), and from 1711 the windows were replaced with Georgian sashes, giving it its current external appearance.

In 1807 George III gave the house to the Royal Naval Asylum, which was to go on to be part of the Royal Hospital School. In response to the need for more classrooms and accommodation, the colonnades and flanking wings were added shortly afterwards. The School occupied the Queen's House for 126 years until the National Maritime Museum took over the building to be refurbished and then formally opened by George VI in 1937 to display the Greenwich Hospital and Caird collections and much more.

From 1990–99 the house was partly refitted and refurnished to give an impression of what it was like as a royal residence in the mid-17th century. It is now used to display the Museum's fine art collection, and for educational programmes, events and corporate entertainment – fittingly perhaps, given the original purpose for which it was built – and the basement includes a display on the history of the Royal Hospital School.

Left: Separate three-quarter-length portraits of Queen Mary II and King William III wearing coronation robes. Mary is surrounded by regalia, crown on table, ermine and orb. She reigned jointly with her husband William of Orange and was instrumental in the establishment of Greenwich Hospital. Her early death persuaded her husband to implement a Royal Charter, which included a statement of intent to maintain and educate the children of seamen.

almshouses where they existed, but the naval wars had been long and bitter, and these resources were not nearly adequate.

The Glorious Revolution of 1688 saw the Catholic James II toppled from the throne and forced into exile, and in February 1689 Parliament formally offered the joint sovereignty to James's daughter Mary and her Dutch husband William of Orange, both staunch Protestants. Two years later, when Chelsea Hospital for soldiers was nearly complete, the commissioners for the sick and wounded were charged with reporting on possibilities for sailors too – and after the English fleet defeated the French at the Battle of La Hogue Queen Mary decided that the welfare of seamen was to be the 'darling object of her life', and demanded that the commissioners, who were giving active consideration to the site of the now ruinous royal palace at Greenwich as the site for the sailors' hospital, should hasten their decision-making.

The Queen's plans were ambitious, and she pursued them with vigour while William was away campaigning in Flanders. But their breadth provoked considerable unease and hesitation, not least in the King himself after his

return. They may well have been modified or simply left to gather dust – except that, in December 1694, Mary caught smallpox. She died, aged 32, just after Christmas, and her husband declared that her memory should be perpetuated in the building of the hospital that she had so fervently wanted. According to Macaulay, the king 'as soon as he had lost her began to reproach himself for having neglected her wishes'.

William therefore issued a charter, backdated to October 1694 so that it could be in both of their names, declaring their intention 'to erect and found an hospital of East Greenwich in our county of Kent for the relief and support of seamen serving on board the ships or vessels belonging to the Navy Royall… who by reason of age, wounds or other disabilities shall be uncapable of further service at sea and be unable to maintain themselves. And for the sustentation of the widows and the maintenance and education of the children of seamen happening to be slain or disabled… Also for the further relief and encouragement of seamen and improvement of navigation.'

Sir Christopher Wren and John Evelyn laid the foundation stone of the Royal Hospital, Greenwich, on 30 June 1696. Raising money proved a constant difficulty, but work on the building continued through the remaining years of William's reign and into that of his successor, Queen Anne, who came to the throne in 1702. The first 42 seamen arrived at the end of January 1705.

There were four main buildings, two on either side of the vista from the Queen's House to the River Thames, named for King William and King Charles on the west and Queen Mary and Queen Anne on the east. By March 1708, numbers of Pensioners had risen to 300 and a further 50 were admitted later that year. The Hospital was growing in size and scope, and now the managing authorities looked again at William's and Mary's original charter.

They had achieved quite a lot of the charter's objectives; but nothing at all had been done about the provision of education and its final stipulation – the improvement of navigation. How were they to do this? On the last but one day of 1712, December 30, they resolved: 'that as soon as the revenue of the hospital shall be sufficient for that purpose, the corporation be at liberty to take in any number of children they shall think fit, not exceeding 100 in the whole at any time and that no child be taken in before the age of 14, nor kept in after the age of 18; and that during their continuance in the hospital they shall be instructed in writing, arithmetic and navigation.' Thus was the Royal Hospital School born.

Left: A Greenwich Pensioner, with peg leg, is pointing to the French flagship L'Orient blowing up at the Battle of the Nile (1798). Amongst others, a Greenwich Schoolboy (with cap on floor) listens intently. Through the years many boys from the School would have had contact with Pensioners, many of them veterans of the Anglo-French wars. For the first seven years, the School provided only for children of Pensioners, but from 1719 onwards the children of poor seamen were admitted.

Far left: The Battle of La Hogue (1692). A copy painted in 1836 by George Chambers Snr from an original by Benjamin West, depicts the destruction of the French fleet, a battle that encouraged William and Mary to support seamen, their widows and children. It hangs in the dining room at Holbrook, a reminder of the School's naval heritage. Interestingly there is a local connection – Vice-Admiral Benjamin Page, who donated funds to pay for this picture, was from Ipswich.

The First School

Since in those days, for those who were lucky enough to receive any education at all, 'normal' school leaving age was 14, it seems that from the start the new school was intended to be vocational. It is not clear when the first boys actually arrived, but according to Dilkes Loveless, Secretary of Greenwich Hospital in the second half of the 19th century and an authority on its history, there were initially ten pupils, living in King Charles Court and clothed in uniforms similar to those worn by the Pensioners.

Queen Anne died in 1714, and was succeeded by George I who, among his early acts, appointed a new Governor of Greenwich Hospital; this was Matthew Aylmer. It was he who now finally did something practical about navigation and the charters' educational aspirations.

James Thornhill had been commissioned some time before to paint the ceiling of the Great Hall in King William Court. This was finished in 1712, and London flocked to see the magnificent result. Money came in from the visitors, a quarter of which was paid over to the porter who admitted and looked after them; the rest was at the disposal of the Governor. He decided to use it to fulfil the charter's promise to 'improve navigation' by teaching it to the young pupils. This was the beginning of the Charity Box, a fund for the support of the School into which were put small amounts of 'windfall' or unofficial income or savings, for example the small fines levied on Pensioners who misbehaved. Two other early and interesting sources of funds for building Greenwich Hospital, were in 1705 the granting of £6,472 from the effects of Captain Kidd, the pirate, who was hanged at Execution Dock, Wapping and in 1716, after the execution of the Earl of Derwentwater for his part in the Jacobite rebellion the previous year, the ceding of his northern estates to Greenwich Hospital in 1735.

Thomas Weston, the 'ingenious disciple' of the Astronomer Royal, John Flamsteed, had a small school in Greenwich standing on hospital

Above: Matthew Aylmer was the second Governor of Greenwich Hospital (1714–20). He was responsible for progressing the early educational aspirations of the Greenwich Hospital charity through development of the School.

Below: The School benefitted from the funds obtained by Greenwich Hospital, which included the seizing of Captain Kidd's effects. The pirate is pictured here in New York harbour and every September there is a re-enactment of a pirate landing close to Holbrook Creek, reminding the School of the origin of the Hospital's most unusual source of funds.

Sir James Thornhill and the Painted Hall

James Thornhill, born in 1675 or 1676, was a bold choice as the artist commissioned to paint the ceiling and walls of the Great Hall within King William Court, taken in 1707 when foreign decorative painters dominated the market. Finances were not at their most healthy either, and Thornhill, who still had a reputation to make, agreed to accept as pay whatever the directors of the Hospital 'should judge he deserved'. The whole tremendous undertaking took 19 years, and after it was finished, the hall was only used for special occassions and so it was opened for viewing by visitors. The 'explanation' of the painting which Thornhill wrote for the directors – partly in one of his frequent attempts to extricate payment from them – was printed, in both French and English, for sale to visitors at 6d each; the first edition of 1,000 had to be reprinted two years later, such was the interest in the painting, and it went on being reprinted for decades. In it he described the plaques that contained the names of benefactors: 'Each table is attended by two charity boys as if carved in white marble, sitting on great corbels, pointing up to the figure of Charity, in a niche, intimating that what money is given there is for their support. … Out of all that is given for showing these halls, only three pence in the shilling is allowed to the person that shows it; the rest makes an excellent fund for the yearly maintenance of poor boys who are the sons of mariners that have been either slain or disabled in the service of their country.'

The original commission charged the artist to include as many references as possible to the glories of the Navy and its achievements in protecting the country and advancing its power. It includes portraits of kings, queens and the great men and women associated with Greenwich Hospital – as well as a self portrait of Thornhill himself. And there are many allegorical figures, including Fame, later used as the figurehead for the School's training ship. After the painting was finished Thornhill's reputation was secure. He had a powerful patron in George I, who in 1718 made him court painter, and in 1720 he was knighted, the first home-grown artist to receive that accolade.

The School has a close association with this Great Hall which helped to fund its formative years and was subsequently such an inspiration to those living alongside it. Since leaving Greenwich, staff and former pupils of the School have often returned for formal events there, most notably on the occasion of the Greenwich Hospital tercentenary in 1994.

Chelsea Pensioners (in red) visit the Greenwich Pensioners (in blue) and view paintings in the Naval Gallery of the Painted Hall. Many are Trafalgar veterans and the women and children represent the transmitters and receivers of knowledge. It usefully represents the passing of information to the next generation and many Greenwich boys benefitted from this process.

property; with funds now available Aylmer approached him to take on the instruction of the sons of Pensioners and nurses in 'the Italian method of book-keeping, mathematics in three languages, drawing, fencing, music as well as a wide variety of languages and navigation'. He accepted only boys who could read and write, as well as pass his entrance tests. This curriculum was unusual and specialist, and as such highly prized at a time when hardly any mathematics was taught in schools, let alone universities.

The Greenwich boys, who attended Weston's Academy as day pupils, were taught high-level navigational skills, with the ultimate aim that they should be 'put out as apprentices to masters of ships and substantial Commanders'. Thomas Weston was clearly a man of some repute; unusually for a mere headmaster, though admittedly one who had also been a highly regarded assistant to the Astronomer Royal, he was immortalised in a portrait in Thornhill's painted ceiling.

Left: James Radclyffe, 3rd Earl of Derwentwater, in an etching by S Freeman taken from a painting by Sir G Kneller. His estates became another source of Greenwich Hospital income and the School has visited this Greenwich landholding for many CCF and outward bound activities. The School retains the Dilston Rapier, associated with the Earl and dated to c1714.

Thomas Weston: the first Headmaster

Thomas Weston worked from early 1699 as assistant to the Astronomer Royal, John Flamsteed, who wrote of him that providence had 'sent me an ingenious but sickly youth (Mr Weston)… [who] by my directions drew the charts of the constellations so well, that as a good designer needed no directions but his draughts to perfect them'. Colleagues reckoned he was Flamsteed's 'principal instrument', as he aided negotiations between Newton and the Astronomer Royal and furthered work on the Greenwich star catalogues. After leaving Flamsteed's service in 1706, Weston set up as a teacher of mathematics.

He died in 1728, just before completing an English version of Galileo Galilei's *Mathematical discourses concerning the two new sciences relating to mechanics and local motion, in four dialogues*. His brother, John, took over the 'Academy at Greenwich' and saw the book through to press; it was published in 1730.

Thomas Weston, the first Master of the Greenwich Hospital School. He taught Greenwich boys who attended his Weston's Academy as day pupils.

Entry to the School was through nomination by the Hospital's directors, who acquired the right in rotation. The original complement of ten appears to have quickly risen to 15 and then 20, though in 1719 it was cut back again to 15 and rules were drafted 'for the regulation of the Royal Hospital boys at Greenwich'. By then it had been decided that they were to be boarders, so that their clothing and their food could also be monitored. A dormitory was fitted out for them on the upper floor of the west side of King William Court, with a fireplace and 20 specially ordered beds costing £1 14s 0d each – though only 17 pewter chamber pots. They were under the care of a nurse and a guardian, part of the latter's duty being to take them to and from school twice a day and oversee them in the evening. They ate in the Pensioners' dining hall, with an allowance of food that quickly had to be doubled to accommodate the appetites of adolescent boys, and 'beer, as much as they will drink'. Those were the days when water was dangerously polluted and light beer was the normal accompaniment to a meal.

The first boy to leave became a servant to Captain Owen of HMS *Advice*; the second, called Jacobs, had clearly shown some academic ability as he became apprenticed as an usher – an assistant teacher – to Thomas Weston. The regular stream of indentures and apprenticeships that followed indicates that Weston's Academy was succeeding in its purpose, and that good employment was being found for the Greenwich Hospital boys who attended. When they left the School, those who needed it were fitted out with clothes and equipment at the Hospital's expense: one Treaby, who was apprenticed for seven years to a Mr LaMotte whose ship was imminently leaving for the West Indies, cost £7 to equip in this way 'that he do not lose this opportunity'.

On his death in 1728, Thomas Weston was succeeded as Headmaster of the Academy by his brother, John. By now the boarding element of the School had expanded; in 1729 part of Queen Anne's Court was converted to provide a second dormitory for 30 boys, and a year later another ten arrived, bringing the overall capacity up to 60. Weston's Academy had to build new day-boy classrooms to accommodate the growing Greenwich contingent.

Above: Thomas Peytner attended the School from 1791 to 1794. It is the earliest image of a named Greenwich school boy. After a naval career he eventually became a lawyer.

The School's Australian connections

ARTHUR PHILLIP – MOST FAMOUS ALUMNI

Widely regarded as the modern founder of Australia, Arthur Phillip *(inset)* was the natural son of a German teacher of languages whose mother later married a naval officer. He joined the Navy on leaving the School and quickly rose through the ranks. In 1787 he set off for Australia in command of the first convict-carrying fleet, with 13 ships and a complement of 772 convicts. He landed at Botany Bay, but moved on to Port Jackson and established his colony (now Sydney) with, 'the finest harbour in all the world'. He became the first Governor of New South Wales, at that time the eastern half of what we now know as Australia, and managed the penal colony, relationships with the local aboriginal people, the farming of new lands and the provision of supplies from Calcutta and Cape Town.

The *Dictionary of Australian Biography* summarises him as 'steadfast in mind, modest without self-seeking [and with] imagination enough to conceive what the settlement might become and the common sense to realise what at the moment was possible and expedient… He was sent out to start up a convict settlement; he laid the foundations of a great dominion.'

Phillip's date of landing at Sydney is today commemorated as Australia Day. He himself returned to England in 1793 and retired from the Navy with the rank of Admiral of the Blue. He continued to support developments in Australia and died in Bath in 1814. He is still honoured at the RHS by the Heads of School attending the annual Arthur Phillip Memorial Service held as St Mary-le-Bow church in London.

DANIEL WOODRIFF – SHIPPING CONVICTS

In December 1767 Daniel Woodriff, the son of a shipwright who had died in 1761, was admitted to the School and, after an apprenticeship and some involvement with trade with Jamaica, was 'impressed' into the Navy in 1778. Within four years he was already in command of HMS *Dependence* and became involved in the War of American Independence, marrying the daughter of an American loyalist. By 1792 he was shipping convicts to Australia, was in charge of prisoners of war and helped suppress a convict insurrection at Port Jackson, for which he was granted 1,000 acres of land at Penrith, NSW. In 1802 he was Commander of HMS *Calcutta*, part of David Collins' expedition to

Inset: Arthur Phillip (1751–53), the first Governor of New South Wales.

Above: Daniel Woodriff (1767–70) – after a life at sea he returned to Greenwich Hospital as a resident Captain.

Left: The Founding of Australia. By Capt. Arthur Phillip R.N. Sydney Cove, Jan. 26th 1788, by Algernon Talmage, 1937.

establish the Bass Straits settlements, and in 1805, while convoying merchants, he commanded an audacious escape for his fleet before his own capture by the French in September near Scilly.

After Napoleon released him he continued his naval career, becoming commissioner of Port Royal, Jamaica, 1814–22. In later life he was made a CB and, rather than becoming a Rear-Admiral, chose to become a resident Captain of Greenwich Hospital. He died in February 1842. All three of Woodriff's sons served with him on HMS *Calcutta* and became naval officers; one of them, Daniel James, helped take charge of *Bellerophon* at Trafalgar when all the officers were either dead or wounded.

WILLIAM COLLINS – FOUNDED HOBART, TASMANIA

This son of a seaman who became a naval officer, explorer and ship owner, attended the School at Greenwich from 1768 to 1771. He was an early settler of Australia, arriving in 1803 and having dealings with aborigines, convicts and bushrangers. He was involved in establishing the site for the settlement of Hobart, and then became its first harbourmaster, owner of the first flour mill on the Derwent River and a pioneer in the local whale fishing industry, establishing Australia's first whaling station. He was also a naval officer and during his time in Australia had direct dealings with many Governors, including Captain William Bligh formerly of the *Bounty*.

HERIOT PERCY BEDWELL – EARLY PIONEER

Born in Romsey in 1832, Heriot Percy Bedwell was educated at the School between 1843 and 1845 and then joined the East India Company. He left the company and arrived in Melbourne in 1853, marrying Margaret Dunn, who had arrived on the *Chance*. They moved to Rushworth where Bedwell bought shares in a gold mine from some Chinese men for £150 and named it the 'Mongolian Reef'. It was profitable for a while, but as it petered out he sold his share to his partners for £50 and in 1859 invested his money in the 1,400-acre Belle Vue Estate, part of William Winter Irving's station. He and his family were among the earliest pioneers in Australia, with nine of his ten children born on the ranch.

JOHN GOWLLAND – MAPPING AUSTRALIA

After leaving Greenwich in 1853 as Captain of the School, John Gowlland served in the Navy during the Crimean War and was awarded one of the first batch of Baltic Medals for his part in destroying the Russians' northern naval base at Riga. As a further prize for his services in the war he sailed the Russian sloop *Anna Maria* back to England. His first posting had been directly to Nelson's former flagship, HMS *Victory,* in Portsmouth Harbour and after the war he conducted mapping missions to South Africa, South America and Canada, where Gowlland Harbour and Gowlland Straits are named after him.

He also mapped parts of Mexico, Hawaii and the Greek islands before settling in Australia in 1865, where he was responsible for updating Captain Cook's original charts of New South Wales and charting the Great Barrier Reef. He undertook the heroic search for survivors of the wrecked brig *Maria,* after which a banquet was held in his honour. On 14 August 1874, while he was mapping Sydney Harbour, a freak wave capsized his rowing boat and he drowned. He has the distinction of being the only RHS boy to have had two snails named after him.

CLIFFORD BERTRAM BATT – JACKAROO AND FARMER

One of the many old boys of the School who led varied and adventurous lives, Clifford Bertram Batt, attended both Greenwich and Holbrook between 1931 and 1935 before joining the Royal Air Force and becoming an air-frame and engine fitter in India. He learned to fly in Rhodesia (now Zimbabwe) and during the Second World War flew transport planes in Burma. After the war he became a jackaroo in Australia, and later owned a copra plantation on 40 of the small Hermit Islands off the coast of New Guinea. On returning to Australia he became a cattle rancher and owned motels on the Gold Coast and a yacht, the *Rudolph Whalen*. In his retirement he entered the *Guinness Book of Records* as the oldest person successfully to swim the English Channel at the age of 67 years and 240 days; his swim from Cap Gris Nez to Dover took 18 hours and 37 minutes in 1987.

HUBERT DESMOND HALL – BRITISH AUSTRALIA SOCIETY

After attending the School at Holbrook, Hubert Desmond Hall joined the Royal Air Force and flew aircraft in the Battle of Britain during the Second World War. His long career in the RAF was most distinguished; he reached the rank of Air Vice Marshal and was much decorated, including being recognised in the Queen's Birthday Honours in 2003 for services to UK/Australia relations.

In the 1990s, as president of the ACT Branch of the Australia-Britain Society, he worked with Sir John Mason to establish the Magna Carta monument in Canberra as a celebration of the close historical and cultural links which exist between Australia and Britain. After a generous donation towards the cost of the monument was received from the British Government

as its centennial gift from the people of Britain to the people of Australia, it was inaugurated in 1997, 700 years after King Edward I sealed the Great Charter. In 2007 Hall attended a ceremony recognising the Battle of Britain victory and the 'shared sacrifice in the defence of freedom' of the peoples of Australia and Britain, and in October 2011 he met HM Queen Elizabeth II at the Australian War Memorial.

Above: John Thomas Ewing Gowlland (1850–53) camping out at Clontarf in 1870, by George Penkivil Slade.

Left: Clifford Bertram Batt (1931–35) was a member of the guard when the School was opened by HRH The Prince of Wales in 1933. He remembered stroking the tail of the Prince's plane when it was parked on the fields. Many years later he reconnected with this plane when he discovered its wreck in Papua and New Guinea.

Opposite: William Collins (1768–71) contributed to the founding of Hobart Town on the Derwent River, Tasmania. Painting by Captain Charles Staniforth Hext.

The fire in the Greenwich Hospital Chapel, 2 January 1779. This hand colour version of a print is by Thomas Furbor, the longest serving Headmaster of the Greenwich Hospital School (1765–1800).

New regulations made it clearer that the main aim of the School was as a 'useful nursery for the breeding up of seamen'. The boys were now to sleep in 'hammacoes', and they had two nurses, among whose duties were to comb the boys' heads regularly to keep them clean of vermin and to ensure that they washed their hands and faces every morning before school and 'their feet every Saturday night before they go to bed'. The best of them were to be apprenticed to 'substantial commanders, using the southern navigation for the better improvement of their talents'.

The opportunities offered by the School for the sons of humble seamen were truly remarkable for the age; yet it was sometimes proving difficult to find suitable entrants who were physically fit, able to read and write and who were orphaned or whose fathers were 'disabled and maintained in the hospital'. The directors widened the field by making places open to the sons of any disabled men, but the boys were still required to have certain basic skills; mere poverty was not sufficient as a qualification.

John Weston died in 1744 to be replaced by his brother-in-law John Rossam, who died in December that same year and was succeeded by Rev. Francis Swinden. At this time it was noted that 2,650 boys had been educated since 1712. However, discipline now became an issue, with many boys running away, though if they came back they were usually readmitted after being duly birched. Numbers fluctuated, but the reputation of the School was growing to the extent that it was mooted that officers' sons could be admitted, though nothing was done at that stage to further the idea. The meticulous accounts of the Charity Box, which had become the Charity Fund, indicate that numbers were still rising, to around 100, and in the 1750s applications exceeded places.

In 1747 the lease of the Academy building expired and it became Hospital property. The new Headmaster, Francis Swinden, took on a

Above: The Queen's House today. The School's asphalt parade ground was relandscaped as lawns in 1935–36. Tourists and visitors to the National Maritime Museum have replaced the pupils and teachers.

John Jervis, 1st Earl of St Vincent – A governor of the School

When Swynfen Jervis, a barrister and counsellor to the Admiralty, was appointed as Auditor of Greenwich Hospital in 1747, he moved to Greenwich and enrolled his son John into Weston's Academy. John Jervis entered the Navy in 1749 and rose swiftly through the ranks, eventually coming to the attention of Admiral Charles Saunders, who combined his active seafaring with the job of Treasurer of Greenwich Hospital. Jervis served on several of Saunders' ships, and then in the 1770s travelled extensively in Europe, visiting ports, dockyards and naval installations and making full notes on what he found. He commanded a ship in the Channel Fleet during the actions against the French during the War of American Independence, and in 1782 was knighted for his services.

By the 1790s he was an Admiral and was given the command of the Mediterranean Fleet, with HMS *Victory* as his flagship; serving under him as captains were Horatio Nelson, Cuthbert Collingwood and Thomas Troubridge. Napoleon was cutting a swathe through Europe, and the Spanish had allied themselves with the French. In 1797 Jervis's fleet was patrolling off Cape St Vincent when the Spanish fleet came into view. Although he was outnumbered almost two to one, Jervis engaged the Spanish and forced them to retreat. The battle was famous for a daring, and disobedient, manoeuvre by Nelson which resulted in his capturing two of the Spanish ships; when this disobedience was later commented on, Jervis said, 'It certainly was so, and if you ever commit such a breach of your orders, I will forgive you also.' He is also famous for his later assurance in a letter to the Admiralty that 'I do not say, my lords, that the French will not come. I say only they will not come by sea.'

The victory was not, in military terms, particularly significant, but it came at a time of great peril when Napoleon was carrying all before him and was threatening to invade England. The boost it gave to morale resulted in Jervis becoming Baron Jervis of Meaford and Earl of St Vincent, with a pension for life of £3,000. The king, Parliament and the City of London heaped other honours on him too, including the presentation of a sword and a gold box which are now in the National Maritime Museum.

St Vincent was known as a strict disciplinarian but also as a fair and generous man who treated officers and men similarly. He was concerned about the treatment of the wounded and the sick, and on the advice of his doctor

Left: Quadrants were a typical prize for drawing. The School has some early scientific instruments associated with pupils and teachers; most notably it displays an ebony, ivory and brass octant inscribed 'Greenwich Hospital School Prize / June 1834' Thomas Hopkirk (taught by Edward Riddle). He went on to become a mathematical tutor and was Principal of the Military Academy at Eltham.

further lease with extra land to accommodate the higher School roll (now numbering 100). But the building was becoming increasingly ramshackle, and in 1758 the directors decided that a new school should be built, and that it would be open only to Hospital boys. The healthy Charity Fund could easily afford to pay for the new building and work began adjacent to Hospital ground on King Street. By 1758 the new building was complete at a cost of £548 and the previous arrangement of sending day boys to Weston's Academy ceased with lessons now conducted in the new School buildings while boys continued to sleep in the Queen Anne building.

While the Academy still flourished nearby, Swinden's joint headship of the new School did not last long after it was built; he left in 1763 to be replaced for just two years by Rev. Braken before Thomas Furbor became Headmaster for the next 35 years. In 1779 Furbor accepted a new arrangement whereby he would be allowed two assistants to help cope with the 150 boys now at the School, and that he would undertake to teach only the Hospital boys. The link with the Academy, in educational terms, was now broken, and its Headmaster

ensured that his ships were supplied with plenty of fresh fruit and vegetables, along with lemon juice to counteract scurvy. As First Lord of the Admiralty, he was determined to combat the widespread fraud and corruption that plagued the administration and conduct of naval affairs everywhere. And he was also directly involved in funding the British National Endeavour charity, which was the precursor to the Royal Naval Asylum and later the Royal Hospital School. While at sea in August 1800, he received a letter requesting his help in supporting the 'establishment at Paddington for the orphan children of seamen who had fallen in their country's service'. He immediately organised a fundraising dinner that evening onboard his flagship for 50 officers of his fleet. He then despatched the mail cutter with instructions to his agents to pay £1,000 to the BNE.

Lord St Vincent retired in 1807, but continued to bombard the authorities with his views and suggestions about the better conduct of naval affairs until his death in 1823, covered in honours. His legacy includes several ships named after him, as well as places in the world newly discovered during those times of far-flung exploration; and of course there is also a boarding house named in his honour at the Royal Hospital School.

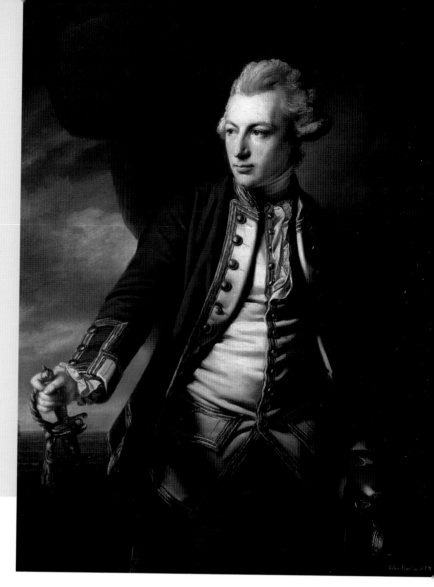

Right: John Jervis, 1st Earl of St Vincent (painted when a Captain by Francis Cotes, 1769), was educated at Weston's Academy alongside Greenwich Hospital boys. He was a staunch supporter of the School and as a Governor nominated children to attend.

shortly afterwards moved to a different location in Greenwich; it later merged with the Burney's Academy.

In 1782 the Hospital authorities demolished the vacated – and tumbledown – Weston building, along with the existing Headmaster's house. A larger three-story school was built with teaching rooms on the ground floor and two floors of dormitories with hammocks for 200 boys above, along with special accommodation for the guardian and nurses. The design included a Tuscan colonnade to provide a place of shelter and it now became a fully integrated boarding school. From now on the boys would come into formal contact with the Pensioners only at mealtimes, which they continued to eat in the Hospital dining room.

Another change was to the rule that, on leaving, boys could be apprenticed only as seamen. It was proving increasingly difficult to place all the leavers with seafarers, so now they could also take on trades connected with the sea, such as rope- and sail-making. One beneficiary of this rule change was Thomas Lancey, who had dislocated his thigh and so could not go to sea, and instead became the head's assistant in 1779, the first example of a pupil teacher. He was clearly talented, succeeding

Furbor as Headmaster in 1800 and publishing two books in 1816, one on the rules of practical arithmetic and the other on finding the time at sea.

In 1782, valuable prizes were instituted to encourage drawing skills. The first prize for 'the best drawing from nature' was a Halley's quadrant valued at three guineas; the second prize was a case of instruments, value a guinea; and the third prize was Robinson's *Treatise on Navigation* 'or something else to the party's own choice'. In those days before cameras, the ability to draw accurately the approaches to identified land and islands, and particularly hazards and safe routes, as well as the new flora and fauna encountered on voyages to distant lands, was a highly valued skill; and it was a map of Denmark that won an extra quadrant for George Moses Wilson in 1801.

The end of the 18th century saw a huge expansion of the Navy in response to war with Revolutionary France and its manpower grew from 16,000 to 120,000 in just four years. This had an inevitable knock-on effect on both the Hospital and the School, which was becoming increasingly unable to accept as many of the sons of sailors killed or disabled in service as were eligible to apply. It was now that a new initiative arose.

The British National Endeavour and the Royal Naval Asylum

'The British National Endeavour for educating, victualling, clothing and apprenticing the orphans of those brave soldiers and sailors who fall in defence of their king and country' was instigated by Andrew Thompson in response to the growing plight of naval orphans. The official foundation date was 1 January 1800. The School was to be funded by subscriptions solicited by Thompson, and it started life in a building in Paddington, London. However, there was a growing suspicion that all was not above board with the funding, and one of the subscribers, the Duke of Sussex – a younger son of George III – investigated. Thompson was duly indicted for deception and fraud and – although he was initially cleared of deception – his involvement with this visionary plan came to an end. He seems to have been a rather murky character, who inveigled his own brother into a fraud for which he was executed. But nonetheless his idea spawned not just the Royal Naval Asylum but also a similar one for soldiers which turned into the Royal Military Asylum and eventually became the Duke of York's Royal Military School.

Whatever Thompson's credentials, the idea itself was clearly too good to lose and the subscribers agreed to carry on with the Duke of Sussex in the chair, though he was later replaced by his brother, the Duke of Cumberland. Nelson was one of the sponsors and Lloyd's Patriotic Fund handed over £40,000 to the new enterprise.

The British National Endeavour did not keep its name for long. In 1801 it became the Naval Asylum and in 1805 the Royal Naval Asylum, and it left its inadequate Paddington headquarters for the Queen's House in Greenwich, which was given to the new venture by the king. Demand for entry to the School had been significant, with a June 1805 appeal to William Pitt, the Prime Minister, for government support which was duly approved; and on 5 October 1805 King George III, influenced by the many recent naval encounters, resolved to make the School 'a royal foundation for 1,000 children'. The new facilities were formally inaugurated on 21 October 1807 (Trafalgar Day), and it is thought likely that that a large Turkish cannon, captured from the island of Kinaliada in the Sea of Marmara by Admiral Duckworth in February 1807, was presented by the Duke of Cumberland to mark the occasion.

Above: HRH Prince Ernest, The Duke of Cumberland, fifth son of George III, was first president of the Royal Naval Asylum. As patron he formally marked its inauguration, presenting the 5.3-tonne Turkish cannon that for 200 years stood at the front of the School in Greenwich and Holbrook.

Left: A drum attributed to the 'Sea Fencibles' (a naval militia 1798 to 1810) is located in the entrance hall to the Royal Hospital School at Holbrook.

Lloyd's Patriotic Fund – nominating children to attend the School

Lloyd's of London began life in the late 17th century in Lloyd's coffee house, where businessmen met to exchange information. It soon became the centre of a new insurance business which rapidly spread worldwide and flourishes to this day. In 1803, a general meeting of the subscribers of Lloyd's established a fund known as 'The Patriotic Fund (at Lloyd's)', a title that persisted until the 1850s, when the name 'Lloyd's Patriotic Fund' was adopted. Although it has extensive connections with Lloyd's, it is an independent charity.

It was founded by Lloyd's chairman, Sir Brook Watson, a colourful character, merchant, soldier, MP and one-legged Mayor of London, having lost his leg at the age of 14 to a shark when visiting Havana, Cuba. The charity was to become a major benefactor of the Royal Naval Asylum, following its early involvement with the British National Endeavour. Its aim was 'to assuage the anguish of the wounded, to palliate in some degree the more weighty misfortune of the loss of limbs, to alleviate the distresses of the widows and orphans and to soothe brow of sorrow for the fall of dearest relatives, the props of unhappy indigence or helpless age, and to hand out every encouragement to our fellow subjects who may be in any way instrumental in repelling or annoying our implacable foe, and to prove to them that we are ready to drain both our purses and our veins in the great cause which imperiously calls on us to unite the duties of loyalty and patriotism with the strongest efforts of zealous exertion'. It was a highly influential charity and its committee boasted four former Mayors of London, the Governor of the Bank of England and the chairman of the East India Company.

The origins of the charity went as far back as 1782 when £6,000 was raised by Lloyd's subscribers for the widows and orphans of seamen drowned in the loss of the *Royal George*. In 1794, £21,281 was raised after the Battle of the Glorious First of June, for distribution among the wounded seamen and the widows and orphans of men who had been killed. Significant funds came in after the Battles of Cape St Vincent and Camperdown in 1797, the Nile in 1798 and Copenhagen in 1801, and it was incorporated as a permanent charity in 1803.

Following Trafalgar, King George III declared 5 December 1805 a National Thanksgiving Day, and the church collections from divine services held throughout the country raised £123,600 which was handed over to Lloyd's Patriotic Fund, which used it to assist with their support for the early embodiment of the Royal Hospital School.

The fund took a keen interest in the education of children of men who had been killed in battle and financial assistance was provided to a number of educational establishments. Most notably, in 1806, a grant of £61,000 in consols was made to the Royal Naval Asylum, which allowed the fund's trustees the 'enduring right' to nominate children to attend the School, with the investment income on the consols funding the children, to be known as 'Lloyd's nominees'. The first was William Jones, who joined on 10 November 1806, followed by a Trafalgar orphan, William Ellis. The fund's association with the School continued after the Asylum merged with the Hospital School, to the extent that in the late 19th century it was nominating large numbers of entrants each year.

The Lloyd's Patriotic Fund continued to have strong links with the Royal Hospital School into the 20th century and after its move to Holbrook. To symbolise these links, in 1962 Lloyd's presented the magnificent Lloyd's Patriotic Fund Sword to the School. It had originally been presented to Commander George Hardinge for distinguishing himself in the capture of the Dutch brig *Atalante* in 1804 when Captain of HMS *Scorpion*; he died in action aged 27 and his family received a posthumous vase in 1808. Only 153 of these swords have been presented. In 1964 the Fund also gave a large donation to the appeal for a new sports pavilion, the foundation stone for which was laid by Lloyd's Deputy Chairman, Raymond Sturge, with the trowel used by HRH The Duke of York (later George VI) when laying the foundation stone at Holbrook in 1928.

The following year, after Sturge became Chairman, the Head Boy was a Lloyd's nominee and along with the Navy Minister visited Lloyd's headquarters in London and presented the Chairman with a watercolour of the School at Holbrook. Sturge then spoke of Lloyd's long connection with the School, citing 637 recorded nominees since 1803. That number has been estimated as in excess of 1,600.

Above: Head boy John de Neumann (1957–65) presents a watercolour to the Lloyd's Chairman in 1965.

Left: The School's treasured £100 Lloyd's Patriotic Fund Sword with scabbard and detailing; presented in recognition of the strong and enduring links between Lloyd's and the School.

The cannon – defender of the School

Bernard de Neumann writes:

To the west side of the main entrance to the Royal Hospital School, Holbrook, stood a large bronze cannon mounted on an iron carriage. It was my purpose to attempt to uncover the history of the cannon, which in my time at the School (the 1950s) was dismissed by military experts as a fake on the grounds that it could not have been part of the ordnance used in the battles for which it carries battle honours. My researches indicate precisely the opposite.

The original markings on the top of the barrel are of Islamic origin giving the weight and dimensions of the cannon and the date of the casting of the barrel: the year 1212 of the Moslem calendar which in western terms is AD 1790–1. Also on top of the barrel is a long inscription recording the presentation of the cannon to the Royal Naval Asylum by the Duke of Cumberland.

The cast-iron display carriage carries a number of plaques, one of which states 'This gun brought from the Dardanelles by Duckworth 1807'; the others are battle honour plaques celebrating naval victories: 'Algiers 1816 Pellew', 'Camperdown 1797 Duncan', 'First of June 1794 Howe', 'Trafalgar 1805 Nelson', 'Nile 1798 Nelson', 'Copenhagen 1801 Nelson', Cape St Vincent 1797 Jervis' and 'St Jean D'Acre 1840 Stopford'.

What appear to be the original decorations on the carriage – a number of 'leafy star shapes' – suggest that it is likely to be original, albeit restored, since they match the patterning on the wheels and appear to have been replaced in some cases by the battle honour plaques.

The gun is certainly one of two Turkish guns captured during a well-documented action in the Dardanelles in 1807 under Admiral Sir John Duckworth. Less clear is when the gun was presented to the Royal Naval Asylum, or the logic of the plaque display. The lack of an inscription giving the date of presentation possibly suggests that it was so obvious that there was no need to record it, though it clearly must have been after the Dardanelles incident. Since the gun was taken in February 1807 and the Royal Naval Asylum moved to Greenwich in November that year, it is tempting to think that it may have been presented at the time of the move.

This suggestion is further supported by the fact that six of the battle honour plaques commemorate the naval battles that led to the establishment of the British National Endeavour and its successor, the Royal Naval Asylum. The gun would therefore serve both as a reminder of the School's foundation and as a memorial to the sacrifices made by the fathers of its first pupils. The Algiers and St Jean d'Acre plaques were clearly added later.

The cannon defended the Queen's House and the training ships until the School moved in 1933, when it took up its duty again in front of the main entrance to the Royal Hospital School in Holbrook, Suffolk. In 2007 it was moved back to its former home and is now on display outside the visitor centre in Maritime Greenwich.

Top: The cannon has always provided a good photo opportunity, for young and old here as seen at Greenwich.

Left: The cannon at Holbrook shortly before it was returned to Greenwich in October 2007, almost 200 years after it was given to the School. It is remembered with affection and still serves as a reminder of the School's royal connections and of the great sea battles that contributed to the founding of the Royal Naval Asylum.

Far left: From the School collection, a framed pen and ink with watercolour of the cannon, dated 1826, and signed by Robert Samuel Ennis Gallon, who lived at Greenwich Hospital until 1840.

The Queen's House had to be repaired and converted for Asylum purposes. Initially 56 moved in during November 1807, with work starting on two new large flanking boys wings on either side, linked to the house by colonnades which ran along the line of the old road, moved north behind the Hospital in 1697–99. Between 1808 and 1815 numbers increased from 337 to 834.

Entrants had to be orphans or motherless, or with a father either disabled or serving on a distant station, and they could join between the ages of five and 12. The conditions for entry were quite clear: 'None shall be admitted except the children born in wedlock of warrant and petty officers and seamen of the Royal Navy; and non-commissioned officers and privates of Your Majesty's Royal Marines'.

And, as a startling innovation, this new boarding school admitted girls as well as boys. Of the complement of 1,000 in its new Greenwich home, 300 places were open to girls who could join up to the age of ten. They were to be taught reading, writing, sewing and knitting and could expect to become domestic servants. They were also expected to mend the boys' clothing, and some might be kept on when they were older to do the domestic work of the School; these girls were lucky enough to continue to receive one lesson a day. They wore straw bonnets, kersey gowns with pinafores and worsted tights and they had dark blue gowns and brown tights for Sundays and special occasions like the royal visit of Prince William, third son of George III (later to become King William IV).

The Goldsmids – major benefactors

Abraham Goldsmid – early benefactor.

In the annals of Anglo-Jewish history, the Goldsmid family is one of the most distinguished. The founder, Aaron, settled in London as a merchant in about 1743, but it was his two youngest sons, Benjamin (born 1755) and Abraham (*right*, born 1756), who expanded the business hugely until, by the end of the 18th century, they occupied a powerful position both within the banking industry and as philanthropists. They had given 20 guineas each to the Marine Society at its inception in 1794, and later became involved in the British National Endeavour. While the nascent school was still in its inadequate quarters in Paddington, they attended a fundraising dinner for it which raised nearly £400, and the two brothers plus one other made the sum up to £1,000. After this, in July 1801, they were invited to join the institution's committee, in return for which they each had the privilege of nominating a child into its care. Benjamin put forward a John Slipe, aged five, whose father had been killed when the *Invincible* was wrecked, and Abraham later nominated James Dickson, the orphan of another sailor lost onboard the ship.

It was at this time that Lord Nelson gave his nomination to Benjamin Goldsmid, who put forward a poor boy named William Hart. A year later the brothers acted as stewards at a dinner attended by about 200 guests, including Admiral Sir Hyde Parker and Nelson. £1,317 10s was collected for the School. The 'Goldsmid friends' continued to give their support, with the accounts showing £162 5s donated in 1803 and £650 in 1804. The brothers were not part of the Royal Foundation that was set up in 1805 to move the School to Greenwich, but the minutes winding up the old committee recorded 'that the thanks of this committee be given to Abraham and Benjamin Goldsmid Esq, and their friends for their most zealous munificent and unremitting support of this institution'. They went on supporting the School, with £2,600 donated in 1806, and were indeed among the greatest individual benefactors to an institution in which they clearly had a strong interest.

Admiral Lord Nelson and his association with the Royal Hospital School

It is not clear when Nelson first became aware of the British National Endeavour at Paddington. He spent most of the years 1798 to 1801 at sea, after which he was ashore until May 1803 when he was appointed Commander-in-chief of the Mediterranean fleet. From then until his death at the Battle of Trafalgar he was almost entirely at sea chasing and trying to provoke the French and the Spanish into battle. It is almost certain that he, like Lord St Vincent, was approached by the founder of the British National Endeavour for his patronage, although the early records of the charity have been lost so this cannot be substantiated. However, in July 1801 he was mentioned in minutes as a patron with the power to nominate children to the School. In early 1802 he was reminded that he had this power and, if he chose not to exercise it, asked whether he would accept the nomination of William Hart. He agreed and the boy was admitted a few days later. In June that year he gave a speech at the charity's dinner at the London Tavern, which raised £1,296 11s, and in February 1803 he nominated Thomas Gravely to the School.

His involvement is therefore beyond question, and he is known to have been fully aware of, and concerned about, the plight of the orphan children of sailors lost in action. When the charity applied for a Royal Warrant in 1804, Nelson and St Vincent were among those named as trustees. His death in October 1805 robbed the charity and the School of his further help; but his continuing influence over the course of events was sealed by the statement by the Duke of Cumberland, less than a month after Trafalgar, that 'the Royal Naval Asylum for the reception of orphans and children of His Majesty's Navy [should] date its existence from the glorious and memorable day of Lord Nelson's victory off Trafalgar on 21 October 1805, of which event I trust it will long remain a monument most honourable to this country'.

In January 1806 Nelson's lead-lined coffin lay in state in the black-hung Painted Hall for three days while the people of London thronged to Greenwich to pay their respects. On the day of his interment at St Paul's Cathedral, the procession escorting his body to the barge on the river included 500 Greenwich Hospital Pensioners, with more Pensioners and the schoolboys lining the route and the river bank.

The boys benefited from a concession which allowed them to choose whether or not they would go on to a naval career. They were taught by a 'quartermaster of instruction' helped by one sergeant assistant for every 50 boys. They rose at 6am in summer and 7am in winter, with an hour to wash, dress and be inspected before lessons began. A drummer was specially appointed to drum them everywhere they went, to meals, to lessons, to prayers and to bed; he also carried out beatings when ordered to do so by the Governor, who was a serving naval officer, usually a captain.

Meanwhile the Hospital School, still a separate entity, had grown to 200 boys, whose education and maintenance were amply provided for through the Charity Fund, which now brought in some £7,000 a year. An audit of the Hospital's finances in the early years of the 19th century suggested that the fund should be merged with the general income of the Hospital, and this was done.

There were now two schools operating on adjacent sites. The Royal Naval Asylum was much bigger than the Hospital School and moreover not only took girls but had amended its entry requirements so that it could accept the children of commissioned officers. That there was a need for this was evident: the long French wars had resulted in many more promotions to commissioned rank from among men who would not previously have been considered, and their families were often in dire straits if they were killed or wounded.

Below: Music cover to an 1843 score by James Harris, Greenwich Hospital School Bandmaster and organist, showing the boys' uniform, with the Queen's House collonades and Hospital beyond.

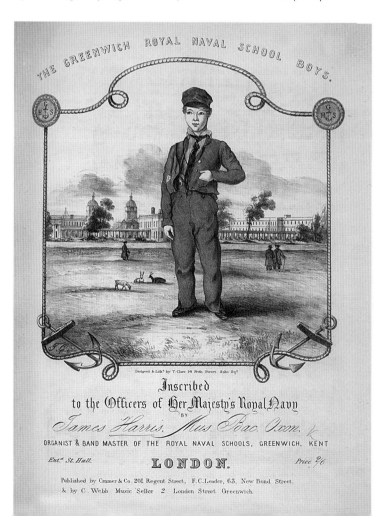

One of 11 similar copies, this painting of Rear-Admiral Sir Horatio Nelson by Matthew Shepperson, 1823 (after Hoppner), was presented to Greenwich Hospital by George IV in 1824. It hangs (2012) in the School dining room, on loan from the National Maritime Museum.

Nelson connections

The School has always celebrated its connection with Admiral Lord Nelson, and observes Trafalgar Day every year. In 2008 a spectacular dinner commemorated the RHS's 75 years at Holbrook; in 2012 over 350 attended the tercentennary dinner and on Trafalgar Day 1924 Admiral of the Fleet Sir Doveton Sturdee gave the School some oak timbers removed from the *Victory* during her restoration for the future framing of a Nelson picture, along with a medallion made from her copper to be inset into the frame. Mr TD Maxwell permanently loaned a model of HMS *Royal George* and a framed copy of *The Times* containing Lord Collingwood's despatch from Trafalgar.

In 1958, the School was given the painting called *England expects every man to do his duty*, which shows the young Nelson and his grandmother 30 years before Trafalgar. The original was exhibited at the Royal Academy in 1883 and later went to South Africa.

On 15 October 2005, to commemorate the bicentenary of the Battle of Trafalgar, a new wood was planted in association with the Woodland Trust on an 11-acre site near the School. Each section of the wood was named after one of Nelson's ships at the battle. The first two oak trees were planted in Prince's Wood and these and a number of subsequent trees mark the positions of the ships at Trafalgar, as calculated long ago by old boy Captain Tizard *(see page 47).* A total of 4,000 trees were planted in accordance with the detailed plans of geography teacher, Lindsay Frost.

The School Heritage Centre exhibits a number of items associated with Nelson and in 2012 a spectacular battle was staged with indoor fireworks and light show at the RHS300 Trafalgar Dinner.

Photo: ANDREW PARTRIDGE

An admirable way to mark a Nelson link

Left: Entitled 'Nelson's farewell to his grandmother,' this chromolithograph depicts Nelson aged 13 in his new midshipman's uniform. The oil painting by Joy is to be found in the main entrance hall of the Royal Hospital School at Holbrook, where the accompanying label states it is the picture exhibited at the Royal Academy in 1883 and reproduced in Arthur Mee's Children's Encyclopaedia. It was presented to the School in February 1958 by the Rev. F Howard Sheldon, Vicar and Rural Dean of Reigate, Surrey.

Right: Junior pupils participate in a Lord Nelson and Lady Hamilton sponsored event. Pupils polished brasses, read flag signals, rowed whalers, sang the Naval Hymn and danced the hornpipe – all to raise money for the Heritage Centre.

The relationship between the two schools was not always good and sometimes even bitter, as evidenced by an Admiralty report confirming that 'in consequence of quarrels that had arisen… certain boys had absconded from the Hospital School, armed themselves with sticks and attacked the boys of the Asylum, in which one of the latter was severely cut in the arm with a knife'. In 1818 the ill-discipline of the Greenwich boys was attributed to the age and infirmity of their guardian, who was blind and had only one hand.

In 1821 the inevitable happened: three Lords of the Admiralty wrote to Lord Sidmouth to request that the king should combine the two schools with the management entrusted to Greenwich Hospital 'in order to produce a more effective and economical system of administration'. On 31 January 1821 a Royal Warrant consolidated the two schools and in April new regulations were issued with the king confirming 'that the School of Greenwich Hospital is now transferred to the Naval Asylum and the funds of the two schools incorporated'.

In effect, the Asylum was to subsume the Hospital School, with the funds of both merged and kept distinct from the Hospital's finances. An inspection of the Hospital School had shown up deficiencies, and it seemed clear that the merger of the two schools under new management and with new aims would be advantageous, both educationally and administratively. All the staff of the Royal Naval Asylum resigned *en masse* at this time, and the new overall Headmaster became William Terrott, who was also the Chaplain. In accordance with the *modus operandi* of the Asylum, a Captain of the Hospital would act as a non-teaching Superintendent, thus establishing the asylum system of dual control that persisted into the middle of the

20th century, with the Captain Superintendent in overall charge and the Headmaster with consequently diminished authority.

The two schools together now numbered 1,000 pupils, 800 boys and 200 girls. Doubts were now expressed about the presence of girls, but as they could be happily accommodated within the Queen's House, nothing was done at this stage to exclude them. The boys were divided into two groups, 200 in the Upper School (senior) and the remaining 600, along with the girls, forming the Lower School. The children of commissioned officers could now be admitted if they were 'real objects of charity'.

The 200-strong Upper School was the old Hospital School under a new name; entry to it remained the prerogative of the Hospital's directors, and there was no automatic right for any individual boy to progress up to it from the Lower School. Its offer of a superior education in navigation and other technical skills, with the prospect of an excellent career at sea, remained a privilege.

Orphans had priority for entry to the Lower School, with the full list subject to the approval of the directors as a body, and there was no educational test. But there was now a firm obligation on Lower School boys to join the Navy; their former right to choose such a career was revoked, and like Upper School boys they had to make that commitment as a condition of entry. Thus the original object of the British National Endeavour – to express gratitude for service given and lives laid down – was subsumed once again into the aim of becoming 'the cradle of the Navy'.

There was no longer a guardian or a drummer. Boatswain's mates, under a boatswain, took charge of the boys and nurses looked after the girls. There were nine teaching staff, three of them for the girls, and pupils who showed aptitude helped to teach their younger schoolmates. Mathematics and navigation remained central to the curriculum.

John and Charles Deane – the RHS's first inventors

Educated at the School from 1807 to about 1812, brothers John and Charles Deane became its first recorded inventors. They both became merchant seamen after leaving school, and Charles then became a caulker, a job which alerted him to the difficulties of fighting fires onboard ship. In the early 1820s John managed to rescue a stable full of horses trapped in a fire by putting on a medieval-style helmet and pumping air to it through a hose. The brothers then developed their 'smoke helmets', but had difficulty marketing them and so, with the help of Augustus Siebe, adapted them for use as diving helmets, loosely attached to a diving suit, to be used for salvage operations. Using their suit and helmet, they successfully recovered a cannon ball from Henry VIII's warship the *Mary Rose*, which had been lost off Portsmouth in 1545, and also salvaged 28 cannon from the wreck of HMS *Royal George* at Spithead. In 1836 the brothers published the world's first diving manual, *Method of Using Deane's Patent Diving Apparatus*, and John went on to become chief submarine engineer during the Crimean War.

Right: *Lithograph by E Wallis showing 'the preparations and mechanisms of Mr Deane's diving operation to explore the Royal George.' The ship sank in 1782 while at anchor at Spithead, and lay 60 feet under water. The Admiralty commissioned two brothers, John and Charles Deane, to work on the possible removal of the wreck. The Deanes had devised a diving apparatus consisting of a weighted helmet, into which air was pumped via a hose from a surface vessel. The diver used a weighted ladder to descend, had a signal line for communicating with the surface and was wearing the newly invented 'Deane's Patent Diving Apparatus, (August 1832).'*

The Greenwich Royal Hospital Schools

The 1820s were eventful years for the School. In 1825 there was another name change; the word 'Asylum' was removed, and the proper titles now became the Upper and Lower Schools of Greenwich Hospital. The name Royal Hospital School was not adopted formally until 1892, but that title was used as an abbreviation from the 1830s on.

At the beginning of 1828, the directors were informed that the Lord High Admiral wished to augment the numbers in the Upper School though the admission of 200 sons of distressed commissioned officers. This office within the Admiralty had been in abeyance but had been revived to provide a position for William, Duke of Clarence, George IV's brother and heir apparent, who had pursued a naval career. He took the job seriously (certainly more so than intended) and was determined to open the navigation classes of the Upper School to more sons of officers.

This order doubled numbers in the Upper School at a stroke, with the consequence that the Lower School could now accommodate only 400 boys, at a time when the demand for places was high and the plight of the children turned away distressing. It had further effects too, one of which was the difficulty of finding suitable places as apprentices for double the number of leavers. The answer was to widen the opportunities open to them; the Royal Navy would now take boys as 'second class volunteers', and there were also openings for those who showed talent in 'mechanical sciences' in the dockyards. Moreover, sons of commissioned officers would now be eligible only for the Upper School.

The other perceived difficulty arising from the increased numbers was simply dealt with. Since 1821 the master teaching navigation had been Edward Riddle, and he announced that he could easily accommodate

400 pupils in the large classrooms newly built next to the Queen's House provided he had a third assistant to add to the two already in place. A decade later his son John, aged only 15, joined the School in this capacity. Edward Riddle was a huge asset to the School. Just 33 years old when he arrived at Greenwich from the Trinity House School at Newcastle, he was already a renowned authority on astronomy as applied to navigation.

In the 1830s the Upper School was riding high. The opportunities open to its alumni were establishing its reputation worldwide, as they

Right: William, Duke of Clarence, brother of George IV and heir apparent – provided more direct royal input into the development of the School. He opened it up to more children and encouraged the study of navigation.

Edward Riddle (1786–1854) and John Riddle (1816–62) – academic rigour

Edward Riddle was born into a poor family in Northumberland, and his obvious intelligence soon brought him to attend a school run by Cuthbert Atkinson in West Woodburn. At the age of 18 he became a schoolmaster, and opened his own school shortly afterwards in Otterburn, where he demonstrated great enthusiasm for higher mathematics, astronomy, optics and navigation. He won prestigious mathematical prizes in 1814 and 1819, and became Master of Newcastle's Trinity House School, where he taught mathematics to Robert Stephenson, son of George Stephenson (of *Rocket* fame, who was himself self-taught, and hence considered his son's formal education, especially in mathematics, to be of considerable importance).

Riddle was erudite by any standard, and a great proponent and enthusiast for his subjects and pupils. It was his contention, contrary to most other teachers of navigation, that pupils would benefit greatly from a proper and thorough development of their subject which included 'concise and simple rules, with their investigations, for finding the latitude and longitude, and the variations of the compass, by celestial observations; the solution of other useful nautical problems; with an extensive series of examples for exercise'. He thus advocated real demonstrable understanding rather than learning by rote. Through his inspirational teaching he kindled huge enthusiasm in his pupils. His most valued work was a *Treatise on Navigation and Nautical Astronomy* (first edition 1824), which provided a complete course in mathematics for sailors, combining theory and practice in a way that had not been attempted before. It became one of the standard textbooks for ships' masters, and went through numerous editions, the eighth and final one appearing in 1864.

Between 1818 and 1847 he also published 16 papers on astronomical subjects, of which the most important were on nautical astronomy and on chronometers. In 1841, at the request of the Admiralty, Riddle's teaching techniques were scrutinised by Augustus de Morgan and Thomas Hall, professors of mathematics at University College and King's College respectively, who rapidly reached the conclusion that they were remarkably effective. Hall and de Morgan reported that the boys had answered all the questions with accuracy and enthusiasm and many, even from among the most ordinary, had the makings of fine navigators. One of Riddle's habits was to awaken his class in the middle of the night if there was some celestial body or event that could be clearly viewed, and by this means he kindled their astronomical curiosity. On his retirement in 1851 he was granted a lifetime pension equal to his full pay; he died in 1854.

Riddle was considered by his contemporaries to be one of the leading teachers of nautical science, and after his retirement many of his friends and former pupils expressed their appreciation by presenting him with his bust in marble, by the celebrated sculptor William Theed. At one time every officer in the Hydrographic Service except one was a former pupil of Riddle, and many of his pupils went on to found and head Board of Trade Schools of Navigation. Others, with highly honed calculation skills, were employed as 'computers' by the Royal Observatory and *Nautical Almanac* while others surveyed the distant lands of the empire: a truly remarkable legacy.

Edward Riddle's only son, John, was educated by his father, and at the age of 15 was appointed an assistant master in the Greenwich Hospital Schools. On the retirement of his father in 1851 he was chosen to succeed him as master. His success in teaching his young pupils not only the practice but also the theory of navigation was remarkable. Like his father, he was hugely enthusiastic about his subject and had a massive influence on his pupils, who benefited from his vigorous mind and rigorous methods and considered him unrivalled as a teacher. He died as the result of an accidental fall from a stool in his classroom while teaching in October 1862, tragically only eight years after his father.

Above: One of the earliest classroom photographs showing John Riddle teaching c1850.

used their skills to explore and survey far-flung lands and chart the little-known oceans; the department of the Admiralty respons ible for the latter work was soon staffed almost entirely by old boys of the School. In 1831 the Greenwich Hospital School medal was introduced for Upper School leavers to encourage good conduct, with a similar smaller medal offered to the Lower School from about 1835. Both carried Nelson's head and the inscription *Palmam meruit ferat* – 'let he who has earned it bear the palm' – which was Nelson's motto, on the funeral car.

But while the Upper School flourished, the Lower School was not meeting the standards required. An inspection in 1840 reported that at least half of the pupils could not read and were therefore unsuitable for a naval career, and that the education the girls were receiving was worth little, as well as promoting unwelcome 'evil communications'. It was therefore decided that the girls' school would close, and that the Upper School would be further subdivided, with the creation of a separate Nautical School.

By April 1841 all the girls were gone, bar one Catherine Brennan, an orphan from the Ascension Islands, who had no family or friends to go to; she was apprenticed to a straw-bonnet maker in Greenwich, with a bounty of £10. The last known 'old girl', Mrs Kirkham (1826 to 1832), is recorded as having died aged 97 in 1914. She had been presented with a medal on Prize Day 1832 by King William IV, and when in 1925 her daughter, Mrs Wilkins, visited the School in

Greenwich, that medal was still in the possession of the family, now resident in Canada. Girls being educated at the School were not to be seen there again until exactly 150 years later.

It was only the brightest who benefited from the teaching of the Riddles, in the even more rarefied atmosphere of the new Nautical School, which was by now the globally recognised leading school in the instruction of navigators. For the rest of the Upper School and the Lower School, the teaching was not always of a comparable standard. Moreover, discipline was harsh. The inspectors were reported as being very unhappy about the frequency of beatings, added to further punishments such as being padlocked to a hammock stanchion with arms held in a strait-waistcoat. The clerk who recorded the names of the boys leaving the School once wrote that they had completed their period of 'servitude' rather than 'education'. Moreover, deaths from the common childhood illnesses of the time were so frequent that a mortuary was built next to the infirmary. Life at the School was, for some, 'nasty, brutish and short'.

To counter this brutality the 1840 inspection decided to abolish the office of Superintendent, in charge of discipline, which would now be left to the perhaps gentler ministrations of the Headmaster. So better, more caring management appeared to be in the offing. However, a new government in 1841 meant new appointments, and tensions within the schools led to a reversion to old attitudes. The office of Superintendent

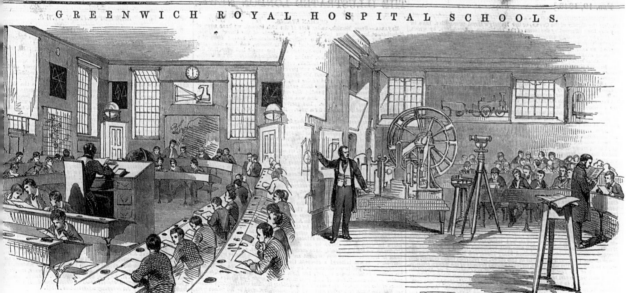

THE ILLUSTRATED LONDON NEWS. [FEB. 19, 1848.

GREENWICH ROYAL HOSPITAL SCHOOLS.

UPPER SCHOOL.—THE REV. J. HILL'S CLASS-ROOM.—MATHEMATICS AND OPTICS.

LOWER SCHOOL.—LESSON ON STEAM MACHINERY.—MR. E. HUGHES, HEAD-MASTER.

Opposite inset: Rev. George Fisher did much to advance scientific studies at the School, including the introduction of astronomy. A collection of scientific instruments used at the School by him and others is held at the National Maritime Museum.

Left: The changes instigated in the early 1840s were significant and the Illustrated London News article dated 19 February 1848 illustrated how school life at the Greenwich Hospital Schools was evolving. There were illustrations of Rev. Hill teaching mathematics and a lesson on steam machinery by Edward Hughes; both these masters drove up academic standards at the School. Other images included gym work, exercising on guns, sail making, blacksmiths and sextant work, the lavatory (washroom), dormitory, marching to the dining hall, dinner and chapel.

George Fisher – Arctic explorer, Chaplain and Headmaster

In 1834 the Rev. George Fisher *(inset)* joined the School as Chaplain and Headmaster. He was a man of distinction – an astronomer and scientist who had been educated at Cambridge and was elected a fellow of both the Royal Society and the Royal Astronomical Society. Having taken holy orders specifically so that he could be a naval Chaplain, he served in that capacity in a number of ships. He was also an Arctic explorer as part of William Parry's unsuccessful 1822 expedition to find a North-West Passage, during which he conducted many experiments which proved of great value to navigators in high latitudes. In 1857 Fisher was awarded the Arctic Medal for his contribution, the only Chaplain to be honoured in this way. A man of questing intelligence, he is credited with introducing the new technology of photography to the School, and it was probably he who took the photograph of John Riddle in his classroom, which is one of a number of such early School photographs. He was also instrumental in the building of the School observatory which Edward Riddle had initiated. Following restructuring of the School, Fisher was appointed Principal in 1856. He retired in 1863, and his pioneering work on educational attainment testing is still widely admired by educationalists 150 years later.

Arctic exploration – the Franklin expeditions

The first known School pupil to be involved in Arctic exploration was William John Samuel Pullen, who was born in 1813 in Devonport and attended the School in the 1820s. After joining the Navy and serving in the Mediterranean, he did surveying work in Southern Australia before rejoining the Navy and being quickly promoted to commissioned rank. He then accepted a position on HMS *Plover* which was due to sail to the Bering Strait to look for signs of the Franklin expedition. He was there for two years engaged on the fruitless search before returning to Britain and again setting out for the Arctic in command of the store ship in Sir Edward Belcher's expedition. His later career was spent all over the world, in action against the Russians, in operations in the Middle East and again involved in surveying work in Ceylon (now Sri Lanka) and the Caribbean. He was promoted first to Rear-Admiral and then to Vice-Admiral, and was granted a Greenwich Hospital pension shortly before he died.

A great many other RHS boys were involved in the Arctic after Sir John Franklin and his ships the *Erebus* and the *Terror* went missing after 1845 as they sought the North-West Passage. In 1852 a schools' inspector praised the RHS for supplying 'a large proportion of officers selected for the present Arctic expeditions', some 42 of which went looking for Franklin's missing party until the end of the 1850s. One of them, Robert Calder Allen (1824–27), who had been educated by Edward Riddle, became Master of the *Resolute* during the search expeditions of 1850–51, in the course of which his crew published at least five handwritten newspapers called *The Illustrated Arctic News*. Similarly, Riddle educated George Frederick McDougall, the accomplished surveyor, artist and author of *The Voyage of the Resolute*.

William Parker Snow (1827–31) was yet another. While working as an author in New York, he claimed to have had a paranormal vision of the whereabouts of the missing Franklin expedition. He was then commissioned to serve on Lady Franklin's expedition in the *Prince Albert*, which inspired a book and after having made his fortune in the Australian Gold Rush he decided to launch another search from Australia. He went on to travel and write extensively about the Arctic, the Falkland Islands, Patagonia, Tierra de Fuego and Australia (the people and the places). He was awarded the Polar Medal and was buried with it on his death in 1895. The Franklin expedition also claimed the life of the father of one of the boys attending the School, Charles Henry Wentzell (1853–56) and his mother lived on to the age of 95, becoming the last surviving widow of the expedition.

Right: Many Greenwich Hospital boys were involved in the search for the Franklin Expedition (inset above). George Frederick McDougall put his skills to good effect, illustrating the journey of the Resolute, *as in this view of 'Sledge Parties departing from the* Resolute *and* Intrepid' *(1857).*

Monitors and pupil teachers

The first 'pupil teacher' at the School was probably Thomas Lancey (1779), who had dislocated his thigh and so was unable to enter the Navy; he went on to be Headmaster from 1800 to 1821. Able pupils were often appointed as monitors to help the teachers, who frequently struggled with classes that were too large. By 1842, each master had 55 pupils to teach in the Nautical School, 90 in the Upper School and 78 in the Lower School. As a result, particularly in the Lower School where entry was not subject to any sort of educational test, many boys left without having received any useful education at all, many of them not even able to read.

The decision was therefore taken to increase the number of monitors, who were chosen from the ranks of the boys, and give them extra instruction to allow them to teach their schoolfellows. This measure, plus the appointment of more masters in the Upper School, considerably reduced class sizes and resulted not just in educational improvement but also in much better discipline.

In the 1850s the monitors were replaced by pupil teachers, selected at the age of 15 'from among those boys willing to adopt the profession of the teacher, who are best instructed and most apt to teach'. They enjoyed a small salary, extra tuition, a separate table at meals and accommodation in the Queen's House. From these beginnings, the School became a well-respected teachers' training institution, supplying numbers of teachers to other schools both locally

(at least 50 went to schools in South East London) and further away. One pupil teacher, Charles Isaacs, stayed at the School for 40 years, becoming Headmaster of the School he'd attended. Similarly, Joseph Evans was an exceptional pupil then pupil teacher who went on to complete his degree at University College, London, before undertaking prominent educational posts in the UK and abroad and then returning to lead his old school into the 20th century.

Yet another was James Baker, who was associated with the School for 55 years, joining the Lower School aged ten in August 1852 before becoming a pupil teacher in 1857 and master in 1861. He was for many years master in charge of cricket and was a great example of long service. Upon his retirement in 1907 he was presented with an album, an inkstand and a purse containing £82 19s.

Many of those who had cut their teeth at the RHS went on to long service and senior positions elsewhere. WHT Pain, who left in 1871, became Headmaster of the training establishment HMS *Fisgard* in 1903 and served for 19 years, increasing apprentices from 47 to 864. Another was Zebedee Scaping, who was said to be known 'in every port and on every sea' after becoming Headmaster of the Trinity House School, Hull. Scaping served an astonishing 55 years in post; he may hold the record as the longest-serving headmaster in Britain or even the world.

In 1883 the pupil-teacher system was abolished and those in post were made up to assistant masters; the last known pupil teacher at the School retired in 1926. They may, however, have made a contribution to the School jargon that survived long after them. When Dan Turner was at the RHS in the 1920s, staff were known not as 'Mr Smith' but as 'PD Smith'. He was told that the PD stood for 'punishment deliverer' – aptly, as he notes – but it is more likely to have been a derivation of PT for 'pupil teacher' or PD for 'pupil demonstrator'.

Above: Zebedee Scaping, Headmaster at Hull Trinity School with an astronomy class in 1873. His time as a pupil teacher at Greenwich prepared him for headship and remarkably he directed this Hull school for 55 years (1854–1909), supporting many boys as they prepared for a life on the ocean waves.

was quickly re-established – and the Lower School boys reacted, on 23 December 1841, by calmly and efficiently breaking every pane of glass in their schoolrooms, dormitories and chapel before parade in the morning. They behaved with perfect discipline for the rest of the day. Their meat ration was stopped until the windows were paid for and 16 boys were flogged, with others running away to escape punishment. That retribution was not more widespread was attributed to the intervention of the one legged Lieutenant John Wood Rouse, who had taken on the reinstated post of School Superintendent. He was well known for his light touch with the pupils and stayed in his post until May 1857 – and it was he who now decided that the education of his pupils would be greatly enhanced if they had a block ship on which to practice naval skills. He therefore set about building what was to be the first of a series of three training ships, the final one of which was *Fame (see page 48)*.

Above: J Hill, Headmaster of the Upper School from 1844 to 1860, retiring in 1870. His son, Rowland Hill, born in the Queen's House, was knighted for services to Rugby Union.

Right: Greenwich Hospital School Silver Medal for 1838 awarded to Alfred Balliston (1834–38), later knighted (1883).

RHS knights – honoured

Sir Alfred Balliston was born in 1823 and attended the School from 1835 to 1838, winning the silver medal in his final year and immediately joining the Royal Navy as a master's assistant. He was quickly promoted to master and, upon reorganisation of his branch, Navigation Lieutenant and eventually Staff Captain, the highest rank to which a member of his branch could aspire. He commanded the royal yachts *Elfin* and *Alberta* from 1849 until his retirement in 1883, when he was presented by Queen Victoria with a 'handsome silver cup, standing 11in high, in a beautiful oak case' bearing the inscription 'Presented by Queen Victoria to Staff Captain Sir Alfred Balliston, in remembrance of his services during 34 years in the royal yachts, 1883', with the royal monogram and the crown star engraved on the other side. He was knighted that same year, having been Serjeant-at-Arms to the Queen and a JP for Hampshire. He died in 1895.

Sir Gilbert Thomas Carter (1858–63) joined the colonial service after leaving school and held several senior colonial positions in the Leeward Islands, the Gold Coast and the Gambia before being knighted and appointed in 1891 as Governor of the Lagos Colonies (modern-day Nigeria). He was involved in wars and conflicts in Africa, played a pivotal role in ending slavery and sourced early African tribal art. He went on to become Governor of the Bahamas, Barbados and Trinidad and Tobago, and designed and built his own retirement house in Barbados. This house, called Illaro Court after one of his Nigerian homes, is now the official residence of the Prime Minister of Barbados. His son Humphrey became the first academic Director of the Cambridge Botanical Gardens from 1915 to 1951.

Other RHS knights include Sir Henry Felix Woods, Sir Joseph Kinsey, Sir Benjamin Martin, Sir Sidney Frew and Sir Philip Enright (see later vignettes).

Right: Photograph presented to the School of Gilbert Thomas Carter (1858–63), later knighted (1893).

The minor insurrection was a salutary wake-up call for the authorities. An inquiry into the reasons for it elicited the information that the boys were protesting about the uninspired teaching and the rigidity of the discipline under which they lived. To the credit of the School administrators, they listened. In 1844 two new appointments were Rev. James Hill as Headmaster of the Upper School and Edward Hughes as Headmaster of the Lower School, both of whom served in their posts for over 15 years and provided further academic rigour and continuity. Perhaps the most significant decision by the Admiralty was the provision of more teachers and monitors – a new institution, of whom four were initially appointed. Their numbers eventually rose to 16, half of whom supported reading classes. In just one year punishments fell from 160 to 28 and boys absconding fell from 28 to eight.

Rev. Canon Henry Moseley, who had for 15 years been one of the inspectors and who was an eminent mathematician, a professor at King's College, London, and a Chaplain to the Queen, later reported on the transformation of the School. The developments were, he said, 'the boldest experiment of which I have knowledge. I consider it the most successful. The masters have been well selected and the chief reason for success is the moral control of the masters over the boys.' Beatings had reduced hugely and the numbers of boys going to sea had doubled. As Moseley went on to report, the Upper School 'is far beyond any other known to me in scientific attainment. I know of none in which the different elements of an English education are more efficiently taught.'

Astronomy: time and stars

It was Edward Riddle who planned and gained approval for the School to have an observatory. Work on it began in 1849, two years before he retired in 1851, the year in which the astronomer Henry Lawson presented his fine 11-foot refracting telescope to the School. The observatory opened in 1859 and was equipped with Lawson's gift as well as instruments given to the Admiralty which had originally been made for the observatory in St Helena. The School's observatory initially had two domes, with a third added in 1864. The School also maintained close links with the nearby Royal Observatory Greenwich and many pupils went on to work in the field of astronomical observation throughout the world.

In 1881 Thomas Lewis, who had been educated at the School, was appointed 'Superintendent of time' at the Royal Observatory. After training as a teacher he entered the civil service as an appointee of Sir William Christie, Astronomer Royal, and was in charge of naval chronometers for 35 years, including most of the Great War. George Biddell Airy had established Greenwich Mean Time which, in 1884, was adopted as the international standard. The School's location effectively on the Prime Meridian at Greenwich placed it at the heart of global time and space in an ever shrinking and globalised world.

Lewis was also a renowned astronomer, writing about double star observations and winning international recognition. He edited the *Observatory Magazine* and was Secretary to the Royal Astronomical Society. He was a close friend of the School's Headmaster, Joseph Evans, also a noted astronomer, who had been both a pupil and a pupil teacher at the RHS. On Evans' retirement in 1920, the formal teaching of navigation and astronomy ended and by 1926 the observatory had fallen into disuse.

THE CANALS ON MARS

Walter Maunder, Superintendent of the solar department of the Royal Observatory, in 1902 and 1903 used the pupils of the Royal Hospital School, with their highly regarded visual acuity and observational powers, to test whether the human perception of canal-like features on the face of Mars was due to the existence of canals there or other visual artefacts.

In *Are the Planets Inhabited?* he describes an experiment designed by himself where the lines are not actual images, but are suggested by markings perceived but not perfectly defined. In conjunction with Evans, the School's Headmaster, he tried a number of experiments on this point, with the aid of about 200 of the boys. They were well suited to this, being keen-sighted, well drilled and accustomed to do what they were told without asking questions; and they knew nothing whatsoever about astronomy, certainly nothing about Mars.

Maunder's experiment involved a diagram based on an astronomical drawing of Mars, but with no canals; only a few dots or irregular markings were put in here and there. The boys were placed at different distances from the diagram and told to draw exactly what they saw. It was clear from the results that the apparent canals were only 'visible' by the boys who were too far away from the diagram to see the separate little irregular markings but could perceive them as what appeared to be a series of straight lines. These experiments were merely the repetition of similar ones that Maunder had made privately 12 years earlier, and they led him to conclude quite firmly that there were no canals on Mars, and therefore no Martians!

In the 1860s the future of Greenwich Hospital itself was the subject of much debate. Numbers of Pensioners had fallen radically in a preiod withour naval warfare and out-pensions became a much preferred option for those who had been injured or grown old in service: the wherewithal to live at home with their families was increasingly seen as a better option than a dull and dreary monastic existence at Greenwich. In 1869 the last of them left, and the main hospital buildings that had housed them lay empty, until in 1873 the Admiralty moved the Royal Naval College from Portsmouth to Greenwich.

This change saw control of the School more completely transferred to the Admiralty, which reviewed the curriculum and introduced further

Left: Former pupil and pupil teacher Thomas Lewis (1867–70) at the eyepiece of the 28-inch telescope at the Royal Observatory, Greenwich. There are records of many RHS boys who went on to work there.

Hydrographers and master mariners

Edward Killwick Calver was educated at the School from 1824 to 1828, after which he joined the Navy and rapidly moved to the Hydrographic Department. He went on to survey and chart the whole of the eastern coastal waters of Great Britain as well as large tracts of the Atlantic and the Mediterranean. He undertook scientific research into coastal tides and oceanic depths and had great influence over the use of tidal waters and harbours. He served a total of 44 years in the department before being elected a Fellow of the Royal Society in 1873. He died in Switzerland in 1892 and is the only RHS boy to have had a couple of sea urchins and a coral species named after him.

Master navigator and former RHS pupil Henry Davenport Sarratt was on hand when, on 14 October 1877, reports were received that Cleopatra's Needle was abandoned and sinking in the Bay of Biscay on its way from Egypt. Sarratt pinpointed the spot where the tow would most likely have been cast adrift and was able to rescue the 3,500-year-old obelisk. It now stands on the Embankment of the Thames as a monument to victory over Napoleon. Sarratt's naval career was a distinguished one. He was involved in suppressing piracy in the China Wars and in the taking of Alexandria in 1882, and in 1863 commanded the *Victoria and Albert II* when it brought Princess Alexandra of Denmark to marry the Prince of Wales, later Edward VII. He was offered a knighthood, which he refused as he felt that on his captain's pay he could not afford the standard of living expected of a man of that rank.

Captain Thomas Henry Tizard, oceanographer, hydrographic surveyor and navigator, was one of the most prominent men in the field during his career. After school, in 1854, he entered the Navy as a master's assistant, and between 1868 and 1879 was employed in survey ships in the Mediterranean and the Red Sea, serving with Captain (later Sir) George Strong Nares. He commanded the first ship to pass through the Suez Canal in 1869 and spent the next three years surveying the Gulf of Suez for the benefit of the increasing number of ships using this route through to the Red Sea. He also discovered the deep, high salinity current that passed through the Straits of Gibraltar.

In 1872 Tizard joined the *Challenger* expedition, commanded by Nares, as Navigating Officer. He was therefore involved from the beginning in the then new science of oceanography, and took an important and leading part in its development. He continued his work in *Challenger* and then *President* until 1891 when he was appointed Assistant Hydrographer of the Navy. In the same year he was elected Fellow of the Royal Society in recognition of his contributions to oceanographical knowledge. After retiring with the rank of Captain in 1896 he continued for some time to write and edit various Admiralty publications, among which the tide tables for the coast of England were perhaps the most important. His final work was to assist the committee appointed by the Admiralty in 1912 to examine Nelson's tactics at the Battle of Trafalgar. An exhaustive examination of ships' logs and journals enabled him to prepare the first plans of every phase of the battle drawn exactly to scale. Tizard died in 1924. His son was Sir Henry Tizard, after whom a secret wartime committee was named.

Top: *The specially designed vessel (and its model,* **inset***) that was located by former pupil, Henry Davenport Sarratt with the encapsulated 180-tonne Egyptian obelisk, Cleopatra's Needle, intact.*

Left: *Cartoon sketch entitled 'Intellectual conversation at the smoking circle', by Captain Thomas Henry Tizard, possibly a self-portrait.*

Far left: *Portrait of Tizard. Many of his oceanographic charts relating to the Mediterranean, Red Sea, Suez, Gibraltar and the Arctic are held at the National Maritime Museum.*

High achievers: 19th-century trade and aid

ESTD 1835

George Steuart

George Steuart & Co is the oldest known company established by a former pupil still trading today, and proudly claims to be the oldest mercantile establishment in Sri Lanka. The company was founded in 1835 by James Steuart, who left the School in 1805 to become an intrepid and highly principled sea Captain. He sailed the Southern Ocean and eventually arrived in Ceylon in 1818 to exploit the immense potential for economic development and commerce there. He initially set himself up as a merchant banker, bought extensive land between Colombo and Galle and became a pioneering importer. The company passed through the hands of his brothers Joseph and George, and after they had left in 1863 the 'coffee crash' saw a move into tea.

At its centenary in 1935 it was proclaimed that the firm had 'weathered the storms of wars and depressions and stood as a shining example of British enterprise and business acumen'. Over the years the company has reinvented itself many times, recovering from the nationalisation of the tea plantations in the mid-1970s and the carnage left at its Colombo head office by the Central Bank bomb in 1996. It is a leader in the export of tea, the distribution of pharmaceuticals, travel and ticketing, airline representation, property development, the assembly of telephones and other electronic products, freight forwarding, insurance, higher education and the recruitment of Sri Lankan professionals for reputable principals overseas. Today's chairman puts the company's success down to the grit and spirit, blended with honesty, that have been handed down by its founder, James Steuart.

Charles Henry Wentzell (1853–56), an orphan of the Franklin Expedition initially pursued a traditional career in the Navy, where he became involved in the quelling of the Indian Mutiny and later the Opium Wars. On leaving the Navy he became a ship's engineer, and later worked for governments all over the world, notably in the cause of famine relief – an early example of international aid. When he returned to India to help those suffering from the Bengal famine in the 1870s he may well have found himself involved with people he had fought against in the mutiny.

A top sportsman while he was at school, Edwin Heather (1875–78) served in the Navy for over 40 years and travelled all over the world, becoming actively involved in suppressing the slave trade. He was Secretary to Lord Kitchener and highly decorated in the Great War. He went on to become Grand Master of the Oddfellows (a longstanding and Friendly Society), working closely with major insurance companies and the government to support the interests of 1.5 million members and manage over £23 million of capital.

HJA Wilkins (1876–80) subsequently gained national and international distinction as a major figure in the cooperative movement. In 1924 he was elected chairman of the Cooperative Wholesale Society, a role which led to him visiting all parts of the world and meeting with presidents and royalty as he fostered commercial relations worldwide. He confirmed that his schooling had taught him 'to recognise that we must be mates if we are to row together across the great seas of life'.

Left: The visit of the Shah of Persia to the Royal Hospital School in 1873. The boys are lined up for inspection. The training ship Fame *is on the right* – Illustrated London News, *5 July 1873.*

reforms, reorganising it into three divisions – the Nautical School Junior Division (full time), the Nautical School Senior Division (targeted at developing naval trades on alternate days) and the Upper Nautical School (which would educate the cleverest boys of any age), recruited by open competition twice yearly. Captain Charles Burney, the new Superintendent appointed in August 1870, introduced Navy uniforms, strict discipline and order; and in 1872 the Admiralty decreed that all boys leaving the School must enter the Royal Navy unless found unfit, in which case they were bound for the Merchant Navy!

A pattern of improvement, decline and reform persisted through the mid to late 19th century with glowing reports alternating with stories

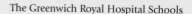

Left: *An 1860s sheet-music cover for 'Les Petits Matelots' as performed by the School band. It shows a divisions ceremony for an unidentified Royal visitor and the viewpoint is from the Queen's House towards the School drill ship, with her yards manned, safety net stretched out below and flying the Royal Standard.*

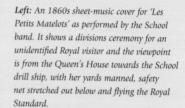

Above: *Attainment and Good Conduct Medal awarded to George F Grant in 1876.*

of punishments and boys running away. A report commissioned by the Admiralty, from a committee which included the able and far-seeing Dilkes Loveless as its secretary and researcher, recommended that the purpose of the School should now move away from feeding boys into the Navy to offering the sons of seafarers the widest education they were capable of receiving, with the aim of fitting them for careers of their own choosing. In the Upper School, the teaching of mathematics and navigation should remain a priority, but only for those who would benefit from it and who intended to use it to ready themselves for a career at sea. The others should receive a sound education, including French and Latin, which would enable them to move on to a variety of callings.

Many of those in the Lower School, the report concluded, failed to profit from the teaching of subjects for which they were not academically equipped. For them, a sound elementary education should lead to the brightest moving on to the more rigorous disciplines of the Upper School, while the others learnt trades. The commitment to join the Navy should be removed, but there should be incentives for those deciding on a naval career including, for the bright boys who became teachers, the encouragement to become naval instructors. Unfortunately, this wise report was too much for the powers that be, and under Burney industrial training became the new approach and the

HEAD MASTER 1870-1891.

NATIONAL MARITIME MUSEUM, GREENWICH.   PROPOSED DAIS. ETC. FOR ROYAL OPENING. 1937.   H.M. OFFICE OF WORKS, PUBLISHED, BEVEDO WESTMINSTER

Left: *Albert Escott, Headmaster from 1870 to 1891.*

Above: *Neptune's Hall, built 1873, provided a multi-purpose space – gymnasium, assembly hall and meeting place – this is the design for its use by King George VI to open the National Maritime Museum on 27 April 1937.*

needs of the Navy remained paramount, with Lower School boys still compelled to commit to a naval career.

A high point at this time was the erection of the gymnasium (Neptune's Hall) in 1873 with a large stage and decorated proscenium arch. It was to become the most-used building in the School, housing assemblies, presentations and speech days, as well as serving as a meeting-cum-living room. It sat in a courtyard formed by an L-shaped western extension of 1862 and south west wing added in 1876 holding the new dining room. In another positive move, in 1874, Captain Burney conceived the idea of naming dormitories after admirals and placing in each an oil painting of its patron. The dormitories which subscribed most to the purchase of the portraits would have first choice of admiral. There was fierce rivalry between dormitories 1A and 2 to gain the first nomination; and 1A was duped into choosing the Duke of Edinburgh, who had recently visited the School, while dormitary 2 secured the prize of Lord Nelson. However, the boys were still formally grouped into numbered companies for organisational purposes.

By 1881 no fewer than 18 trades were being taught, ranging from carpentry through to bricklaying, sock mending and laundry repair. But there was no movement between specialities; a boy working in the laundry, for example, never moved on to learn another skill, even to the point that one boy would be taught exclusively to heel a shoe

while another did the sole. Conditions were appalling: 1,000 crammed into accommodation that had been a tight squeeze for 800, and lighting so poor that many boys were rejected for the Navy because they were short-sighted.

The navigational education was still good, but as the Headmaster of the time, Albert Escott, reported, the opportunities for his boys were few and far between. Indeed, in the early 1880s a number of Admiralty committees considered closure of the School, suggesting that the state could in future be relied on for the necessary education for the Navy. However, nothing came of this and by the mid-1880s the School had turned a corner and instigated further improvements. Of the 300 who left in 1885, 167 went to sea, and two years later it was reported that 'from among these boys will come some of the best petty officers of the Navy'. Between 1874 and 1930 the School could go on to claim over 10,000 entrants to the Royal Navy.

A useful development in 1886 was the arrival of day boys from Sir William Boreman's school, a local foundation also dedicated to the education of seafarers and 40 years older than the RHS. Its entrants had to be Greenwich-born and the sons of seamen, watermen or fishermen; their £10 a year was a welcome addition to the School's finances. The small improvements in conditions that various committees had put in place now resulted in more recruitment to the Navy.

The Boreman Foundation

William Boreman (d. 1686) was appointed kepper of Greenwich Park in 1660, on the restoration of the monarchy, and knighted the following year. He later became Lord of the Manor of Greenwich, and founded a school there in 1672 on the north side of what is now Greenwich High Road. It was called the Greenwich Collegiate School, and initially admitted 20 boys who would receive an education with a naval bias. Samuel Pepys advised on matters of uniform, attendance times and curriculum. In his will of 1684 Sir William bequeathed the school, adjacent land and other property interests to the Drapers' Company, who still maintain the charity today. With this valuable endowment the school remained on the same site for some 200 years, educating both collegers and fee-paying day boys.

By 1773 the school was in serious financial difficulties and was closed for several years. It reopened in 1778 and functioned successfully until 1874 when its site was compulsorily acquired for the extension of the South-Eastern Railway. After a few years as a day school, in temporary premises, in 1886 a new scheme of the Charity Commissioners provided for Boreman Foundationers to be educated as day boys in the Hospital School with their distinct badges and 'greencoat' uniform.

The Boreman boys joined the Upper Nautical Division of the Hospital School, adding £1,000 a year to the coffers through their fees. They always remained separate from the rest of the School, and not just because they were day boys who went home to their families at the end of each day. As a Boreman boy who was one of the 100 who were at the School from 1919 until 1923 recalled, 'We wore a badge on the right arm with the Boreman coat of arms and "Boreman Foundation" on the cap ribbon. Apart from this our uniform was identical with that of No 9 Company of Greenwich School [the Upper Nautical]…'. They were organised into four classes and taught separately, though their curriculum was very similar to that of the Greenwich boys.

Many Boreman boys went on to distinguished service at sea and elsewhere, though they were under no obligation to become seafarers at the end of their school years despite the requirement to express the intention of doing so at enrolment. This was perhaps one of the differences in status which caused bad feeling between the two camps at the School. Letters held in the archive from both sides record battles and harassment, fuelled by differences in uniform and education and exacerbated by the resentment felt by the resident Greenwich boys that their counterparts were able to be with their families and enjoy 'civvy' life. As Dan Turner said, they were 'able to go "outside", without suffering what those who were left behind had to endure'.

Towards the end of the 1920s, when it was known that the School was soon to leave Greenwich, the

Above: Sir William Boreman with (inset) the brass plaque from the reception hall at Holbrook.

Below: A Boreman Boy jacket along with various badges and cap tallies – donated by former pupils who were very proud to have attended the Royal Hospital School as day pupils.

numbers were reduced and the last Boreman Foundation boy, George Frederick Berry, left in December 1931 to join HMS *Fisgard* as an engine room artificer apprentice. He was on the *Prince of Wales* when she was sunk in December 1941, and either drowned or ended his days as a Japanese prisoner of war.

There was a later link. In 1965 the Drapers' Company, as trustees for the Boreman Foundation, agreed to sponsor not more than two seafarers' sons a year, with a preference for boys from Greenwich. This idea had come from HJ Hoare, who had been a Boreman boy in 1892. He had been an enthusiastic and energetic treasurer of the school's Old Boys' Association, and now gave the School a replica of a portrait of Sir William Boreman and a plaque celebrating the connection. The foundation itself still provides awards for the education and training of young people resident in Greenwich and Lewisham.

The Royal Hospital School

In 1892 the name that had been used informally for the School since the 1830s became its proper title – and royal interest and involvement in the Royal Hospital School in the final decades of the 19th century was marked with a series of prominent royal visits. In July 1886 Prince Albert Victor completed the School inspection, and this was followed by a visit in Queen Victoria's Golden Jubilee year of 1887 by the Prince of Wales's second son, George – later to be King George V – who was a naval man and an alumnus of the Royal Naval College. The Prince of Wales himself came in 1889 with his wife and three princesses.

In 1894, to celebrate the bicentenary of Greenwich Hospital, a special train took the Superintendent (Commander George Huntingford), Headmaster (Mr George Pulsford), the staff and over 1,000 boys to Windsor, where they paraded on the east lawn of the castle and marched past the Queen, who took their salute. Before being given refreshments, they formed up 'in open interval formation in front of the Queen and performed a series of dumb bell practices and pole drill to musical accompaniment by the band of the School'.

The School was beginning to feel the winds of external change, as education became more widespread and indeed, from the 1880s, compulsory. Local Education Authorities were introduced in 1902, which put the funding and management of local schools on a sounder footing. All this meant that there were many more well educated boys from among the general populace who could compete for the places in institutions like the Royal Navy, which had previously been filled only from specialist schools.

Nevertheless, the Royal Hospital School continued to act as 'the cradle of the Navy', with the proportion of boys going on to a career in the Navy or the dockyards rising from 28 per cent in 1886 to 76 per cent in 1906. But although the bulk of the boys leaving the School were still going into the services, it was often into more menial occupations than they might have expected in earlier years. The boys in the School band were an exception: half of the 60-strong complement were assured of places in the Royal Marines. But meanwhile the curriculum was being broadened to take account of new technologies and to equip the boys for the increasingly competitive world outside their tight boundaries.

The sons of commissioned officers were no longer eligible for entry to the RHS, except in special circumstances, and for the Lower School the orphans of Warrant Officers, petty officers and seamen had priority, followed by the sons of serving men and after that the sons of Pensioners. In 1895 the Lower School had applied to be classed as

Postcard photograph of the Buckingham Palace inspection of the School by HM King Edward VII.

G.P.&O.S.(COPYRIGHT). 196.

a 'public elementary school', which made it eligible for a government grant, and in 1905 the regulations of the Upper School too were revised in order to qualify for public funding – though in the event there were too many criteria that the School could not meet. One of these was the anomalous status of the Headmaster who, although he had to supervise education in the whole School and himself teach in the Upper Nautical, was still subordinate to the Superintendent.

In July 1907, *The Royal Hospital School Magazine* was launched and old boys were encouraged to write in with their stories and experiences. That the School was engendering a sense of loyalty among its alumni is evident from the magazine for July 1915 which included responses from men serving in no fewer than 174 ships. In 1909 the celebratory publication '*Souvenir Album of the Royal Hospital School Greenwich*' further promoted the School with a fabulous series of photographs showing views of the buildings and boys at Greenwich.

The School continued to enjoy strong links with royalty. On 20 March 1908 the Prince and Princess of Wales and Prince Albert visited the School, with the band greeting them at the front gates with the National Anthem. A pupil called WJ Windsor demonstrated sail-making to the royal visitors and the two 'houses of Windsor' went on to meet again in 1915 when the prince visited Dunkerque and asked directions from Windsor to HMS *Excellent*, and then again in 1928 when the prince met him on a visit to the TB colony at Papworth Hall in Cambridgeshire.

And then on 9 July 1909 the whole School of 1,040 boys accompanied by 50 staff were invited to Buckingham Palace by the King. After they were greeted by the King and Queen, Princess Victoria and Prince Christopher of Greece, the band played the National Anthem and the School marched to '*A Life on the Ocean Waves*', followed by a gymnastic display and a dozen boys dancing the hornpipe.

Above: Invitation to attend Buckingham Palace on 9 July 1909, along with details of those attending.

Below: After the salute, march past and indian club drill, 12 boys danced the hornpipe. The king complimented 'the lads' on their smart and healthy appearance.

R.H. SCHOOL, GREENWICH.
INSPECTION BY H.M. THE KING
AT BUCKINGHAM PALACE ∽—
—∽ JULY. 9, 1909. ∼

The Royal Hospital School Magazine

The Royal Hospital School Magazine was published every term from 1907 on, and ran to 75 editions through to the School's move to Holbrook in 1933. It helped to establish the School within its historical context and created a deep sense of belonging. It was circulated to all naval ships and establishments and old boys were encouraged to relate their experiences and memories of their schooldays and beyond.

Its editor for some years was NS Amess, who joined in 1920, taught maths, ran the First XI football team for 23 years, at Greenwich and at Holbrook, and was at the School until 1957. The final edition of the first series of School magazines, number 75, was published in March 1933 as the School prepared for its move to Holbrook. In it the Chaplain looked to the future: 'Let us think of Holbrook with its green fields stretching down to the river, its sunlight and unsullied air, its spacious quarters, the new life which is to begin there and say God be with the new school as he has been with the old.' And Captain Edmund Cooper-Key, the Superintendent, wrote that he was 'very confident that in addition to all the baggage and paraphernalia that will be taken to the new anchorage the grand old traditions of the School will not be forgotten – traditions that have bought success to a large number'.

The Royal Hospital School Magazine was in abeyance until April 1935 when it was relaunched, but the onset of the war saw its disappearance again until 1950, when Major Arthur Buckley reintroduced it as one of the major innovations for which he was responsible. He was keen to forge strong links with the old boys and started reunions again in 1951. The magazine was a powerful vehicle for this renewed relationship.

Since then the magazine has continued publication each year, recording sporting triumphs, academic achievements, house rivalries, individual pieces of literary and artistic work and much else. Its spirit is perhaps summed up by the tributes paid to their School in the 2002/3 edition by two members of the editorial team. Paul McCaffrey wrote, 'If enjoyment, variety, a feeling of achievement, a sense of belonging and a tradition of continuity are worthy goals in the lives of young people, then life at the Royal Hospital School must surely contribute to the attainment of these goals'; and Simon Warr is quoted as believing that 'A school is nothing if it merely teaches what the world is. It must teach what the world should be, and could be, if only we would make it so. Judge its value by that.'

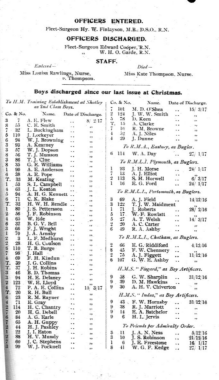

The Easter 1917 edition of The Royal Hospital School Magazine. *It had been running for 10 years.*

1920s.

1930s.

1950s.

1960s.

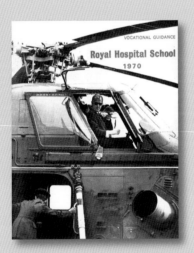

1970s.

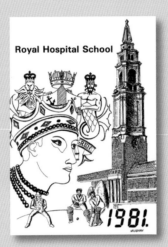

1980s.

1990s.

2000s.

Today, *The Royal Hospital School Magazine* (now known simply as *The Magazine*) is predominantly an organ of record and an important part of the School archive. Editors have worked hard to ensure that it is as full an account as possible of each successive year. While the house reports are written by the pupils, staff write the formal academic and sporting reports, and it always includes a full staff list and as much information as possible on all leavers and alumni. While there are many informal photographs, the editorial team always ensure that formal and sports team photographs are included; with the academic life, music and sport reviewed in detail. The magazine is an accurate summary of the year passed and all issues from 1919 to present are available to view using the School's on line digital archive.

Above: Naval crown used on the front of a short run of pre-war magzines produced at Holbrook.

Right: The 2009/10 edition of The Magazine, *with contemporary sailboarding cover.*

Antarctic Exploration – links to the Scott and Shackleton expeditions

The School played an important part in the epic explorations of the Antarctic in the first decade of the 20th century. The first old boy to be involved was Ernest Edward Mills Joyce, who was at the RHS from December 1886 to May 1891. He was wrecked in 1901 and ended up in Simon's Bay, South Africa, where he joined Robert Falcon Scott's Discovery Expedition (1901–04), completing a 70-day sledge journey over the Great Ice Barrier. The crew received the Silver Medal of the Royal Geographical Society and the King's Silver Antarctic Medal.

He then became a member of Shackleton's Nimrod Expedition (1907–09) to the magnetic and geographical south poles, before joining him again for the Trans-Antarctic Expedition of 1914–17. An expert in dogs and sledging, he was tasked with laying storage depots on the Ross Ice Shelf, which the team achieved in appalling conditions, losing three men before they reached a safe base camp, where they waited for several months for Shackleton to reach and rescue them.

During their time at the camp, Joyce organised expeditions to mark the grave of one of those who had died and – unsuccessfully – to try to find the others. Although he was a difficult and bombastic man who regularly fell out with his colleagues, they all acknowledged his determined heroism in ensuring that the weaker members of the expedition were looked after and brought to safety. In 1923 his bravery and endurance

Left: Sir Joseph Kinsey noting compass bearings taken by EA FitzGerald. He acted as attorney for both Scott's and Shackleton's expeditions. Scott wrote on 24 March 1912: 'My dear Kinsey, I'm afraid we are pretty well done – four days of blizzard just as we were getting to the last depot. My thoughts have been with you often. You have been a brick. You will pull the expedition through, I'm sure …. I should have little regret in leaving the world, for I feel that the country need not be ashamed of us – our journey has been the biggest on record, and nothing but the most exceptional hard luck at the end would have caused us to fail to return. We have been to the S. pole as we set out. God bless you and dear Mrs Kinsey. It is good to remember you and your kindness. Your friend, R. Scott.'

were recognised with the presentation of the Albert Medal by King George V, and his name lives on in Mount Joyce in Antarctica.

Another RHS hero of the Antarctic was Thomas Williamson, who served with Scott on his Discovery Expedition and was one of the search party that set out in November 1912 to find whatever was left of Scott's later and final ill-fated Terra Nova Expedition. Williamson kept a log in which he recorded that on 12 November at 6am the party spotted what they thought was a cairn, but that it turned out to be a tent three-quarters buried in snow. As he wrote, 'It was a great blow to us and I must own I shed a few tears, and I know the others did the same… although we knew full well for months past that we should meet with this sort of thing… I did not go over for quite a good time for I fear I could not look at this most pitiable scene. But when at last I made up my mind I saw a most ghastly sight, three sleeping bags with frozen bodies in them.'

Scott's diary was read out to the men, confirming both that he had been beaten to the South Pole by Amundsen and that two of the final party of five who reached the Pole had died on the way to the final camp; Edgar Evans had been badly weakened by falls and died near the foot of Beardmore Glacier and Lawrence Oates had walked out into a blizzard to his death with the immortal last words 'I am just going outside and may be some time'.

All the members of the search party signed a note recording how Scott and his two remaining companions, Edward Wilson and Henry Bowers, had died, and sealed it into a cylinder. They then piled snow over the tent and erected a cross over what was now the polar explorers' tomb, before setting out further south in the hope of finding Captain Oates's body. The journey took them two days and they found only his empty sleeping bag. In 1929 Thomas Williamson presented the School with the skis and sticks he had used on this expedition.

Also associated with both Scott's and Shackleton's Antarctic expeditions was Sir Joseph Kinsey, who taught at Dulwich College for nine years after leaving the School and then emigrated to New Zealand in 1880. He founded the very successful shipping company Kinsey & Co, and acted as the New Zealand agent for all the British expeditions to the Antarctic in the early years of the 20th century. It was his firm that fitted out the *Aurora*, which was the store ship carrying the supplies that were being laid out across the Antarctic – by, among others, Ernest Joyce – for Shackleton's trans-Antarctic expedition. After successfully landing several consignments of stores, the *Aurora* was caught in a vicious blizzard and swept out to sea trapped in pack ice, where she drifted for several months before making it back to New Zealand for repairs. Meanwhile, the expedition had had to be abandoned after Shackleton's own ship, the *Endurance*, was crushed by pack ice in the Weddell Sea. After Shackleton himself reached New Zealand, he sailed on the *Aurora* back to the Antarctic to pick up the survivors of the store-laying party. Kinsey received the Scott medal of the Royal Geographical Society in 1914 and was knighted in 1917.

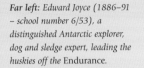

Far left: Edward Joyce (1886–91 – school number 6/53), a distinguished Antarctic explorer, dog and sledge expert, leading the huskies off the Endurance.

Left: Joyce by George Marston, official artist to the Shackleton expeditions.

Below: During WWI boys were seconded to the offices of Admiral of the Fleet John (1st Earl) Jellicoe, when he commanded the British Grand Fleet. A number of his belongings were given to the School and the design centre and ceremonial dining hall are named after him.

The outbreak of war in 1914 had a profound effect on the School. Six teachers enlisted immediately and others followed. Many boys had fathers serving at sea, and the older boys would soon be joining them. The cricket pitches were turned over to the growing of vegetables, and the Admiralty requisitioned pupils to act as messengers so that reservists could be released for active service. Boys worked closely with Admiral Jellicoe and Prince Louis of Battenburg (later Mountbatten), First Sea Lord, both of whom would in future visit the School. Zeppelins were a threat, and during an air raid the boys lay fully clothed on their beds in case they had to evacuate quickly to a nearby shelter; fortunately, their buildings escaped any damage.

Oswald Tuck

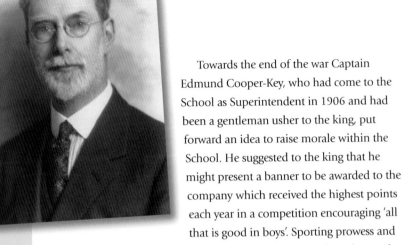

Born in 1876 and educated at the RHS, Oswald Tuck's career began at the Royal Observatory in Greenwich from 1892 to 1896. He then entered the Royal Navy to teach astronomy and navigation on the training ship HMS *Conway* on the River Mersey. He was appointed a Naval Instructor in 1899 and sent to the Far East, where he served first in HMS *Goliath* and later in HMS *King Alfred*. While there he began to learn Japanese during two periods of leave spent travelling around Japan and, in 1902, he took on a Japanese servant, Takego, with whom he continued to practise the spoken and written language. In 1906 he was appointed Japanese interpreter to HMS *King Alfred* and authorised to teach Japanese to fellow naval officers. He also took on translation work and acted as an interpreter for the admiral, making speeches for him on official occasions. In 1907 he began his translation of the secret Japanese naval history of the Russo-Japanese War, and was appointed assistant to the naval attaché in Tokyo.

After Tuck returned to the Admiralty in London in 1909 he continued his translation of the secret history, but was then appointed to naval intelligence during the Great War. After the war he became the archivist in the Historical Section of the Admiralty, retiring as head of the section in 1937. When the Second World War broke out he moved to the Ministry of Information and became a press censor in Japanese, mainly vetting journalists' reports. On the declaration of war with Japan, he was recalled by the Admiralty to teach intensive six-month courses in Japanese to students recruited to decrypt Japanese military cyphers at Bletchley Park. His courses were a great success, with his students learning Japanese in a far shorter time than had been previously thought possible. After the war, he continued teaching Japanese and translating at the Royal Naval College, Greenwich, where at the age of 70 he was the oldest serving Captain. He died in 1950.

Towards the end of the war Captain Edmund Cooper-Key, who had come to the School as Superintendent in 1906 and had been a gentleman usher to the king, put forward an idea to raise morale within the School. He suggested to the king that he might present a banner to be awarded to the company which received the highest points each year in a competition encouraging 'all that is good in boys'. Sporting prowess and academic distinction were to receive points, as were good conduct and efficiency. Smartness on parade and well kept dormitories also counted, and marks could be deducted for misconduct.

The king approved, and the Superintendent went to Buckingham Palace on 20 July 1918 to receive the banner; a party of boys should also have been there, but the flu epidemic intervened. The gift of this banner was a great honour – 'a mark of appreciation of the service given to the Royal Navy for the boys of Greenwich Hospital School'. It is a distinction unique to the School. No 5 Company were the first to win the competition and stated, 'We are confident that the honour will be keenly competed for in the future'. Being declared the winners and becoming the 'Banner Company' was quite a privilege: not only were the boys distinguished by wearing lanyards, but they were always the leading company on parade and on special occasions led the School in banner flying. The competition was to persist at the RHS in more or less its original form until 1993.

In 1919 the question of a war memorial for those who had died in the conflict was mooted. Numbers and names were initially difficult to determine, but eventually a window was placed in the chapel and 151 names were engraved on an oak board which was displayed in the

Right: Former pupil, pupil teacher and Headmaster (1899–1920), Mr Joseph Evans.

Left: The oak war memorial to those who fell during the Great War – Lest we forget. It was located in the Great Hall to the Queen's House and bore the names of 151 boys and three teachers.

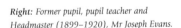

THE ROYAL NAVAL SCHOOL, GREENWICH
AL MARINE LIGHT INFANTRY)

Great Hall at the Queen's House. It was later calculated that at least 442 boys, and three masters, had given their lives in the war. On 6 July 1921 the School attended the service to commemorate the end of the Great War at St Paul's Cathedral in the presence of the king and queen.

1920 saw the retirement of both Edmund Cooper-Key, the Superintendent, and Joseph Evans, who had been a boy and a pupil teacher at the School, and who had returned from a teaching career elsewhere to become Headmaster in 1899. This was the end of an era in other ways too; from now on neither navigation nor astronomy would be studied at the School. A few years after its bicentenary, the Royal Hospital School finally moved on from the intentions of its founders.

During the 1920s the School continued to maintain its traditional function as 'the cradle of the Navy', though boys found it more difficult to find positions on leaving and in 1931 training schemes were established to help them find employment. There were many formal engagements; for example attending the Royal Navy and Military Tournament at Olympia on a number of occasions and the boys lining the route for HM King George V and Queen Mary to visit the Royal Observatory in 1925. Royal interest continued with prizes distributed by future King's HRH The Prince of Wales in 1928 and HRH The Duke of York (with the Duchess of York) in 1931. But a new era was about to dawn, as the result of a hugely generous gift from the greatest benefactor the School had ever known.

Far left: Early 20th-century colour postcard of the boys.

Below: Edmund Cooper-Key retired as Captain Superintendent in 1920.

Below left: Model of a naval cutter made by boys at the School in 1914.

Bottom: The King's Banner paraded in the School at Greenwich (1931). Entitled 'The Cradle of the Navy', by artist William Barnes Wollen, it was bought by the Director of Greenwich Hospital, Arthur Smallwood, for exhibition in the School at Holbrook.

GIFFORD SHERMAN READE AND HOLBROOK

Gifford Sherman Reade, who was born in Cape Town, South Africa, in 1845 into an old Suffolk family, had made a large fortune in tea in India and had then settled in New Zealand. He always had a great love of the sea, and was full of admiration for the Royal Navy, not least because of the protection it offered to his merchant fleet during the hostilities of the Great War.

As he and his wife were childless and not in the best of health, he wrote in 1916 to his great friend, Agnes Weston, asking her to communicate with the Admiralty and find out if they would be willing to accept his Suffolk estate, plus an ample endowment, as a legacy of gratitude. Miss Weston, who was known as 'Mother' and was later to become Dame Agnes, had cared for seamen in her 'Sailors' Rests' at Portsmouth and Plymouth for 40 years. She now acted as a go-between and, after making it clear to the Admiralty that the Reades wanted their gift to be 'for the benefit of the Navy and our sailors', told the Reades that the First Lord of the Admiralty would be happy to accept and suggested Greenwich Hospital as the proper beneficiary.

The Hospital's Director, Charles Stansfield, went to inspect the property, which consisted of about 850 acres with a long frontage on the River Stour and a house with 19 bedrooms (and one bathroom). He initially decided that it might be suitable as a school for girls, though several other ideas for the use of the gift were considered. Reade's first choice was to found a school to which boys from all parts of the empire would be sent, which he thought would strengthen their ties with the mother country. The impracticability of this idea was realised when the vast distances which separated the countries of the empire, and the slowness of travel between them, were considered. It then took six weeks for a fast mail boat to get to Australia, a constraint which also applied to the correspondence between the Admiralty and the Reades, which was painfully slow.

The letter of thanks from the Admiralty in January 1917 quoted William's and Mary's charter to show them how the Hospital benefited sailors and their families, and added that income was often insufficient to meet the heavy demands made on it. But even before he received this letter, Reade had sent Miss Weston a signed and witnessed codicil to his will leaving his estate at Holbrook to the Admiralty 'for the exclusive benefit of Greenwich Hospital'. He also bequeathed half the residue of his fortune to the Hospital, but with the proviso that it must be left to accumulate for at least 11 years after his death before it could be used.

At the end of the war, with his health now improved, Reade decided to stay in New Zealand, and in 1919 offered to give the Holbrook estate to the Hospital at once. The legal formalities took two years and the deed of gift was duly executed on 22 July 1921. No immediate plans were made for its use until, in 1922, Arthur Smallwood, now the Director of Greenwich Hospital, had an inspiration. The buildings at Greenwich now used by the School were inadequate for their purpose, and the accommodation there was both too small and increasingly unsuitable for the education of young boys. He therefore proposed that the Royal Hospital School should move to Holbrook, to a new purpose-built school with plenty of space and fresh air.

Reade was informed of the Admiralty decision to relocate the Greenwich school to Suffolk, and when plans of the proposed new buildings were sent to him he heartily approved, but expressed concern lest any financial stringency on the part of Greenwich Hospital might lead to any curtailment of the scheme. In early 1924, preliminary site work started.

Sir Aston Webb was appointed as architectural advisor, having previously designed the Duke of York's Military School in Dover, the Royal Naval College at Dartmouth,

Left: Dame Agnes 'Aggie' Weston, a naval philanthropist known as the Angel of the Waves. She died in 1918 shortly after introducing the idea of a bequest to the Admiralty on behalf of her friend Gifford Sherman Reade.

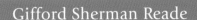

Gifford Sherman Reade

The Reades were a well established land-owning family in Suffolk, and in 1845, when Gifford Sherman was born, his father was in the Bengal civil service. He, however, was born in South Africa, though the family uprooted to India to join their father when he was still a baby. Six years later they returned to England to live with their grandmother in Holbrook, and the young child learned to enjoy all the pursuits that were available to him in the Suffolk countryside. He became a keen fisherman and a crack shot, as well as a sailor and rider.

When he was 19 he joined his uncle in India to help build up a tea plantation on 3,700 acres of jungle in Assam leased from the government. It was a remote and primitive place, 35 miles from the nearest river station on the Bramaputra River. It took a while to develop, but by the time Gifford retired the whole area had been planted and large numbers of staff were employed. He married his wife, Margaret, in Calcutta when he was 42.

He was well known for his skill with a gun in an area where tigers were common. On her first night at the plantation, Margaret heard a tiger prowling outside her window; her husband promptly shot it. The same thing had happened to him on his first day at the plantation many years before, when he saved his terrified dog from another tiger which was threatening it in the kitchen of his house.

By the early 1900s he was in failing health, and a combination of long-term asthma, malaria and a hunting accident persuaded Gifford and Margaret Reade to return to Holbrook, where he became involved in the Navy's shore-based establishment, HMS *Ganges*, at nearby Shotley. Now a wealthy man with a large fortune made mostly in India from tea, jute and coal, and from his fleet of merchant ships, he continued to lead an active sporting life and travelled all over the world. He was in New Zealand when the war broke out in 1914, and as he could not actively serve decided to stay there until it was over. He never returned permanently to England, and died in New Zealand in December 1929, aged 85, surviving his beloved Margaret by five months.

Their grave in Hillsborough Road cemetery, Auckland, overlooks Manukau Harbour, and the curb stone bears the inscription: 'Mr Reade gave his family property and large fortune to the Admiralty for the benefit of the Navy, in memory of its services during the Great War 1914–1918'.

A similar inscription is found in Holbrook church, where his three brothers and other family members are buried. Each year at the annual Holbrook parish meeting, the Headmaster, as a representative of Greenwich Hospital, receives the rent of one Suffolk reed as the token by which the village rents from the Hospital Reade Field, the recreation ground in the heart of the village.

Below: Half-length seated portrait of Gifford Sherman Reade, commissioned after his death. The corresponding minute sheet (14 February 1930) has Arthur Smallwood, Director of Greenwich Hospital, writing: 'As Mr Reade gave the Holbrook site and as his fortune bequeathed to Greenwich Hospital should ultimately produce income sufficient to endow the School, it seems fitting that some memorial to him should be placed in the School'.

Above: Gifford (with Elephant Gun) and Margaret Reade in India with their favourite elephant, Sarah.

Inset: Coloured chalk portrait dated 1852 of Gifford (left) and brother. Confirmed 'to be placed in the new School at Holbrook as a memorial of the donor to the estate'.

Gifford Sherman Reade (1846-1929)
Who in 1921 gave this Estate to the Trustees of Greenwich Hospital for the benefit of Officers, Non-commissioned Officers and men of the Royal Navy or Royal Marines or of their widows, children or dependants and later left the whole of his large fortune for the same purpose.

the Admiralty Arch at the end of the Mall in London and Christ's Hospital in Horsham. Six architects were selected to prepare plans and they duly visited the School site, presenting their designs at an exhibition in July 1925. Herbert T Buckland and William Heywood of Birmingham were confirmed winners and appointed as architects, and by 1928 J Gerrard and Sons Ltd of Swinton, Manchester, were appointed as general contractors for what was to be the largest building project in Suffolk, half a mile long end to end and in the Queen Anne style.

Reade then wrote to Greenwich Hospital suggesting that the coloured plans of the new school at Holbrook be exhibited in Auckland and other important imperial centres to foster recruitment to the Navy. A clay scale model was constructed (with two variations of a chapel and two of a boarding house) and it was shipped to Auckland for his inspection and approval. By 1927 it was clear from tenders received that capital cost would be high and so Smallwood, to avoid his ambitions being severely reined in by the Admiralty, travelled to see Reade in the hope of persuading him to make a gift to the new school during his lifetime.

Long discussions ensued with no progress on an immediate donation, as Reade was determined to build up a substantial trust fund for the School. The main legal difficulty was his intention of tying up the estate for generations with successive periods of accumulation, but this was finally obviated by the elimination of all such provisions from the will except as regards the first period of 11 years. The will was therefore preserved from the grave risk of being found invalid, while Reade's wishes in regard to the policy of continual conservation over long periods were embodied in a letter and the Admiralty reply, the terms of which – to preserve them and prevent them from being forgotten – were ordered to be brought before every successive Admiralty Board. After this Reade duly wrote to confirm that he proposed to alter his dispositions in order to leave the whole of his fortune, instead of half, to Greenwich Hospital, subject only to sundry small life annuities.

So by 1928 sufficient funds were available to allow work to start in earnest, albeit on a slightly smaller scale than Smallwood had initially hoped; there would be no chapel in the immediate future and houses for the staff were also deferred. Given the colossal number of bricks required, the contractors built a wharf and a 2ft-gauge railway along the sea wall but, although they planned to use steam power, it never materialised. They did purchase a 27-year-old engine named 'Hampstead' that had been used on building the Charing Cross, Euston and Northern Line tube.

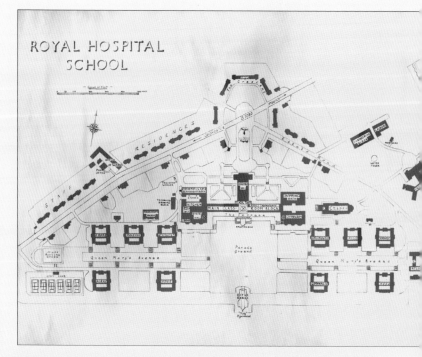

Above: An amended version of the Buckland and Heywood design for Holbrook – originally 14 boarding houses were planned. The other three would have been located where the bowling greens and grass tennis courts (between the houses on the front rank) are found today.

Below: An accident on Stutton Road, 1932, with the staff houses in the background. There are six albums of photographs that tell the complete story of the construction of this magnificent building project from green pasture to final completion.

HMS *Ganges* – the naval neighbour

HMS *Ganges* was a Royal Navy shore training establishment (stone frigate) that was a close and friendly neighbour of the RHS from the School's early years at Holbrook until *Ganges* closed in 1976. The establishment began life as the second ship named *Ganges,* which was an 84-gun second-rate ship-of-the-line experimentally built of teak. She was launched in November 1821 in Bombay, and commissioned in Portsmouth in 1823. Years later her hulk was to become the original accommodation of HMS *Ganges*, the Naval Training Establishment at Shotley.

Prior to Gifford Sherman Reade giving his estate at Holbrook to the Admiralty in July 1921, and on his last visit to Holbrook House, he engaged with officers from HMS *Ganges* to learn of its aims and discuss the future of the Navy. Before it was decided to build the RHS on the land he

donated, officers from *Ganges* used the estate for shooting, and *Ganges* boys used to row, sail or hike there and camp near Holbrook Creek.

Ganges was the first step of the formal route by which many former pupils from Greenwich and Holbrook joined the Navy as 'boys, second class' on their way to becoming seamen. In the 1950s the School band was sometimes invited to play music for *Ganges* divisions, and the Captain often took the salute at RHS divisions on a Sunday.

During the time that the two establishments were near neighbours, *Ganges* supplied much equipment to the School on 'permanent loan', including weapons (rifles, bayonets and cutlasses), boats (whalers, cutters, sailing dinghies and ancillary equipment), and no doubt other seamanship items. After *Ganges* closed in 1976, her figurehead was lent to the RHS and was placed opposite the School's cannon at the main entrance. The trainees at *Ganges* competed in a range of sports and took part in 'Nore Command' competitions, as did the RHS – and competing against teams of men tended to make RHS teams formidable compared with other school teams.

Left: HMS Ganges figurehead shortly before it was returned to the HMS Ganges Museum at Shotley.

Right: The assembly hall under construction, October 1931.

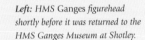

No. 196   6 OCTOBER 1931
ASSEMBLY HALL

The Royal Hospital School: Celebrating 300 Years

On 28 October 1928 HRH The Duke of York, later King George VI, laid the foundation stone with a guard of 110 boys attending from Greenwich. He celebrated the occasion with the benefactor by sending a cable to Gifford Sherman Reade:

With the approval of His Majesty I have this day laid the foundation stone of the new Royal Hospital School at Holbrook. Your gift of this fine open site is indeed a fitting symbol of your admiration for the work of the Royal Navy. It is my earnest hope that every success will attend your endeavour to increase, for the years to come, those benefits which were first inaugurated by Royal Charter at Greenwich over two centuries ago.

The massive foundation stone came from the quarries on the Isle of Portland which Sir Christopher Wren had used to build Greenwich Hospital. In a cavity under it was placed an oak casket made from a beam of the Queen's House; it contained a copy of that day's *East Anglian Times* and one each of all the coins of the realm, all newly minted. Winston Churchill later said that 'we shape our buildings and afterwards our buildings shape us', and this mighty building has influenced many lives.

An aerial view of the construction work shows the scaffold-clad RHS tower growing and the ceremonial mast in place.

HM King George VI (then HRH The Duke of York) inspects the School ceremonial guard that travelled from Greenwich to Holbrook for the foundation ceremony (1928).

Below: Preparing to lift the tower pinnacle. Some say this was fashioned out of an old sea mine.

On 12 January 1929 the necessary alterations were made to Reade's will and the April School magazine confirmed that, in addition to the gift of the estate, he had recently arranged a large sum of money as an endowment, designed for the support of the School. The endowment would be held for at least 11 years from his death with £100,000 of this put aside and reinvested permanently for four periods of 14 years. In the magazine Reade stated that he had gained his affluence from his own endeavours. 'I had to struggle to get on my feet in the first place,' he explained. 'I lost money from the start. I had to buy my experience. Then I concentrated. I relied on my own business instincts, and I began to prosper.'

After Gifford Sherman Reade died in New Zealand on 5 December 1929 Smallwood sought permission to use capital to reinstate the chapel and the staff houses in the knowledge that the bequest would eventually replenish the coffers. By 1931 the new School buildings were completed at a cost of £1,100,000 and it was ready for occupation in 1933.

THIS STONE WAS LAID BY HIS ROYAL HIGHNESS
THE DUKE OF YORK. K.G. K.T. GCMG. GCVO.
ON THE 26TH DAY OF OCTOBER 1928
IT WAS TAKEN FROM THE QUARRIES
IN THE ISLE OF PORTLAND FROM WHICH STONE WAS
RAISED ON WARRANTS OF SIR CHRISTOPHER WREN
FOR BUILDING THE ROYAL HOSPITAL AT GREENWICH
IN THE YEARS 1700-1701

Above: The ceremonial presentation key used in the foundation stone laying ceremony. Symbolically, the Portland stone above was carved and inscribed to form the impressive centrepiece foundation, today comprising one wall of the School reception hall.

Left: The Duke of York surveys the large clay model on display, with the invitation to the foundation event (inset).

Below: The trowel and mallet used in this same ceremony, today located in the School reception hall above the foundation stone.

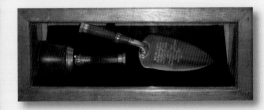

THE ROYAL HOSPITAL SCHOOL.
HOLBROOK, SUFFOLK.

LAYING OF FOUNDATION STONE
BY
H.R.H. THE DUKE OF YORK,
K.G., K.T., G.C.M.G., G.C.V.O.
ON
FRIDAY, 26TH, OCTOBER, 1928.

PART II

HOLBROOK: CHANGING TIMES

The New School

On 23 March 1933, the Royal Hospital School at Greenwich formed up in companies for the last time. There were two drum rolls, the band struck up a march and one by one the companies paraded out of the gate, with the Drum Major tossing his mace over the gate and catching it on the other side. They left behind dormitories, classrooms, gymnasium and dining hall empty and echoing, and they also left behind the remains of *Fame*. They took the beakhead to Holbrook, complete with figurehead and bowsprit for mounting on the end of the small bore rifle range.

The last month at Greenwich saw many traditional elements of the School routine being performed for the last time, among them the Sunday morning chapel service. To this, King George V and Queen Mary were invited, and although they could not come, the King's Private Secretary confirmed that 'you may rest assured of the king's and queen's unabated interest in the welfare of the Royal Hospital School, and of Their Majesties best wishes for its continued prosperity in its new home'. Old boys, friends of the School and the Mayor of Greenwich were in attendance at the last march past of the boys.

Left: The Drum Major leads the band from Greenwich for the final time (23 March 1933).

Left: *The DH84 Dragon built by De Havilland landed on the playing fields with HRH The Prince of Wales on board. It was sold in 1938 and in 1951 crashed in New Guinea.*

Below: *After inspecting the band, HRH The Prince of Wales moved to the saluting base to review the ceremonial displays and march-past.*

Previous pages: *Looking east down Queen Mary's Avenue towards Nelson House. In 2007, 66 holm oaks were planted to replace the original 24 donated in 1938 by Queen Mary and other members of the royal family and the Admiralty.*

Above: *Mr Bushnel and the boys are packed and ready for departure, with the training ship Fame in the background.*

The estate – a wonderful place to live, learn and work

The original Holbrook estate, as gifted by Gifford Sherman Reade, was 850 acres in extent, much of which was set aside to be farmed for the benefit of the School. Fifty acres were laid out from the beginning as playing fields. The buildings overlook the estuary of the River Stour at the back, and are laid out in a triangular shape with the road from Ipswich to Stutton and beyond running along the curved northern edge, lined with staff houses.

A large assembly hall and dining room, an infirmary (with a mortuary), a gymnasium and a covered swimming pool were part of the plan from the start, and the vast parade ground behind the main building was originally equipped with a rigged mast. Holbrook House was rebuilt on a smaller but nonetheless lavish scale and set aside for the use of the Superintendent – later the Headmaster – and 11 boarding houses were constructed, with space left for two more which were never built. Five of them – St Vincent, Raleigh, Drake, Blake and Howe – were positioned to the west, five more – Collingwood, Anson, Hawke, Hood and Cornwallis – to the east, and Nelson was built to a separate design closing the east–west axis of the site. Nelson's arms appear in its pediment, and the central cupola is topped with a weather vane which is a model of the *Victory*. Originally used to house new boys – as Trafalgar Quarters had done at Greenwich – Nelson went through a number of permutations before becoming (in the 21st century) a mixed house for the upper sixth. At the opposite end of the site, Blake and Drake are now houses for new boarders and day pupils, and Raleigh is a dedicated day pupils' house from year 9 onwards.

The ten standard-design houses are built in an H-shape, each wing being originally laid out with dormitories on the top floor and a day room, a boot room, a washroom and a well ventilated cloakroom for raincoats and sports clothing on the ground floor. The ground floor of the cross bar contained accommodation strictly partitioned for an unmarried housemaster and the house matron, while on the floor above were offices for the matron and the housemaster and a communal shower room for the boys. There was also a further single-storey cross piece containing lavatories. Between the two cross pieces was a muster yard flanked by colonnades. Today, housemasters and mistresses have the benefit of spacious new accommodation filling in the bottom part of each H, and there are also generous flats provided in each house for other resident staff.

Classrooms were laid out on either side of the main building with its bell tower; they were built with open arcades at the front through which cold winds would whistle before they were glassed in. The estate was almost entirely self-sufficient: surrounded by its own farmland, it was built with its own water supply, sewage treatment plant, fire station, post office, engineering shop and laundry. The infirmary had an operating theatre, X-ray equipment and dental facilities, as well as the mortuary, which has rarely been called into use.

The chapel was not part of the original contract because it was believed that it could not be accommodated within the budget; but Arthur Smallwood, Director of Greenwich Hospital, decided to recommend that capital should be released to build it, so it was completed only a year after the School moved to Holbrook.

Now the site occupied by the School grounds is 200 acres with much of the surrounding land and property now let. The main building and the chapel are listed Grade II*, and many of the other buildings are Grade II. In addition to the controlled listed building status exerts over both alterations and maintenance, modern building regulations and health and safety rules make the continued management of the whole splendid estate a daily challenge – one that is tackled by the Estate Manager, Mike Beard, and his 37 staff, who include electricians, plumbers, carpenters, decorators, gardeners and ground staff.

Above: A warren of underground pipework and services.

Right: Matrons still play a key role in looking after the pupils.

Right: RHS pupils riding past Holbrook Creek, with an impressive view of the Holbrook estate. Tower, domes and belfry decorate a range of school buildings set in majestic grounds that sweep down to the sea wall, salt marshes and River Stour beyond.

Below right: Clockwise (from top left) – an impressive display of grounds maintenance vehicles; original industrial driers still going strong; chippies shaping an oak door for the Heritage Centre; sports kits, sponsored by the School's affiliated Royal Navy vessel, HMS Dauntless, hanging pristine clean in the laundry.

There were very few changes to the original buildings before the early 1990s when the first improvements to the boarding houses were initiated, but since then large sums and a great deal of effort have gone into making the whole School more comfortable and compliant with current legislation. In addition to the main School buildings and the boarding houses, there are around 90 staff residences, some on the campus and some along Stutton Road. There are miles of underground pipes, with heating systems for boarding houses and the main School buildings to be maintained, and the School's own water supply and sewage farm to be managed.

The loosening link with Greenwich and the need for the School to be increasingly self-financing have meant that reductions in the numbers of maintenance staff have been inevitable. But the original vision of the School remains undimmed, and the beauties of the campus and the individual buildings continue to inspire those who live, work and study here.

Staff memories

Jean Sage has a long association with the School. In March 2012 they visited to share their memories with some of today's staff and pupils, who also photographed, filmed and recorded them.

Jean Sage is the longest-serving known member of staff. She arrived in May 1933, only a few weeks after the School moved to Holbrook, to be between-maid to the Captain Superintendent, Captain Evan Bruce-Gardyne, at Holbrook House. Her duties included lighting the fires, making the beds, scrubbing the steps and helping the cook – and she remembers many of the distinguished guests who visited, including the Archbishop of Canterbury who came to dedicate the new chapel in 1934. She also recalls the Prince of Wales's annoyance when he arrived to find that his valet had forgotten to pack his jacket, so he had to have his tea in shirtsleeves.

Jean left for a year or so, but returned in 1939 as the family cook. She stayed until 1945 when Bruce-Gardyne retired to Scotland and she had her own children to bring up. Her husband, Francis Sage, also worked at the School, in the gardens and kitchens for 34 years. After the children were grown up in 1965 she started again at the School, working in the kitchens and doing some of the cleaning work until she retired in 1977.

Peter Page also worked at Holbrook House as its gardener, starting in January 1944 and – with a single break for his national service in 1948–49 – he stayed at the School until 2010, living in house in the grounds until after his wife's death. He therefore worked for the last Superintendent of the School, Captain Bruce-Gardyne, then for the next three incumbents who combined that role with the headmastership and then after that for every Headmaster from Norman York to Howard Blackett. He made himself useful until well into his formal retirement by cutting flowers for the chapel and pulling vegetables for Holbrook House, though its garden has long since ceased to be separately staffed, and is now looked after by the School's ground staff.

Peter Page arrived a year before Bruce-Gardyne retired, and remembers the upheaval when the family and their belongings were being packed up for the move – and he himself was ordered to ride the family pony, Jazz, to the station where horse transport was waiting for it. He had never been on a horse before but managed the trip safely.

Left: Long serving gardener, Peter Page and employee from the year Holbrook opened, Jean Sage – return to the School to meet pupils and recount memories.

Below: Early pre war photograph of Holbrook House walled garden. There are tales of headmasters cultivating tobacco and pupils developing green fingers. A 1970s gardening club report confirmed they had 'plucked the lush harvest of broad beans, turnips, parsnips, cauliflowers, curly kale, lettuce, radishes and leeks'. Nearby Wall Farm had for many years belonged to the School estate and boys were from time to time involved with cultivating and farming the land around the School.

He remembers treating the Holbrook House garden as his own and growing more or less what he chose – including tobacco, up to the limits laid down by excise regulations, and grapes for wine making. His work was rewarded not just by an MBE but also by a medal from the Royal Horticultural Society presented to him at the School after 40 years' service, followed by a bar after 50 years. His wife also worked as a nurse in the School infirmary, both before and after having children and up to retirement age.

Above: A double-decker delivers the boys to Holbrook, April 1933.

Below: Stanley Robert Hewitson BSc MBE, the Headmaster from 1920 to 1939 and 1940–45. He managed the School through its transition from Holbrook to Greenwich and the difficult war years.

The mayor told them, 'Don't leave your tradition behind you; carry it with you and hand it on to those who will follow you at Holbrook.' The last School magazine to be published at Greenwich had the Headmaster Stephen Hewitson, in post since 1920, promising that 'the new school will not only worthily uphold the high traditions of the past, but gain new and even better laurels. Everyone attached to the School must strive to make this ideal a success.'

On 27 April 1933, a school train from Liverpool Street and then 16 double-decker buses took the boys to their new home, and as they spilled out in front of the School at Holbrook they formed themselves into their usual numbered companies. But there were changes to come. As they marched off to the main hall they were divided into

two columns, with the juniors (those aged under 13½) on one side and the older boys on the other. Entering the building they passed long tables where they were issued with new clothes: naval uniform was in future only for special occasions. Jackets, shorts and jumpers were handed out, along with socks with coloured bands indicating both the house – no longer the 'company' – to which they were now to belong and also whether they were juniors or seniors.

Nelson House was the reception house, where the intake of 'New

Jacks' who joined twice a term would spend six weeks, and the five junior houses on the east side and five senior houses on the west side (all now named after distinguished admirals). There were 80 boys in each house, divided into two wings, each with its own dayroom and dormitory. The dayrooms actually had chairs to sit in – there were none at Greenwich – and though the beds in the dormitories were the same, there was much more space between them and each boy now had his own locker. And a huge innovation was that each house now had its own matron. The School jargon for a visit to the infirmary had previously been 'going up home' since only there was there 'anything in the shape of the care of a mother'. Now their resident matrons would get to know the boys and look after them, and the infirmary could be kept for the really sick, who were said to be 'kept up'.

The royal family continued their interest in the School, which was formally opened by HRH The Prince of Wales (later King Edward VIII) on 26 July 1933; he piloted his own plane to the School and landed on the playing field to meet the pupils and 1,800 guests. Boys manned the yards on the newly rigged ceremonial mast and the rest stood on the banks to the parade ground. In January 1936 a party of 60 boys represented the School at the funeral of King George V, bearing the banner presented to them by the king in 1918 and lining up behind the troops, while back at School the choir sang patriotic hymns and the band played the 'Last Post' and 'Reveille' as the funeral service was broadcast in the assembly hall. On 12 May 1937, Coronation Day, the whole School assembled to plant a Coronation Oak and afterwards listen to the broadcast in the assembly hall before an afternoon production of *The Rotters* by the Cameron Repertory Theatre, the distribution of souvenir beakers to every boy at a special tea and the declaration of 'open gates for all' – the freedom to walk to Holbrook in the pouring rain!

When Queen Mary visited in 1938, she was impressed with the buildings but also recognised the need to have pictures on the walls and some trees to liven up the approaches. She donated the money needed to plant two oak trees and these were later augmented by a further five from the royal family and 17 from the Admiralty. This avenue of 24 trees became known as Queen Mary's Avenue; sadly, most of them were blown down in the 1987 hurricane. In 2008, a fundraising appeal was launched to replace them. Sixty-six holm oaks were planted along Queen Mary's Avenue and sponsor boards erected on both the east and west sides listing all those who kindly donated a tree. Not only do they contribute to the aesthetics of the Royal Hospital School and provide something that generations to come will enjoy, but they also contribute to the ecological heritage of the site.

Jack Judge – Greenwich and Chelsea Pensioner

Born in 1913, Jack Judge is unique among Royal Hospital School alumni in that he benefited from both Greenwich Royal Hospital and Chelsea Royal Hospital. He attended the RHS from 1924 until 1928, and then joined the Royal Navy and served in several ships before he contracted tuberculosis, which led to his discharge from the Navy as medically unfit. He soon found himself missing the camaraderie of a service life, which he had of course lived from the age of 11, and so, in order partially to regain it, he joined the Territorial Army and rapidly threw himself into their training activities. On the outbreak of war in 1939 the TA was assimilated into the regular Army, and Jack served throughout in a number of theatres. At the end of the war his commanding officer noticed that he had never undergone a medical during his time in the Army, and so he was sent to the medical officer who quickly spotted his disease. He was therefore discharged with a pension and, much later, after his wife died, he applied for, and received an in-pension at Chelsea Royal Hospital. He therefore lived his days out as a Chelsea Pensioner.

To mark the tercentenary of the Chelsea Hospital in 1982, the in-Pensioners were encouraged to promote and participate in unusual or innovative events, and Jack Judge, with his unique service (for a Chelsea Pensioner), in the Royal Navy, applied to go to sea on a warship. One day the phone rang in the sergeant's cabin on his ward, and he was summoned to see the Governor. Startled and with some trepidation, he reported as ordered, to be told that the First Lord of the Admiralty had written congratulating him for his idea and inviting him onboard one of the Royal Navy's ships for a short voyage. He

attended the next RHSA weekend at Holbrook resplendent in his Pensioner's uniform and arriving by conventional means, but he departed from Ipswich docks onboard HMS *Grafton*, bound for Portsmouth.

Above: Jack Judge attended Greenwich Hospital School (1924–28) and Chelsea Hospital as a Pensioner.

The School was inspected by the Board of Education in October 1933. The inspectors were impressed by all they saw and considered that 'given the right conditions, this school could take a prominent place in English education'. Full recognition and government grants had always up to now been refused because of the School's particular focus, and refusal continued pending a full inspection.

This took place in the summer of 1934, and made a number of recommendations: more practical training for the less able boys; further academic development as the School settled down; and attention paid to the ways in which, in accordance with naval discipline, boys were 'marshalled from one occupation to another'. The inspectors were concerned that 'the striking orderliness of the boys' lives needs careful watching lest it should crush or suppress individuality'. The dichotomy in management between the Superintendent and the Headmaster was noted as being a possible cause of friction. But they agreed that the School should be

recognised for grant-giving purposes, though a grant itself was not forthcoming until 1937. However, the inspectors' desire to see the syllabus broadened was not immediately acted upon, and both the quality of staff and, later, the shortage of teachers during wartime limited the academic range further, with no languages, art or music, and science confined to the Upper Nautical Division.

The splendid chapel was finished in 1934 and dedicated by the Archbishop of Canterbury, Cosmo Lang. In the same year Arthur Smallwood retired, having been a hugely energetic and persistent force in the establishment of the new school. He was commemorated in a very special way. A statue of St Nicholas, the patron saint of seafarers and children, had been commissioned for over the entrance to the chapel; the sculptor was asked to give the saint Arthur Smallwood's features.

In 1936 the Director of Greenwich Hospital felt that the time had come to seek the benefit of outside advice on how the School should be run; he proposed a 'committee of inspection' to be chaired by a retired admiral, with members including a nominee from the Board of Education and the headmaster of a public school. They were to meet once a year and report on matters of principle rather than detail, with the aim of keeping the School abreast of both naval and educational requirements.

Left: Philip Newell served on the pre-war Committee of Inspection and the Bruntisfield Committee, and later became the Director of Greenwich Hospital. He is seen here with HM Queen Elizabeth The Queen Mother in 1968 receiving the Suffolk Reed, which is presented to the School by the Holbrook village council as a 'peppercorn' rent for the Reade Field.

The committee members were told that the School was maintained by the Hospital as 'a charitable benefit for the sons of naval ratings, past and present, and as a nursery for the Royal Navy'. Moreover, its objective was 'to prepare boys for entry to the lower deck'. That the RHS was not out of the same mould as other schools was vividly brought home to Philip Newell, then Headmaster of Gresham's School, who had accepted a place on the committee. To quote from his 1984 history of Greenwich Hospital, at his first meeting 'I still remember clearly the shock on hearing that while all boys at the age of ten had promised to join the Navy on leaving the School, their attainments and the Navy's needs were both so small that only half were taken. In these magnificent buildings, the Board of Education's grant was for little more than elementary education. Two other recollections are clear: small boys in disciplined groups of 30 or more being herded at the double from place to place; and an item from the Superintendent's report... that the majority of boys preferred the old to the new: supervision by naval pensioners rather than young civilians. It was a shock to learn that the 11 housemasters with 80 boys each under their care were, in fact, the most recently recruited teachers... rather than, as was traditional, chosen with care after long experience of their qualities.' Moreover, the housemasters were rather less important in the life of the houses than the matrons, and the accommodation on offer to them was minimal, with no room for wives. Initially they were all unmarried and when, several years later, the first married housemaster was appointed, his wife had to live in the village.

Newell was certainly not alone among non-naval newcomers to the School in finding the strong naval traditions and connections surprising. Educationally, the School was divided into Junior Division for the younger boys, Senior Division for the older boys and the Upper Nautical Division for the brightest, most of whom ended up taking the artificer's examination to enter the Navy. Seamanship remained central to the curriculum, taught by the company officers, and all the PE teachers were ex-naval instructors. Great emphasis was placed on all the boys being able to swim, and they also had shooting lessons in the rifle range.

Although no ship to replace *Fame* was built at Holbrook, the beakhead and figurehead were re-erected on the south end of the rifle range overlooking the playing field. Close by there was a rigged mast at the bottom of the parade ground, and the timetable included regular PE sessions when the boys had to climb up the rigging. A number of naval pensioners also worked in the School, manning the stores, the kitchen, the bakery and the quartermaster's office.

The stories of boys who were at the School during the 1930s and 1940s indicate that, although some things had changed, systems, routines and discipline were very much as they had been at Greenwich. Naval uniform was no longer worn every day, but the boys still marched everywhere, and they still cleaned their own houses every day before breakfast – which, like supper, was taken in the houses during the war years since the dining hall could not be blacked out. The routine on Saturdays was to clean the whole School according to rotas organised by

Left: Queen Mary leaving the chapel in 1938, escorted by Captain Superintendent E Bruce-Gardyne RN DSO.

Duncan Alexander Croall Scott-Ford – the RHS traitor

On 3 November 1942 Duncan Alexander Croall Scott-Ford was executed for treason at Wandsworth Prison. Aged just 21, he was the youngest person – and one of only two independent school pupils – to be executed under the terms of the 1940 Treachery Act. The other school that can claim this dubious distinction is Harrow.

Born in 1921, Scott-Ford was sent to the RHS after his father, a sick-bay attendant in the Navy, committed suicide. He attended the School between 1933 and 1936, and joined the Royal Navy in 1937. After questionable liaisons with a temptress in Dar-es-Salaam and prostitutes in Egypt, he was court-martialled over financial irregularities, dishonourably dismissed from the Navy and imprisoned.

On his release back in the UK, he managed to join the Merchant Navy and sailed to Lisbon on the SS *Finland*. While there he was approached by men who later turned out to be German agents and who offered him money in exchange for information about ship movements. He appears to have given them very little useful information, but he foolishly signed receipts for the payments they gave him, which enabled them to blackmail him. Before his final voyage back to Britain in August 1942, they asked him to provide information on his convoy's course, speed and distances, as well as details of the Royal Navy escort ships. He duly wrote notes on his convoy during the voyage, which were discovered after he was questioned when he reached port.

He was found to have been involved in espionage, with covert meetings confirmed with a German agent called 'Rutherford' in which 1,600 escudos changed hands in exchange for information. He appears to have quickly decided to confess about his contacts in Lisbon and was despatched to London to stand trial for treason, for which he was sentanced to death. He made no appeal against conviction or sentence and was hanged by Albert Pierrepoint on 3 November 1942, a mere two weeks after the trial.

Several posters designed to warn sailors about the dangers of loose talk were produced to prevent similar cases. The slogans 'Loose lips might sink ships', 'Keep mum, she's not so dumb', 'Somebody blabbed, button your lip' and 'Bits of careless talk are pieced together by the enemy' all featured on placards with naval themes after his death.

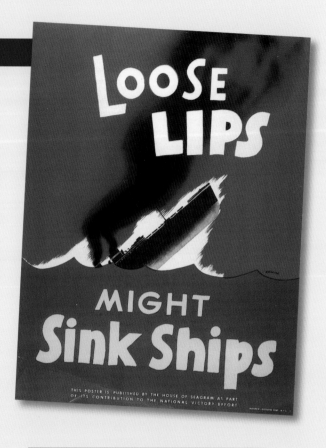

Above: Duncan Croall Scott-Ward (1933–37, Raleigh) was hanged for treason in 1942. His example drew attention to information campaigns designed to limit the possibility of people inadvertently giving useful information to enemy spies; for example as here 'Loose Lips Might Sink Ships' or when referring to potential temptresses in port – 'Keep Mum, she's not so dumb.'

Below left *and* **below:** *Wartime precautions against air raids – sandbags around the old infirmary (later the music school) and boarding up the ground floor windows of a boarding house.*

the Chief Petty Officer boys (CPO's, equivalent to prefects in other schools). There was drill every day and lessons were followed by games and sport, including swimming in the School's own indoor pool. Sundays saw the boys parading in 'number one naval rig', which had to be spotless.

The system of food distribution remained as it had been at Greenwich, which meant that the junior boys at the foot of the tables were served last and invariably got the smallest portions. Discipline remained harsh and was often implemented by the PO boys who, except in the most serious cases, were left very much alone by the housemasters to keep control of their fellows. Although they were not officially allowed to inflict corporal punishment, a blind eye was usually turned, and some of them even retained the instrument of torture known as a 'stonicky' – a short length of rope with a large knot, typically a 'turk's' head' at one end.

The approaching war stimulated discussion about evacuating the School from its vulnerable position on the east coast, but nowhere suitable could be found so it remained, albeit with much preparation for wartime conditions. Pupil numbers were reduced, the upper playing fields became a vegetable patch as the School sought to become self-sufficient, the grounds were seeded with anti-glider traps, camouflaged trenches were dug by the boys, the ground floor windows were protected from bomb blast by large boxes of sandbags which reached up nearly to the top of the glass, the

buildings were blacked out where possible and half of Nelson House was converted into an emergency hospital. The other boarding houses ceased to be merely junior or senior houses, and a mix of ages was dispersed through each house, possibly to help spread the risk to the different age groups in the event of an attack on the School.

Fortunately none of these precautions were needed and the School remained virtually unscathed: the only damage was three broken panes of glass in the chapel from a nearby parachute mine blast. Hitler, it seemed to a commentator, managed to do less damage than the boys of 1841 who had broken every single pane of glass in the chapel – though an alternative theory is held by long-serving RHS gardener Peter Page. He recalls meeting a German family after the war whose son had been in the Luftwaffe and who told him that German pilots had been specifically ordered not to bomb the School as it was wanted for a headquarters building after the invasion. They had also, it seems, used the tower to provide them with a bearing on their course to various bombing raids. Whatever the truth, as a boy who was there at the time recalled, 'The only association we had with the war was watching the bombers returning from their daylight raids over Germany, often limping home badly damaged. The American Air Force also used to practise dive-bombing targets in the middle of the river at the bottom of the playing fields.'

Wartime stories – just a few, from so many

COLDITZ – THE GREAT ESCAPE

John Wilkens (1923–25) is the only known RHS boy to have been held prisoner in Colditz. He was captured when serving as a telegraphist on the submarine *Starfish*, which was depth-charged 64 times by German minesweepers while on patrol off Heligoland in January 1940. The submarine was flooded so extensively that she struggled to the surface only by abandoning her drop-keel – a measure of extreme desperation. *Starfish* then sank and her officers were taken onboard the minesweepers.

Wilkens tried three times to escape from his first prison camp and enraged his guards by telling them that he and his fellow prisoners would not unload coal trucks into an armament factory. The confrontation lasted all day, after which he spent six weeks in solitary confinement before being sent to Colditz as a persistent escaper, accused of inciting fellow prisoners to mutiny. He learned to speak German and worked as an interpreter. He also invented a type of immersion heater – two tins and a wooden handle plugged into a light switch to provide an immediate source of hot water. In August 1941 the first camp Olympics were held and he confirmed that 'The British came in last place in every event cheerfully, to the dismay of the other participants who took the competition deadly seriously.' An accomplished musician, he played the clarinet in the Colditz band which he formed to accompany the concert party, often playing fortissimo to muffle the sound of tunnels being dug beneath them. He was all set to escape in January 1942, but fell ill, his place being taken by Airey Neave. The following June, after being transferred to Stalag 344 at Lansdorf, he escaped from a working party and made his way to Ulm, where he was caught at the railway station. He was eventually freed by the 5th Armoured Division in April 1945 and after the war was an active member of the Colditz Association.

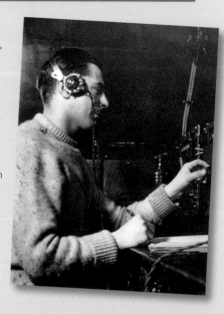

SUBMARINERS' STORIES

The first enemy U-boat to be captured, in June 1940, fell into the hands of a former RHS pupil Bill Moorman, who attended the School from 1917 to 1921. While commanding an anti-submarine trawler *Moonstone* in the Red Sea he captured the Italian U-boat *Galileo Galilei* after firing depth charges and a surface engagement. He towed the prize to Aden to great acclaim and later received the DSC as well as being mentioned in despatches. The marine artist Norman Wilkinson painted the incident in a work entitled *Catch of the Season*.

A key member of the famous 'cockleshell heroes' wartime mission, Royal Navy telegraphist Raymond Quick, who was educated at the RHS, died in 2011 aged 95. He was the last surviving submariner to have taken part in Operation Frankton, a mission which Winston Churchill claimed had shortened the Second World War by six months. In 1942 ten Royal Marines – who became known as the 'cockleshell heroes' – were launched from his T-Class submarine

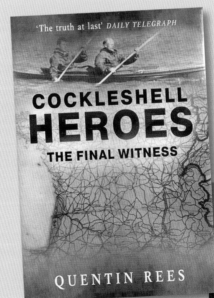

'The truth at last' *DAILY TELEGRAPH*

COCKLESHELL HEROES
THE FINAL WITNESS

QUENTIN REES

Left: Two photographs of Colditz POWs. John Wilkens was incarcerated in the infamous Oflag IVC, better know as Colditz. He was involved with a number of escape attempts. As a member of the band he was involved in masking the sounds of those preparing to break out. Unfortunately, he missed out, falling ill just before he was about to embark on his bid for freedom.

Above: *Raymond Quick (1930–33, company No 5/33) was radio operator on board HMS Tuna.*

Left: *Quick provided memories for Quentin Rees's book* Cockleshell Heroes: The Final Witness, *his testimony encouraged by offering him rum-soaked raisins. He was the link to the outside world from inside HMS Tuna and holds a significant place in history, as the man who sent the message 'Operation Frankton completed'.*

HMS *Tuna* in five tiny 'cockle' canoes to attach limpet mines to shipping in Bordeaux harbour.

Admiral Louis Mountbatten described it as the most courageous and imaginative of all the raids ever carried out by the armed forces, and they crippled the enemy. However, two of the men drowned and six were executed by the Germans. Their bravery was commemorated with a permanent memorial in Bordeaux, which also reflects the role of HMS *Tuna* and her men.

Quick's wartime role as Chief Petty Officer telegraphist won him the DSM, but not for Operation Frankton. It was for his 'outstanding coolness, cheerfulness and skill' while serving on HMS *Tuna* in five arduous patrols and a brilliant and successful attack on a German U-boat on 7 April 1943. However, he thoroughly detested *The Cockleshell Heroes*, the 1954 movie. The modest hero said he was 'scared out of his wits' most of the time, especially when his submarine was forced to spend 36 hours at the bottom of the Mediterranean, off Cyprus, avoiding Nazi hunters. He expressed amazement that he survived the war, having sailed in a succession of five submarines, all of which were lost after he was transferred, and concluding hostilities safely on board HMS *Tuna*.

THE ARCTIC CONVOYS – RUSSIAN MEDALS

Paddy Donovan (1932–36) received the 'Russian Order of Patriotic War' for his role in the Russian convoys, specifically action at the end of 1942. He was replaced on HMS *Chequers* by Prince Philip, and then saw action in the Korean War before taking part in mine-sweeping operations during the Suez crisis. He was awarded the MBE in 1968. At least three other RHS boys were awarded the same Russian medal, and the School is likely to be able to boast the largest number of former pupils who hold it.

Above: British Arctic convoys carried vital war materials to Russia. Ice, gale-force storms and constant threat of attack from German-occupied Norway meant this was an incredibly dangerous journey and a number of RHS boys were decorated with the Russian Order of Patriotic War (right).

Hugh Thomas Henry Moore
13.04.1909 (1920–24).

George Caleb Lewington
10.10.1914 (1926–29).

Leslie Victor French
20.11.1922 (1935–38 St Vincent).

Alan Charles Cooper
21.12.1922 (1934–38 Blake).

RHS BOYS LOST IN THE *HOOD*

On 24 May 1941 HMS *Hood* sank with the loss of 1,415 lives. Many former pupils from the Royal Hospital School were onboard, as well as the School's Assistant Chaplain, Rev. RJP Stewart, who was appointed to the *Hood* just prior to the war and went down with his ship. To honour the loss of her son, and in accordance with the swimming blue he had gained at Cambridge, Mrs May Stewart donated the 'Stewart Cup' for 220 yards freestyle. The Cup was first competed for in 1942 and his mother was present for nearly all of the first 30 races before her death in 1972; her daughter presided thereafter.

After the war many orphans from HMS *Hood* were educated at the School and were usually placed in Hood House. A scale model of the *Hood* is to be found guarding the west side entrance.

Right: Many HMS Hood orphans attended Hood House (name above entrance).

Inset: Penknife given to Hood House by a sailor who served on HMS Hood prior to its sinking.

Below: Sinking of the Hood on 24 May 1941 – an unknown number of former RHS boys were lost.

SINKING THE *BISMARCK*

Benjamin Martin, born in 1891 and educated at the RHS, was the first boy from the School in modern times to reach flag rank in the Royal Navy and the first officer in 87 years to become a Rear-Admiral on the active list from the lower deck. He joined the Navy in 1907 as a boy, first class, and was appointed to warrant rank as a torpedo officer in 1915 and then to commissioned rank the following year. He was given his first command in 1924 and by 1935 was a Captain. In 1939, just before the outbreak of war, he was given command of HMS *Dorsetshire* on the China Station.

He was still in that post in May 1941, on convoy duty, when the ship was summoned to take part in the operations against the German battleship *Bismarck*, arriving just in time to deliver the final torpedo attack which sank the ship. Captain Martin was awarded the DSO for this action. He moved on up the ranks, being promoted to Rear-Admiral in 1944 and then taking command of operations in Burma during the war in the east. For his work there he was knighted, and on retirement after the war was promoted to the rank of Vice-Admiral.

Above left: Sinking of the Bismarck on 27 May 1941 – old boy Sir Benjamin Martin (1901–07, School No 7/7) (top right) commanded the final Dorsetshire torpedo attack.

Above right: Rev. Patrick Stewart, Assistant Chaplain (1940–1) went down with the Hood *and since 1942 has been remembered by pupils competing in the Stewart Cup for swimming.*

News Chronicle

BROWN & POLSON
CORNFLOUR AND CUSTARD

WEDNESDAY, MAY 28, 1941   RADIO PAGE 2   ONE PENNY

No. 29,058

BISMARCK: THE FIRST FULL STORY

Air and Sea Chase Lasted Four Days, Covered 1,750 Miles

Churchill Gives News From Bits Of Paper

CANADIAN PLANES CAME FROM NEWFOUNDLAND

A FLEET SAILED UP FROM GIBRALTAR

NEXT TWO DAYS ARE VITAL IN BATTLE FOR CRETE

1,000 Saved from Ships Lost In Battle of Crete

The Winds of Change

The move to Holbrook had not, as the committee of inspection found, inspired any immediate or basic change in the aims of the School or the approach to educating its pupils. But the war years and their aftermath stimulated rapid and fundamental developments in society as a whole, and the Royal Hospital School was not exempt – and it was fortunate in the new Director of the Hospital, Norman Macleod, who took office in 1942. Although his tenure was short before he was summoned back to the Admiralty, he initiated a wide-ranging and far-seeing discussion on the future route the School should travel, with the establishment of the Bruntisfield Committee, which held its first meeting on 5 April 1943.

I was in Drake from May 1942 to about August 1946. I recall Sister Paton as a true matron who looked after us well and, like most of the staff, helped to instil values which served me well in life. In my imagination I can still hear her crackle as she bustled about the surgery, but the starch was in her uniform; she had a soft centre!

Gary Cooper was Drake's housemaster when I joined and I still remember both him and his wife with great affection. The night we arrived we new boys inadvertently joined a 'clear lower deck' in the dormitory at which Gary administered six of the best to a person who shall remain nameless as I believe the offence involved possession of another's property, a very serious naval offence. English masters feature largely in my memories. The teacher I recall drumming English into me was Mr Snee who taught us not only grammar but how to spell unusual words like 'mnemonic'. He also delighted in telling us boys, always hungry in those days of rationing, about the pre-war seven-course dinners he used to attend. He caned me once for getting involved in an ink pellet fight in class (I came off worst) and then sent me home to his wife for removal of ink stains from my flannel so that I would not invoke the displeasure of Sister Paton.

John Coleman (1942–46)

Left: *RHS boys took great pride in their appearance. 'Gidge', cap tally and collar – all in place.*

Opposite top: *RHS Works Department outing to Southend-on-Sea, 1948.*

Macleod recognised that the RHS, as it stood, was an elementary school, offering an education far below secondary level: 'As things are,' he wrote, 'I could not advise the father of a bright boy to send him there.' He believed its future should be as a good secondary school with a nautical and engineering basis, and with pupils required to offer a higher standard of educational attainment on entry. But the crux of the problem was its mission, under the original charter, to accept naval orphans regardless of their educational potential: 'Destitution or misfortune or even the services of a whole line of naval ancestors can never constitute a claim to higher education if the ability to profit from it is lacking.' His suggestions would move the School further away from acting as a source of supply

ROYAL HOSPITAL SCHOOL, HOLBROOK.
WORKS DEPARTMENT STAFF OUTING TO SOUTHEND-ON-SEA - 4th SEPT. 1948.

I took the entrance exam for the School at the Cripplegate Institute, London, in January 1945. The invigilator was Nobby Lumsden, who told us that should a V1 'doodlebug' pass overhead during the exam, we were not to panic – simply to bite on our rubbers and duck under our desks. As if on cue, a doodlebug materialised about ten minutes later, the rocket motor stopped (not a good sign) and we all dived for cover while Nobby remained standing like an admiral about to go down with his ship. The bomb exploded about a mile away, the whole building shook and Nobby calmly told us to get on with our exam. Those of us who passed were labelled by name and by house and then trucked off to Liverpool Street station, where our mums tearfully said farewell to us before we boarded the train for Ipswich, each of us clutching a suitcase, a gas mask and a sandwich to keep us from starving to death on the journey. It was dark by the time we got to Ipswich, where we were met by Gary Cooper, who loaded us into a couple of trucks (presumably the School couldn't afford a bus) for transport to Holbrook. When we got to the School, we were all tired, scared and frozen stiff (the ground was covered in snow). Gary Cooper and a couple of senior boys wheeled us into the kitchen, where we were given huge mugs of Pusser's cocoa and slab-like corned beef sandwiches before being split into groups and marched off to our respective houses, there to remain until released.

One of our English teachers was Baggy Shawell. He salvaged the Sirius, sailed her into the creek and virtually rebuilt her with a great deal of help from those of us lucky enough to be invited to slap on the paint and varnish. I vividly remember once stepping from Sirius into the dinghy tender, only to find that the dinghy wasn't there! In spite of the fact that he giggled like a girl, Baggy was enormously popular as a teacher. If we didn't feel like parsing a sentence, we had only to mention Africa and he was off on safari for the rest of the lesson.

My first housemaster in Drake was 'Baldy' Kneebone, whose deerstalker hat we pinched and put on the guy for the first fireworks night bonfire after

the war. Our chief collaborator on that occasion was the house matron, Sister Paton. She was a pretty tough little lady. She terrified a succession of housemasters and none of her boys was ever allowed to get constipated. Who could ever forget her infamous 'black mixture', administered for every ailment from boils to sluggish bowels and as a punitive mouthwash for anyone caught swearing within earshot of her surgery?

My favourite masters? Hugh Grant-Scarfe, who taught English and gave religious instruction to us Catholic lads. He kept bees in his back garden. I was helping him one day when we both got badly stung. Still, it was worth it. I finished up being spoiled rotten for two days in the infirmary. He encouraged me to write and, after I left the Royal and Royal Australian Navies, I made a pretty good living as an industrial journalist.

And who could forget 'Piddler' Pine? If he caught you drifting off in class, he'd frighten ten years growth out of you by sneaking up behind you, grabbing your ear and bawling 'On the form, you maggot!' He could also capture your attention (and your collar) by wielding the window pole like a boat-hook. In 1955, while still serving in the RAN, I revisited the School with an uncle who was also an old boy, of Greenwich vintage. We stayed overnight at the old pub in Stutton. When we went down to the bar for supper, we saw half a dozen RHS teachers, among them 'Bandy' Ship and 'Piddler' Pine, then retired. He hadn't spotted me, so I came up quietly behind him and barked 'On the form, you maggot!' Piddler didn't even flinch. He just turned around, looked me up and down and said, 'Sherval, isn't it? Have you come back to buy us a drink?' That was an early start to a very late night.

John Sherval (1945–49)

RHS politicians – representation

The earliest known active politician who was a boy at the School was George Julian Harney, who joined in 1828. He later became a leading member of the Chartist movement and in July 1845, when Karl Marx and Friedrich Engels visited England, an appointment was made for them to meet him. His campaign for universal suffrage, his committed republicanism and his support for the use of general strikes led to him being arrested on many occasions. Marx and Engels both wrote articles for the newspaper he edited, the *Northern Star*, and in 1848 he published and prefaced the first version of the *Communist Manifesto* available in England. After supporting the north in the American Civil War, he emigrated in May 1863 to the USA where he worked in the Massachusetts State House before returning to Britain for the last 20 years of his life.

In 1882 the RHS's first Member of Parliament, albeit for Canada, was elected. Edgar Crow Baker attended the School until 1860 when he joined the Royal Navy. He married in 1869 and emigrated to Canada where he became a prominent accountant, real estate agent, conveyancer, notary and one of the wealthiest men in British Colombia. He entered politics as an Alderman for Victoria and in 1882 was elected to the Canadian Parliament as a Conservative. He resigned in 1889 and died in 1920. Another old boy, Walter Owen, became chairman of London County Council in 1948 after a successful career as a solicitor and in local politics. It was said of him that he was involved in politics 'not for the opportunity of power but to better his fellow men'.

Perhaps the most notable RHS politician was Harry Pursey, who was born in 1891, was educated at the RHS and the Royal Naval College and began his career as a boy seaman. He saw action in the Great War, was mentioned in despatches and commissioned, and eventually reached the rank of Commander. After retiring from the Navy in 1936 he worked as a journalist in Spain during the Spanish Civil War, and was elected as the Labour Member of Parliament for Kingston-upon-Hull East in 1945. He served as an MP for 25 years, retiring at the 1970 general election and being succeeded in his seat by John Prescott.

After his death in 1980, his obituary in *The Times* described him as 'the first naval officer promoted from the lower deck' to enter Parliament – and while he was there he was untiring in his pursuit of what he saw as the damaging changes that had been imposed on the School since the move to Holbrook, and the post-war decisions made by the Admiralty on its future direction. Having used his maiden speech in 1945 to complain that a boy of his own lowly origins would not now get a place at the School *(see page 85)*, he subsequently seized on the occasion to repeat his complaint when, by a law passed in 1885, Greenwich Hospital's finances had to be put annually before the House of Commons. By the 1960s it was clear that the requirement to scrutinise the finances was a waste of Parliamentary time, and had become, as one MP put it, 'a Pursey benefit night'. In 1967 the 1885 enactment was repealed.

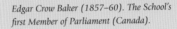

Edgar Crow Baker (1857–60). The School's first Member of Parliament (Canada).

George Julian Harney (1828–31). Radical politician and associate of Marx and Engels.

for the Navy and towards becoming an institution for providing the best possible education for sons of seamen.

He proposed that entry should continue to be limited to the sons of seamen, though the sons of Warrant Officers promoted to commissioned rank could now be admitted. But there was no longer to be a stipulation that pupils would join the Navy after leaving, though they would be expected to have the capacity to reach the educational standard required if they chose to do so. The staff would be graduates, and the syllabus would broaden to include a variety of technical subjects in addition to those normally taught in good secondary schools. Boys with claims on admission but who failed to meet the standard should receive grants for training at other institutions.

The most controversial and close-fought of Macleod's suggestions was that the roles of Superintendent and Headmaster should be amalgamated. Under the current regime, the Superintendent was in total charge and the Headmaster merely one of a range of junior officials under him: some sources claimed that he ranked as low as 25th in seniority after the Superintendent, the Chief Naval Officer and the two Naval Instructors allocated to each house. It was abundantly clear to most of those involved in the discussions that under those circumstances no suitably qualified man would take on the onerous task of reorganising the School and, in the words of the subsequent advertisement for the post, 'raise it to the level of the best technical and secondary schools in England'.

The debate split along service lines, with the Admiralty preferring the command to remain with a naval officer and the civilians wanting a scholar, though they were prepared to concede that the chosen man should have naval connections. In the event the civilians won, and upon the retirement of Captain Bruce-Gardyne, who had steered the School successfully since the transfer to Holbrook, the dual control system was replaced by a single professional Headmaster. In April 1945 the first appointment to the role of 'Superintendent Headmaster' was AJ Price, who had served in the Royal Navy in the Great War and was already a headmaster at the age of 46.

But external events intruded. The Labour Party victory in the post-war general election resulted in an early piece of legislation which instituted new secondary education classifications: grammar schools for the more able and 'secondary modern' for the rest. There was also pressure on the School to maintain the admission of fatherless boys regardless of their educational standard; the war at sea had left an unprecedented number of these boys who, under the previous regime, were entitled to the benefits of Greenwich Hospital and its School.

A new Member of Parliament, Harry Pursey, a former RHS pupil, used his maiden speech to complain that 'a boy of my origin would not get in today'. His view was that the new school had become 'one of the greatest charitable scandals of the century'. Having once taken 1,000 boys, it had now reduced its numbers to fewer than 600: 'Do not take the cream who could go elsewhere and fail to take those for whom it was founded.'

The Admiralty's response, without consulting the Headmaster or the advisory committee, was that the RHS should fall within the 'secondary modern' category and that 90 per cent of the compassionate cases should gain entry. This was not the school that Price had expected to join, and he gave notice to quit. He was succeeded by his assistant, Major NE Lee, a Territorial Army man who remained in post until 1951 and, when the formalities of an occasion demanded, wore his Army uniform, thereby provoking comments about a naval school led by an Army officer. Yet another inspection was undertaken, which concluded that it would be too expensive to maintain a grammar stream

Right: Former Bursar and Housemaster at Wellington College, Major Norman Edward Lee OBE TD MA BJSc, Headmaster of the RHS (1946–51).

Stanley Lawrence McArdle

On the morning of 31 January 1953 the ferry *Princess Victoria*, with 174 passengers and crew members on board, was caught in a severe gale off the Northern Irish coast, and eventually capsized and sank with the loss of 121 lives. The SOS calls resulted in several lifeboats and ships being sent to the area, including the Royal Navy's HMS *Contest*, but they were delayed by the severity of the storm and by the time they reached the stricken ferry she was on the point of sinking. Her captain had waited too long to give the order to abandon ship, so many of the lifeboats could not be used and by the time the rescue vessels arrived many of the passengers had fallen into the sea and drowned.

Onboard the *Contest* was Lt Cdr Lawrence McArdle, who had attended the Royal Hospital School from 1934 to 1938. Along with the rest of the crew he helped to pluck small groups of survivors from the sea, and he was awarded the George Medal for an act of conspicuous bravery which saved the life of one man. McArdle went on to enjoy a distinguished naval career and ended as a Rear-Admiral.

Right: Captain Superintendent Evan Bruce-Gardyne DSO RN was the last Naval Superintendent (1933–45) at the RHS. His son, Jock Bruce-Gardyne, was raised in Holbrook House and became a Conservative MP and after this a life peer and Baron.

The Admirals – top ranking

The RHS can boast at least ten old boys who went on to become admirals. The earliest was Arthur Phillip, who has been covered elsewhere, as have William Pullen, an Arctic explorer involved in the Franklin expedition, Benjamin Martin, who sank the *Bismarck* and Stanley McArdle, who was awarded the George Medal. The RHS is distinct as a school in educating the largest number of boy seamen who have risen to flag officer.

Another was Admiral Sir Henry Felix Woods, who was born in Jersey in 1843 and educated in the Upper School in the 1850s, finishing top of his year and being appointed an assistant master. He became a Navigation Lieutenant in 1867, but then was attached to the British Embassy to the Ottoman Empire and eventually, with Queen Victoria's consent, joined the Imperial Ottoman Navy with the rank of Admiral. The authorities were so impressed with a floating lighthouse he constructed to make the Bosphorus easier to navigate that he was adopted by the Turks and, among other roles, put in charge of coastal defences and eventually the Turkish fleet. He became known as Woods Pasha, was well respected and became *aide de camp* to Sultan Abdul Hamid, whom he represented at the coronation of King Edward VII, the occasion at which

Above: Admiral William Whittingham (RHS 1870s) pictured with two of his three sons – Clive Alan (centre) and Harold Edward (right), later knighted.

Left: Admiral Sir Henry Felix Woods KCVO (RHS 1850s), was a colourful character. He became a Pasha in the Imperial Ottoman Naval Service. This photo of Woods landing from an imperial caïque at Seraglio Point in Turkey is from his autobiography, Spunyarn: From the Strands of a Sailor's Life Afloat *and* Ashore: Forty Seven Years under the Ensigns of Great Britain and Turkey.

he received a knighthood. He published his own memoirs in 1924 entitled *Spunyarn*; and a brief extract describes his part in one of the many royal visits paid to the School in the 19th century:

'I was a main "royal yardsman", being one of the smallest boys in the School, and I well remember the pride with which I ran aloft to take my station in "manning yards" when the Princess Royal came with her fiancé, the Crown Prince of Prussia, to visit the School. The prince, in his uniform, looked a very handsome fellow, but what struck me about the Princess Royal was the enormous size of her crinoline, only recently in fashion. This was the first occasion on which one of those voluminous garments had come across my vision, and I gazed with wonder at the manoeuvres required to get her in and out of her carriage.'

Admiral William Whittingham, born in 1862, was at the School during the 1870s. He served in the Sudan and in Canada, was with the Grand Fleet during the Great War and was a staff officer in Scotland, retiring with the rank of Engineer Rear-Admiral. He kept in contact with the School, and in 1918 wrote, 'On one or two occasions I have visited it as a stranger and have gone to my old dormitory and walked around the old well remembered buildings.' After retiring from the Navy he served in local politics and education and his three sons were all quite remarkable medical students. Clive was killed by shellfire in Belgium in 1917 and William was gassed in the trenches in 1918, leaving Harold to scale the heights denied his siblings, becoming Air Vice Marshal Sir Harold Edward Whittingham, Honorary Physician to the King.

Admiral George William Baldwin was at the School in the 1880s and won the silver medal in 1885. After joining the Navy he saw action in the Benin Expedition and served throughout the Great War. He then became chief engineer of the Invergordon naval base, before being posted to Malta and finally to Devonport Dockyards and retiring in 1926 as a Rear-Admiral.

Admiral James Figgins left the School in 1902 and entered the Royal Navy as a boy, second class. He soon became a Warrant Officer, and was one of the first to be selected as a mate when that rank was established. He served with distinction through the Great War and in 1933 was the first officer to be promoted to Captain via the rank of mate. He commanded several ships during the Second World War and was for a time naval officer in command at Lowestoft. He ended his service as a Rear-Admiral.

Admiral Sir Sidney Oswell Frew (1903–05) joined the Navy as an engine room artificer. After reaching the rank of mate during the Great War he became an Engineer Lieutenant and then served for many years in submarines. From an early stage in his career he was involved in secret and experimental work, and his promotion from Lieutenant Commander to Commander in only three years was remarkable, particularly during the inter-war years when the Navy was being severely reduced in numbers. He introduced the German schnorkel to Royal Navy submarines and wrote extensively on naval steam engines. He became a Rear-Admiral and a Grand Officer of the Order of Orange-Nassau before being knighted in 1949, the year of his retirement. A division of HMS *Fisgard* was named after him.

Admiral Sir Philip Enright, who attended the School from 1907 to 1910, is the only man in the modern history of the Navy to have risen from boy seaman to full

Admiral. He joined the Navy as a boy, second class, at HMS *Ganges* and later attended the Royal Naval College. He reached commissioned rank in 1922 and served in a wide variety of stations until in the Second World War he became Captain of the Mediterranean Fleet. After the war he was for a while naval aide-de-camp to King George VI and was promoted to Rear-Admiral. He was Admiral Superintendent of the Devonshire Dockyard until May 1953, and a few months later, on the day of his retirement, became a full Admiral. He had already been knighted the year before.

That year, 1952, also saw him return to the School for Speech Day, and in 1958 he came again to unveil the memorial book in the memory of old boys who had given their lives in the service of their country. He died in 1960.

Above: Admiral George William Baldwin (RHS 1880s) received the Most Honourable Order of the Bath in 1926.

Right: Admiral Sir Philip King Enright (1906–10) on return to the RHS to unveil the Book of Remembrance in 1958. He rose from boy seaman to full Admiral and he gave his medals (inset) and sword to the School and was knighted in 1952.

Recognising gallantry and service

Among the thousands of RHS boys who joined the Navy and served their country in the wars of the 18th and 19th centuries, there must be many who were officially recognised for their valour and gallantry, but their names are lost in the mists of time. Even after the Great War, when the School actively sought to search out and commemorate all the RHS boys and masters who had given their lives, whether decorated or not, only 154 names could be found, and it was recognised at the time that this was certainly an incomplete record. The names of those who could be identified were inscribed on an oak tablet which was installed in the Queen's House at Greenwich, and a memorial stained-glass window was also placed in the chapel. The tablet travelled with the School from Greenwich to Holbrook.

In the 1950s further attempts were made both to complete the Great War data and to identify those killed in the Second World War. This resulted in the conclusion that at least 442 boys and three masters lost their lives in the First World War and at least 765 in the Second. But it was also decided that there would never be a definitive tally of the RHS dead of both wars, so to commemorate them all, known and unknown, the School commissioned a beautifully bound and illuminated vellum book which was placed in the chapel. Illustrated by Margaret Raisbeck and bound by Sydney Cockerell (Royal Coronation Binder) it gives a brief history of Greenwich Hospital and its School and continues:

Here are no names. The diversity of their service and sacrifice defies our search. Let us honour all who enriched our heritage by their bravery and crowned it by giving their lives.

Left: A page from the Book of Remembrance recognising those lost in the 1939–45 war.

Below: An early design for the RHSA Memorial Cross dedicated in 2012.

Young men who had been at the School made an enormous contribution to both wars; at least 11,000 of them served in the Navy during the Great War, including six Sperring brothers who had attended the RHS between 1891 and 1913 and who all survived the war. One of them is known to have been in Russia during the revolution, and another received the Croix de Guerre for heroism. The numbers of those lost in the Second World War include only those known to have died while serving in the Navy; no numbers could be reliably established for those who had served in the Army, Air Force or Merchant Navy.

and a sixth form in a school where the majority were unlikely to benefit; so there should either be high entrance standards, with those unable to achieve them supported elsewhere, or boys who turned out to be academically able should eventually be sent to grammar schools to complete their education.

Additional funds now became available from a number of sources – the introduction of the boarding schools allowance for those posted overseas, some local authority funded grants and access to some of the carefully protected Reade endowment – and so the School was at last able to support and develop greater educational aspirations. At the same time it was realised that the surge of war-created orphans would soon subside. The Admiralty therefore eventually decided to go along with the most expensive option and allow the grammar stream to continue. At the same time a more conventional governing body was created, though still reporting ultimately to the Admiralty. By 1946 candidates had already started to be entered for School Certificate examinations, and this entry grew with the introduction of the O level in 1948.

The naval tradition had not faltered, however. In 1949 Royal Marine Major Arthur Buckley joined as Chief Naval Instructor, and he maintained the traditions that had been built up over the centuries, albeit now with more than a nod to the modern world. He introduced new daily ceremonial and a School flag. He also worked hard with the School band to improve their performance and output, restarted and edited *The Royal Hospital School Magazine* and forged stronger links with old boys. But inevitably the concentration on seamanship was gradually being reduced, not least because the rapid development of naval technology demanded new skills and the old ways of operating ships at sea were passing.

On Major Lee's retirement in 1951 he used his final report to describe positively the breadth of education now offered by the School. Soon afterwards, HRH Princess Elizabeth went to Greenwich to open

Of the many honours awarded to people associated with the School, which include both medals for valour and recognition at the highest levels in the honours lists, two can perhaps stand for all. One was the George Cross awarded to John Babington, Headmaster between 1951 and 1955, for a conspicuous act of bravery while working in bomb disposal during the war, work for which he was also awarded the OBE. The other was the award of both the Edward Medal and the Carnegie Hero Fund Medal by George V in 1921 to RHS old boy Donald Adolphous Brown who, while working as a foreman at Woolwich in1919, had single-handedly dragged a case of exploding rockets out of the depot, preventing a serious incident. He was notable in other ways too. The mixed-race son of a Guyanan sailor, he married Adelaide Knight, a disabled woman who campaigned vigorously for women's suffrage along with Emmeline Pankhurst and her daughters. The couple educated themselves, worked hard for their beliefs – she was imprisoned for her suffragette activity – and were spirited in their opposition to the prejudice they faced, she for her disability and he for his colour.

Awards for life saving have also featured heavily among medals given to RHS schoolboys. One of the earliest and most notable was the Royal Humane Society Silver Medal for Saving Life, awarded in 1834 to John Felstead, aged 14, who jumped into the Thames to rescue a young man who had fallen in and got into difficulties. This was the highest medal awarded by the society at the time.

The School still possesses honours boards featuring other Royal Humane Society medals and certificates granted to RHS boys. They include 14-year-old AEH Robertson, who in 1900 saved the life of a nine-year-old boy by jumping off the pier at Hurst Castle into deep water and a roaring tide, while that same year

WHT Bicknell saved a three-year-old at East Cowes. The last award recorded was in 1945 when David Kendrick, aged 13, rescued three-year-old Anthony Feltham from a pond in Portsmouth.

Those awards have their echo today in the life guard training undertaken by many pupils. This has been a focus at the RHS since 1948 when Stanley Good, Hawke housemaster from 1937 until 1960, introduced the Life Saving Club. The training given then, and still now, was and is at a serious level, and those who gain the difficult qualification have a skill that stands them in good stead for the rest of their lives.

Top: John Babington GC OBE RNVR, Headmaster (1951–55), was awarded the George Cross for 'great gallantry and undaunted devotion to duty' in defusing bombs during World War II.

Left: Lifesaving class from August 1927 in a photograph by F Sharp (official sports photographer in the 1920s). The shield presented by the City Livery Club for swimming and lifesaving. Royal Humane Society Awards recognising boys involved in lifesaving.

Above: *Donald Adolphus Brown's (1885–89) entry on the register of candidates for admission to Greenwich Hospital School.*

Inset left: *The Carnegie Hero Fund Medal*

ROYAL HUMANE SOCIETY AWARDS.

1893 AUG. 10TH HORACE SMITH, AGED 13, CERTIFICATE. WHILST BATHING AT BOGNOR ASSISTED TO SAVE W. GOODYER, AGED 19.

1894 AUG. 29TH DAVID BREBNER, AGED 13½, CERTIFICATE. SAVED ANNIE DUKES, AGED 14, BY JUMPING IN HIS CLOTHES INTO THE BASIN AT DEVONPORT DOCKYARD.

1903 AUG. 13TH ARTHUR T. SQUIBB, AGED 12¾, CERTIFICATE. SAVED THE LIFE OF GEORGE TRUEMAN, AT LANGSTONE HARBOUR.

the converted East wing of the National Maritime Museum, in which the Upper Nautical Division had formerly been taught. Her route through the old School grounds was lined by boys from the Royal Hospital School who were given a full tour of the Museum afterwards.

The new Headmaster in 1951 was John Babington who, although his term of office lasted only four years, had a considerable effect on the School's transition from the old to the new. The aim as stated by the governing body of giving 'every boy an opportunity of obtaining the best education appropriate to his ability and aptitudes' required more staff and more facilities, for which the money was not easily available. But it was during his time that the first RHS boys were admitted as officer cadets to Dartmouth, and the first A Level pass and the first university place (AN Hughes) were gained. Significantly, perhaps, these academic advances came in the same year, 1953, that the rigged ceremonial mast at the bottom of the parade ground was declared unsafe and taken down.

Coronation Day in June 1953 was a very special day at the School. While 40 pupils attended the procession at the Victoria Memorial and 12 marched in the Ipswich naval group, the whole School listened to the broadcast. A celebratory pageant of empire was produced: the first historical part included a re-enactment of the laying down of Raleigh's cloak for Queen Elizabeth I, supposed to have occurred at the School's former home in Greenwich, and there was a similar reconstruction of Sir Francis Drake's bowls match – all to the accompaniment of 'Greensleeves'. The second part saw 52 peoples from all over the empire represented by boys in fancy dress paying homage to HM Queen Elizabeth II, with empire flags and a recording of the Queen. Heralds, trumpeters, narrators, band and choir all played their parts in this epic performance. To round the day off the films *Henry V* and *Royal Destiny* were shown in the evening. This same year Admiralty approval was granted for the School to have its own flag, the blue ensign defaced by the arms of Greenwich Hospital, a unique honour among schools.

Babington was the last Headmaster also to be Superintendent; when he resigned in 1955 this position was abolished altogether. And as a further departure, fees were introduced, with help for those who could not pay. Second Master Norman Lumsden assumed the headship for one term, pending the new permanent appointment. He had joined the School in July 1919 and was most deserving of the MBE he received at Buckingham Palace later in the decade. He was highly committed and his favourite phrase was 'To hell with the principles! What is the problem?'

Norman York joined in January 1956 as the new Headmaster. He was a scientist, a Cambridge rugby blue and an Army man.

His brief was to raise educational standards and introduce a more academic syllabus, though there was to be no cutting of the link with the Navy. Inevitably, however, pressures on the timetable caused by the introduction of more subjects led to lessons in seamanship becoming fewer. From 1958 the two grammar streams received no seamanship instruction after their first year, and its place in the curriculum declined even further in the early 1960s when the introduction of the CSE meant that the less academically inclined boys were also now able to take public examinations.

Left: George Hardy OBE. He was a housemaster and Deputy Headmaster (1958–85), initiated CCF and renewed the HMS Victory *weather vane on top of Nelson House.*

Below: Norman Arthur York, Headmaster (1956–74) and his wife Mary. A good leader who induced confidence in his staff and a feeling of moral obligation to follow him.

HISTORICAL STUDIES

Royal Hospital School 1974

Above: The 250th Anniversary Luncheon held in the School dining hall in 1962. The toast to 'The School' was proposed by the Earl of Stradbroke, who commented favourably on the School's healthy surroundings, its fine buildings, superb chapel, great traditions and the bearing of the boys.

A counter to the move away from naval training came with the establishment on 1 May 1960 of the Combined Cadet Force unit, where activities took over one of the games afternoons. As Bernard de Neumann remembers, this was mainly the initiative of Nelson's housemaster, George Hardy: 'We became the first school to have a Navy section instead of an Army section for basic training. Hardy threw himself into establishing our CCF, and undoubtedly faced off a lot of opposition from the naval staff.' It rapidly became popular and, with 12 officers and 350 ratings, was soon one of the largest in the country. The School also participated enthusiastically in the new Duke of Edinburgh's Award scheme.

In 1959 Rev. Jack Holland, the first civilian Chaplain, arrived; he stayed ten years and was another staff recipient of the MBE. And a break from tradition occurred when Earl Mountbatten visited the School on 23 July 1960 and, at the end of the parade, surprisingly ordered the boys to break ranks so that he could informally address them all, stating 'This parade is extremely good. I have actually never

seen a better one.' A tape recording was made of his speech in which he stressed that 'boarding schools give a unique opportunity for the formation of character'. This message was further reinforced by the *Illustrated London News* article on the education of British youth. It featured the Royal Hospital School and images of laboratory work, the library, gym, dining hall, canoes, chess, the main entrance and *Fame*.

The houses were remodelled in the early 1960s, providing refurbished boarding quarters and new flats for house staff, many of whom were now married men with families. In 1962 the 250th anniversary of the School's foundation was celebrated, with the First Sea Lord, Sir Caspar John, host and principal guest on Speech Day. This milestone was also marked at Greenwich with the unveiling of a bronze plaque commemorating the previous use of the buildings now forming part of the National Maritime Museum. And funds were raised from old boys and the Lloyd's Patriotic Fund for a new sports pavilion to celebrate the anniversary. Two years after the bicentenary Earl Jellicoe presented the prizes on Speech Day, donating his father's sword and a punishment book relating to him; this event was attended by Miss NC Reade, the last surviving link the School had with a relative of its great benefactor.

In 1964 Philip Newell became the new Director of Greenwich Hospital. Having taught at Uppingham and Repton he had become Headmaster of Gresham's in 1935 and served as a founder member on the Admiralty Advisory Committee for the School in 1938 and on the important Bruntisfield Committee from 1943. In all these capacities he had a significant influence over the School and its progression towards becoming a mainstream educational establishment. That progress was being made in this respect was confirmed by the first place at Cambridge secured by a pupil; this was RL Toase in 1965 who went to St John's College to study mathematics and physics. And the visit of the Chancellor of the Exchequer, Jim Callaghan, reaffirmed the changing nature of the School, when he stressed that it was not now just designed 'to produce boys for the Royal Navy, but to develop their talents in whatever direction they lay'.

By 1968 the banner given to the School by George V some 50 years earlier had become worn and tattered. HM Queen Elizabeth II agreed that her grandfather's gift should be replaced, and delegated the presentation to her mother, who came on Speech Day for the ceremonial handing over of the new banner. Her Majesty's visit was also marked by the naming of the common room in the new – and at the time still unfinished – sixth form block in her honour. She had presented the prizes at Greenwich alongside her husband in 1931 and was the only guest of honour to have visited both locations. The Headmaster declared

Top: *HM Queen Elizabeth The Queen Mother, accompanied by Headmaster Norman York on the occasion of her visit, 15 July 1968.*

Above: *The coronation cushion, made from tapestry used in Westminster Abbey for the Coronation of King George VI in May 1937 and used on her visit to open the sixth form building in 1968.*

Left: *The Queen's Banner, received by Head Boy, ER Newman, on the cover of The Royal Hospital School Magazine, 1968.*

Far left: *The Queen's Banner is renewed and rededicated in 2006. Here, HRH The Duke of York represents it to Deputy Heads of School, Thomas Wood and Claire Kester.*

Royal Hospital School 1968

that he was proud of the royal foundation and recalled the interest which the sovereign and the royal family had always maintained in the School. Her Majesty stressed that 'you who are here are, indeed, heirs of a great tradition, a tradition of service and loyalty, of which you must be justly proud'. During her visit she was involved in the presentation of a cushion linked to her coronation and to mark the occasion of her visit asked that the boys should be granted an extra week's holiday.

The board bearing the inscription remembering that day is a single piece of mahogany that had been stored for nearly two centuries at Greenwich in case new doors should ever be needed for the 1789 chapel. It stands on a stone corbel carved by Tudor craftsmen for the Palace of Placentia and reversed and reused in the building of the Hospital's King Charles Wing in 1664; a Luftwaffe bomb had dislodged it during the war and it had lain ever since among other stone salvage in the Queen Anne undercroft at Greenwich. So in the mid-20th century at Holbrook the School acknowledged its formidable links both with Greenwich Hospital and with its predecessor royal palace on the site.

By the 1970s the sixth form numbered over 100 pupils and there were new laboratories and lecture rooms. In addition to cadetships in the Navy, the Army and the Royal Air Force, many more boys were going on to university, gaining 18 places in 1972, including four to Cambridge. Norman York retired in 1974 with his work for the School rewarded by the award of a CBE. His vision for the future had seen him presiding over massive strides forward in the educational and sporting attainment of his pupils, as well as the growth of musical, artistic and theatrical activities and moves away from the severely imposed discipline of the naval tradition. He had provided stability and wise and determined leadership during challenging times of transition.

At his final Speech Day all six Greenwich Hospital directors with whom he had worked during his time at the School were present, and his farewell party was attended by over 250 staff. His retirement had been prompted by ill health, and he was to live for only three more years. But as Philip Newell wrote of him, 'He became Headmaster at a critical stage, when a man was needed with vision to see how to adapt to modern needs magnificent buildings created in the 1930s for an orphanage giving little more than elementary education. When he retired the laboratories and workshops were second to none and his sixth formers were regularly gaining university places. But his concern was always for the under-privileged, the orphans and the less able in the community.'

His successor was Norman Worswick, who had previously been a housemaster at the RHS before moving away to headships in other schools. He maintained York's modernising approach and his eight years' headship saw much consolidation of all the achievements of his predecessor. He greatly encouraged music in the School, with the establishment of new brass and wind ensembles and a string group and chamber choir supporting a growing orchestra. His tenure also saw the modernisation of the boarding houses, with study bedrooms for the older boys and bunk-bed desk units, and the old communal showers replaced with

Above: Headmaster Norman Worswick (1974–83). From the first he exuded the air of a firm disciplinarian who knew where he wanted the pupils to go and the standards to which he wanted them to aspire.

Left: An original stone corbel from the Palace of Placentia in Greenwich (*inset*) was presented by HM Queen Elizabeth The Queen Mother in 1968 to symbolise the School's roots there.

Her Majesty Queen Elizabeth the Queen Mother on the occasion of her visit 15th July 1968 graciously consented that this room should be called

THE QUEEN ELIZABETH ROOM

The stone on which this board rests came from the Palace of Placentia the first Royal gift to found Greenwich Hospital and hence to endow this School

cubicles. Nelson House, which had become the upper sixth house, was equipped with bed-sitting rooms and a bar to help the boys bridge the gap between school and university. However, a show of hands at a staff meeting about the possibility of the School going co-educational resulted in a 70 per cent vote against.

His final term in 1983 was marked on 7 May by a disastrous fire in the chapel caused by an electrical fault in the organ. The Robson organ, that had been at Greenwich since March 1821, moving between chapel, dining room and gymnasium before its transfer to Holbrook in 1933, was totally destroyed and the pulpits and some of the choir stalls were badly damaged. Worse damage was done by the smoke which totally engulfed the building, but at least its appearance spurting out of the vents high in the roof alerted two sharp-eyed senior boys who quickly raised the alarm. It was two years before the new organ was installed.

Also in 1983, a year after the Falklands War had ended, the white ensign flown by HMS *Glamorgan* during that conflict was presented to the School to join that flown by HMS *Superb* in the 1914 Battle of the Falkland Islands. As Philip Newell graphically records, 'No fewer than

East Anglian Daily Times, Saturday, June 23, 1984, No. 35,971, Price 18p

The Archbishop of Canterbury Dr. Robert Runcie and the Bishop of St. Edmundsbury and Ipswich, Rt. Rev. John Waine, with the headmaster of Royal Hospital School, Holbrook, Mr. Michael Kirk. Today Dr. Runcie will conduct an open-air service in Bury St. Edmunds. Read about the Archbishop's Holbrook visit on Page 14. *Picture by Jeremy Turner.*

Left: *Headmaster Norman Worswick is joined by HRH The Duke of Gloucester in 1983 to survey the damage following the fire that destroyed the School's historic organ.*

Above: *Presentation of the white ensign flown by HMS* Glamorgan *during the Falklands conflict (1983).*

Top: *In 1984 The Archbishop of Canterbury, Robert Runcie, celebrated the dedication of the Chapel of St Mary and St Nicholas 50 years before, accompanied by new Headmaster Michael Kirk (1983–95).*

Above: Matthew March, who lost his caravan in the great storm of 1987. During his 40 years at the School (1971–2011) he was a history teacher, sports coach, housemaster, Registrar and Senior Master. On his retirement he presented the trophies on Sports Day.

Right: The 1987 edition of The Royal Hospital School Magazine *illustrates the damage to the trees along Queen Mary's Avenue – some of these trees had been given by the royal family in 1938.*

57 boys in the School had a parent serving in the South Atlantic at the time of the hostilities. Among the many old boys on active service there, one was twice rescued from the cold sea by the same hand. He knew it well; its owner had been with him in the same house at Holbrook.' The naval link and tradition clearly continued.

High-profile visitors continued to visit the School. HRH The Duke of Gloucester opened the squash courts, HRH Prince Michael of Kent came as president of the Royal Patriotic Fund who sponsored pupils at the School and the Archbishop of Canterbury, Robert Runcie, preached in the chapel on the occasion of the 50th anniversary of its dedication. But the School was about to enter a new phase.

I remember 1987, when the hurricane hit and we had no electricity for a week. It was a wonderful, magical time and we were excused prep as it was October and so got dark early. The food was pretty awful though, as the only cooking implement that worked were the huge gas-powered boilers. They made a sort of stew most days, but instead of proper meat I seem to remember whole sausages floating around in a greasy mess.

In the houses we were given lanterns and candles and experimented with making toast and heating up biscuits. One not so welcome side effect was that we were only allowed cold showers as the fuel oil was needed to run the emergency lights. This was really annoying when we needed to sleep as they burned quite brightly. Naturally any attempt to cover them was met with punishment (possibly the only demonstration of health and safety evident during the whole event).

The hurricane was still blowing very strongly when we got up in the morning, though most of us had been up half the night as it seemed that the windows might be blown in any minute. On the way to breakfast we struggled against the wind and our badgie decided that it would be safer to go to the dining hall through the corridors – though the colonnades had not at that time been glassed in, it was still better than no shelter. As we passed the chapel there were tiles flying off the roof and after breakfast it was announced that chapel would be in the assembly hall that morning.

The destruction was awesome. Matthew March, housemaster of Nelson, lost his caravan – all that was left was the base. Trees were felled left, right and centre, and instead of sitting in a classroom during naval instruction Les Dryden took us to Alton Water, where every boat had been knocked from its trailer, so we spent an hour righting them. After a week of this it was announced that we were being sent home early, except for the choir, as they were performing at the annual Seafarers' Service in St Paul's. As a member of the choir I was expected to stay but luckily my mother refused to make two trips to pick up my brother and me, so I escaped. I had similar luck after the Easter holiday the next year when the whole of the south was snowed in and so those of us from Pompey or Plymouth got to stay at home for an extra couple of days while those poor northern and Scottish lads had to return on the correct date.

Richard Hardcastle (1985–90)

The Modern Era

The new Headmaster was Michael Kirk, whose brief was to continue to improve and modernise the School, and this at a time when numbers of applicants were dropping dramatically as both Royal and Merchant Navies contracted. He introduced two fundamental changes within his first few years. The first was the announcement in 1986 that corporal punishment was to cease. The second was to initiate the process whereby, in 1990, an Act of Parliament amended the School's constitution.

Henceforth the Royal Hospital School would be able to admit both girls and boys, and they could join regardless of any seafaring connections within their families. This final break with the terms of William's and Mary's charter was carefully debated, and assurances were given that the children and grandchildren of seafarers would always have preference

over others. So the School was now on track to become a fully fledged independent public school, able to recruit from a wider pool of potential pupils. However, the Earl of Arran stated that there was 'no intention to alter the School's naval ethos' and Lord Callaghan confirmed that 'he was happy to see that steps are being taken to maintain and, I hope, expand the School so that it will continue its great traditions'.

The decision to readmit girls to the School 150 years after they had been ejected was a recognition that the challenges posed by changes in society and education at the end of the 20th century had to be faced. The School's governors at the end of the 1980s realised that it would be increasingly difficult to maintain the viability of the RHS as a large, wholly boarding establishment for pupils of secondary age, with naval backgrounds and with a comprehensive range of ability including a large sixth form offering a variety of subjects at A Level. The policy of

Right: Michael Kirk was appointed Headmaster in 1983. Towards the end of his tenure (10 May 1994) he accompanied HM Queen Elizabeth II on the occasion of the tercentenary of the foundation of Greenwich Hospital. Being inspected on parade at Greenwich, with the 1811 West wing of the old school behind, are WO2 Les Dryden RM, Head of School, James Leason and Deputy Heads of School, Jessica Weller and Karl Vidak.

Kirk introduced girls to the School and during his 12 years in office it had transformed itself – becoming a co-educational independent school open to all.

Left: Girls are now fully integrated into the Ceremonial Guard – here relaxing prior to a parade. There is strong competition for places in the Guard who perform high quality precision drill on ceremonial occasions.

Below left: The School has been co-educational since 1991, girls are also fully involved in the school community – here pictured at a wild west event in the Jellicoe Room, featuring hoe down, line dancing and fancy dress contest.

restricting entry to the sons of seafarers was no longer an option, even if grandsons were added to the equation. Admitting the sons of members of the other armed forces, an open entry without any sort of service qualification at all and the admission of day boys were all considered. But opening the School to girls gradually became the preferred option, not least because of the pressure being brought to bear by parents.

It was a brave and expensive decision. Not only would boarding houses have to be modernised to suit the girls, but also changing rooms in the sports buildings and accommodation in the infirmary – and the boys would feel rightly short-changed if their houses were not also upgraded. A programme of gradual improvement of all the houses was therefore instituted, which was completed by the mid-

1990s. The curriculum needed little immediate change, though it was recognised that new subjects would eventually have to be introduced. The girls' uniform was carefully thought through – including the welcome decision that they should wear WRNS uniform on parade – and the food on offer in the dining hall was augmented by a salad bar and other new menus acceptable to both girls and boys. The whole transition was overseen by Hazel Anthony, the first Senior Mistress, who had run a boarding house at her previous school and now joined the management team.

I was the last of the dying breed of Howe boys before the girls took the house over in 1993. In my third year under the watchful eye of Noel Smith (housemaster) we moved to Blake while Howe was being converted for the girls. We all felt jealous at the time and asked 'why should the girls get all the new furniture and rooms etc', though eventually all of the houses were converted to what they are today. I went on to become Head of House in St Vincent, but was always a Howe lad to the end.

Alex Shaw (1990–97)

I was considered to be a bit of a toff when I was there (I suppose I was a bit plummy) and I was called 'Vodes'. It was ages before I discovered that this was short for Vodafone, in the days when mobiles were only for the very rich.

Vicky Riding (1991–94)

Changing perspectives – as time marches on

MONTY CALLOW AND DON HAWKLEY

That the RHS has changed fundamentally in the last 20 or so years is obvious – and who better to document that change than Monty Callow. He was a boy at the School from 1967 to 1974, returned to teach biology in 1979 and has lived through the developments that have seen the RHS turn from 'the cradle of the Navy' to an independent school with HMC status.

He was typical of entrants in the late 1960s, in that he came from a Portsmouth naval family of moderate means, and his fees were paid by Greenwich Hospital. Yet he was also a talented scientist and benefited from the highly academic education on offer in the 'U' stream. He remembers a sixth form at least 40-strong of whom the majority went on to good universities; he himself did a degree in biochemistry.

He also remembers a school about which he uses the word 'brutal'. The 'red light' system at meal times was still in operation for part of his time there, the dormitories were cheerless places where the beds were all made up with naval precision, there were communal showers and there was no private space. Parents were often based overseas, so most boys could not go home; the RHS was their home, and although everybody had a named legal guardian in the UK, most of the boys did not see their parents or any family members for months on end. Their friends were at school and their life was based there. Discipline was mainly maintained by the prefects – or Petty Officer boys, as they were still known – with little adult supervision; the prevailing attitude was that the senior boys would sort out any troublesome issues that arose.

While Callow was still a schoolboy, concerns about the School regime began to be raised, particularly by David Owen when he was Harold Wilson's Naval Secretary, and small changes were implemented; for example the move to a cafeteria system at meal times. However, it took the liberalising influence of Michael Kirk to start the process of digging away at decades, if not centuries, of naval heritage – and it is arguable that the need to move the School forward was over-speedy for some traditionalists, both within the common room and outside at the Admiralty and Greenwich Hospital.

Don Hawkley is another long-standing member of staff who has seen and experienced the changes since 1978 when he came to the RHS to teach art and PE. Both he and Monty Callow have been housemasters and, like everyone else among the staff, have joined fully in all the sporting and extra-curricular activities. Don Hawkley coached first XI cricket for 34 years, as well as the girls' first XI hockey from their first arrival in 1991 until 2008, and has also been involved in careers advice and Personal, Social, Health and Economic Education (PSHEE).

Although both recognise that the School is a very different place today from what it was 30 years ago – and admittedly feel that some of the things they loved about the old place have gone forever – they both feel honoured and privileged to have been, and still to be, part of the Royal Hospital School. Until the houses were modernised, both staff and pupils lived in accommodation which offered little of the comforts of home, but they all joined fully in the full time boarding school environment – and this was because the staff were motivated by the boys to whom they were more than just schoolmasters. They felt – and feel – that they could really make a difference to the young people in their charge, to whom they were much more *in loco parentis* than is usual, even within the norm of the boarding school tradition.

Above: Don Hawkley, art teacher (since 1978) and Head of PSHE is pictured at L'Orangerie in Paris on the 2009 School Art Trip. He is a skilled ceramic artist.

Left: Monty Callow (1967–74, Drake), biology teacher (since 1979) with a talent for outdoor pursuits.

Above and left: *Tom Wood (2000–07, Drake), business studies teacher (since 2011) and talented athlete. He was a member of staff accompanying pupils on South Africa Tour (2012).*

Below: *On the right, Charlotte Anderson (1998–2005, Blake), RS teacher (since 2010) and talented staff cricketer and England mixed hockey player. On the left, Rebecca Nutton, one of a series of the College of William and Mary (Williamsburg) graduates who have since pursued a career at the RHS.*

TOM WOOD AND CHARLOTTE ANDERSON

This feeling that the RHS is a place apart from other independent schools is echoed by two young members of staff who have returned to the School to teach after being pupils. Tom Wood (2000–07) did a law degree and now teaches business studies, and Charlotte Anderson (1998–2005) has returned to teach religious studies. They are both resident tutors and enjoy the improved accommodation now on offer in the houses, and they love the happy environment in the School and the endless buzz of activity. Both feel, from their own experience and from what they see on offer now, that the School really nurtures its pupils and encourages them to follow their dreams and achieve their full potential.

Both were at the School during Nick Ward's headship, and witnessed the results of the changes made by his predecessor and the ongoing developments during his time. They were part of the School when the naval connections and the militaristic approach were being quietly toned down, and they saw fundamental changes in the house system while they were pupils.

Schools tend to generate loyalty among those who enjoyed and benefited from their time there; but the Royal Hospital School is perhaps unique in that it has weathered major changes in both environment and ethos over the last few decades and yet can boast a real sense of belonging among both the older hands and the more recent recruits.

RHS centenarians – honoured on our 100th page

Even in the early days Greenwich Hospital could boast very elderly men among its Pensioners – perhaps not surprising given the quality of the accommodation and food offered to fortunate naval veterans. One John Worley, who had spent 70 years at sea before coming to the Hospital, was the model for 'Winter' in James Thornhill's painted ceiling, and even at the age of 96 years was in constant trouble with the authorities for getting drunk and using foul language.

In the modern era, the School has produced at least three old boys who have topped the century mark. In December 1941, as Hong Kong was falling to the Japanese, Jim Fallace was leading one of the last machine-gun sections in the naval dockyard. Having left the School for the Navy in 1917, he resigned in 1929, went to China and joined the Shanghai and later the Tientsin police, learning to speak four dialects of Chinese. At the outbreak of the Second World War he went straight to Hong Kong to join the Royal Marines again, but ended up in the Hong Kong Navy, blowing up minefields. After his heroic efforts to defend the harbour he was imprisoned in one of the infamous Japanese camps and in September 1942 was force-marched to a prison ship, which was torpedoed and limped on under tow with prisoners dying by the hour in the locked holds. When the ship eventually sank Fallace managed to escape, swimming three miles towards the Chinese shore before being picked up by a Chinese junk with only about five other survivors and nursed back to health by local islanders. He made his way back to allied territory and lived to 102 years of age.

When Jack Strath died in September 1991 at the age of 107, he was the oldest recorded Royal Hospital School boy. He served in Victoria's Navy, served in the Great War and offered to serve in World War II. When serving in the Pitcairn Islands, he rubbed shoulders with descendants of the Bounty mutineers and listened to handed down family tales of the hardships faced by Fletcher Christian and his men. During the 1914–18 war, he took an active part in the capture of German West Africa and the bombardment of Turkish forts in the Dardanelles. When the war came along again in 1939, he at once volunteered to return to sea. However, the Admiralty turned him down on the grounds of age – he was then 55. Ironically, Jack Strath outlived many of those who returned from active service.

In June 1999, aged 98, Fred Bunday returned for a visit to the school he had left in 1916. His father had been a pall bearer at Queen Victoria's funeral in 1901, and he himself was the School's last known surviving veteran of the Great War, during which he went down with three ships. Only the year before he had been honoured by President Chirac with the Légion d'Honneur, France's highest honour open to a foreign national, for his services during that war. He also served throughout the Second World War, and was the longest-serving freemason in the country, having been initiated into the Lord Kitchener of Khartoum Lodge in 1926. He was thrilled to see 'so many children proud of their school and its traditions', and went on to celebrate his 100th birthday on 28 November 2000, before dying just over two years later.

Below left: Fredrick Henry Bunday (1912–16, Company 7/5), who reached 102 years.

Below: Jack Strath (1896–99, Company 2/32), who died at the age of 107.

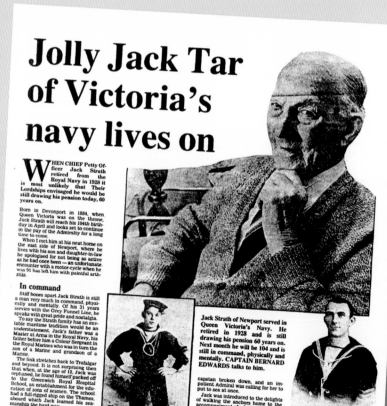

Above: Admiral of the Fleet Lord Lewin of Greenwich, pictured here in the Painted Hall close to the spot where Lord Nelson's body lay in state. He had a long-standing association with the School, opening the converted sixth form boarding house, Nelson, in 1989; taking the salute on Speech Day in 1993 and as a Patron of the Friends of the Royal Hospital School. This painting by John Wonnacott hangs in the NMM.

Right: Nicholas Ward, Headmaster (1995–2004). As writer, broadcaster, School governor and parent Libby Purves wrote – a man of 'irrepressible optimism, and a constant, bubbling, mischievously humorous appreciation of the oddities of school life. You felt that he was having fun, loving his job, proud of the School.'

Girls were initially admitted at age 11, 12 and 13 and in the lower sixth, and their first house was Hood, which opened with a full complement. It was followed in 1992 with, first, Cornwallis and then Howe: and the final conversion Blake. Acclimatisation naturally took a few years. Some of the boys resented these interlopers into their male territory – one referred to being 'contaminated by the female sex' – and complained about the perceived preference given to girls and the privileges they enjoyed. The first girls clearly put themselves under pressure to do well in competition with the boys and to show that they could offer value to the School. Their smartness on parade was noticeable, their work ethos was considerable and they joined in enthusiastically and on equal terms in all the activities available. But there were inevitable challenges and tensions on both sides, new rules of engagement had to be introduced and the staff – particularly perhaps the long-standing male members of the common room – had to learn new sensitivities. One member of staff remarked, 'I've never taught girls before, but they are just the same as boys, aren't they?'

There were all sorts of new questions that had to be asked, particularly in the early days when girls were hugely outnumbered. The decision was made that there would always be more than one girl in a class, but they would still be heavily in the minority, so it was difficult to know where to seat them. And for teachers who had always addressed boys by their surnames, the dilemma was what now to call the girls. Old habits die hard, and it took a while for first names to become the norm. The boys did, however, quickly accept that having girls in class 'might improve classroom behaviour and so improve results'.

Prior to girls arriving, Nelson House was closed for a year and converted into a new university-style residence for the upper sixth boys; Admiral of the Fleet Lord Lewin of Greenwich was principal guest at the opening of the house. He was a great supporter of the School and patron of the newly formed 'Friends of the Royal Hospital School' association. New building during the 1990s included the expansion of the existing Jellicoe Centre into a centre for art and design, reopened in 1992 by HRH The Duke of York, and the Jubilee Pavilion, opened in 1993 by HRH The Duke of Edinburgh, with the word 'Jubilee' referring to the year being the 60th anniversary of the move to Holbrook, a milepost that was celebrated by the guard performing in the Royal Tournament in Earls Court.

The anniversary was also marked by a major event held at the School on 23 May 1993. This 'fly drive' occasion echoed the landing of HRH The Prince of Wales on the fields to open the School six decades previously. Over 10,000 visitors and 2,000 cars attended an event which boasted over 47 display aircraft and over 200 vintage motors, as well as commercial and military vehicles and motorbikes. A private air traffic control system oversaw old Tiger Moths and Huskies landing on the playing fields and Wing Commander Wallis's James Bond Wallis Autogyro swinging through the air to the appropriate theme music. There was a parachute drop from a helicopter and abseiling down the tower, plus diving demonstrations in the pool and a sail-past by local yacht clubs. The splendid day ended with the sunset ceremony led by the band and the guard.

The Diamond Jubilee of the move to Holbrook was followed a year later by more cause for celebration, with the tercentenary of the foundation of Greenwich Hospital. This was duly marked on 10 May 1994 by the whole School parading in the grounds of the National Maritime Museum in Greenwich in the presence of HM Queen Elizabeth II. The birthday on 4 November of the Hospital's founder, William III, was chosen for a further commemoration, a splendid banquet in the Painted Hall. HRH The Duke of York was the guest of honour, accompanied by Admiral of the Fleet Lord Lewin, the First and Second Sea Lords and the Secretary of State for Defence, Malcolm Rifkind, who recognised that 'great themes of royal interest and naval tradition run like a golden thread throughout the past 300 years'.

Prince Andrew's speech indicated the excitement he felt at the School's plans for the future, particularly recognising that 'International exchange programmes… are of vital importance if we are to build understanding among nations. Special tercentenary scholarships are being created through the generous sponsorship of trusts and institutions… designed to bring students from different parts of the commonwealth to the sixth form. It is an imaginative move which deserves to be applauded.'

Michael Kirk's last term as Headmaster, in 1995, coincided with the 50th anniversary of VE Day, commemorated at the School with a 1940s themed day and the performance of the choir at the celebrations in Hyde Park in front of members of the royal family, heads of state from elsewhere and the BBC. Back at School pupils had late breakfast and dressed in 1940s fashion, ration books were issued with an afternoon of fun activities, including a visit to the VE air display at Duxford and rambles, beetle drives, soap box races and historical films followed by street parties, the sunset ceremony and lighting of the beacons.

Kirk's departing message reaffirmed the RHS's commitment to its traditions: 'Every school has to have something that is special to it, whatever its background, and here [the sea] is our tradition, which it is important to maintain while we are opening the School to non-seafarers and gradually becoming better known in the independent school world.' He believed that the parades, the sailing and the flag ceremonies were all valued and appreciated by parents whether they

were connected to the sea or not, and that they made RHS stand out among other schools with a more conventional history.

Nick Ward, the new Headmaster, quickly reaffirmed this view, and further believed that 'remembering our seafaring heritage is important and, as well as the ceremonial, we should look at more practical ways of doing this … aiming to become the leading school in the country for activities to do with the sea.' An immediately practical step was taken in 1996 when the Holbrook Coastguard was formed, run during term time entirely by RHS pupils. Fully affiliated with the national body and with a fully operational watch station, it covered the coastline from the dry dock in Ipswich round the Shotley peninsula to Manningtree. It survived until 2008, when it was disbanded because of changes in regulations imposing age limits on participation.

The nine years of Ward's headship saw the School both consolidating and developing. Most notably, RHS became a Headmasters' and Headmistresses' Conference (HMC) school, recognition of its transformation into a mainstream independent school. The influence of the girls continued to grow, with girls taking their due places in every year group (though the School has, by design, never reached 50/50 parity in numbers). The band and the choir continued to perform at prestigious events including, in 1995, the choir singing a specially written anthem 'That they go down to the sea in ships' in front of HM Queen Elizabeth II and HRH The Duke of Edinburgh at the annual Seafarers' Service in

Above left: In June 2001 a spectacular musical extravaganza was staged at the School – followed by sunset ceremony and fireworks over the River Stour.

Above right: Television presenter Frank Bruno brought a televised 'It's a Knockout' competition to the School in August 2000, which helped raise funds for the RNLI.

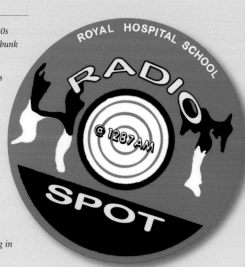

Left: New boarding facilities – during the 1990s pupils had their own dedicated 'Cubbies' with bunk bed, wardrobe, desk, drawers and poster space.

Right: In June 2000 School Radio Hotspot was launched, broadcast on 1287 kHz medium wave. John Humphries (BBC News), Jenni Murray (Woman's Hour) and Jeremy Paxman (Newsnight) all provided pre-recorded messages of support. Griff Rhys Jones, neighbour and friend of the School, helped open this facility.

Below left: HRH The Duke of York has attended Speech Day, as special guest, on the most occasions. He first visited the School in 1992 and he has since maintained a close relationship with the School, regularly dropping in and always taking a real interest in pupils.

St Paul's Cathedral and, in July 1996, the band appearing at the Royal Tournament once more, with 625 seats filled by those with a connection to the School. Then in November 1997 the choir were again in London, performing two anthems at the British Legion Festival of Remembrance at the Albert Hall. There were two performances on the day, the first attended by a 7,000-strong audience in the hall and the second broadcast all round the world by the BBC

As Patron of Greenwich Hospital since 1996, HRH The Duke of York continued his constant support, presenting the prizes on Speech Day 1996 and confirming that 'the royal family has a very close connection to the Royal Hospital School, with very many of my family over the years being involved with it'. in 1998 he opened a new floodlit all-weather sports ground named after him and again attended Speech Day in 2001.

The School's extracurricular programme was also developing strongly during the late 1990s. In November 1999 a highly professional James Bond fashion show was staged, with catwalk extravaganza and accompanying band, and in June 2000 the School's own radio station made its first transmission. Radio Hotspot's first production manager was Rose Heiney, whose parents Paul Heiney and Libby Purves attended the inauguration, along with the School's close neighbour Griff Rhys Jones. Later in this same year Andrew Motion, the Poet Laureate, talked to the School about his role as the poet of the nation and about his faith in the value and relevance of poetry; and former pupil and parent Richard Todd delivered a lecture entitled 'Sets, drugs and crocks of gold', a richly entertaining and informative survey of the British legal system. Over the years an outstanding series of general studies lectures and special speakers have been arranged, with

Mary Whitehouse, Bruce Kent, Sir Robin Knox Johnson and Tim Yeo, the local MP, all keynote speakers.

The status of the School as a boarding establishment was now recognised by the election of the Headmaster as chairman of the Boarding Schools Association, the leading organisation for training and support of heads and staff in boarding schools. Academic achievement continued to blossom; in October 2002 a record six Oxbridge places were taken up by RHS pupils. And the continuing benefit, to some alumni at least, of co-education was evidenced by the 2004 wedding in the School chapel of the first Nelson House couple to get married – Thomas Pratt and Victoria Clark.

Nick Ward left at the end of the summer term in 2004, and was succeeded by Howard Blackett, who was already a well-established and experienced headmaster, previously at Dover College. His arrival coincided with a fundamental change in the relationship between the Royal Hospital School and Greenwich Hospital. In May 2004 an Admiralty directive stated that it was 'not consistent with the objectives of the founding charter that 90 per cent of the Hospital's net disposable income should be used for the benefit of the School'. There was no question that Greenwich Hospital would continue to support the School, but there was a stated aim that the percentage of the Hospital's income that was used for the School's benefit should reduce to 50 per cent by 2015, with the 'stretch' of 40 per cent by 2012.

In 2004 most of the over £6 million pounds that were given to the School by the Hospital went on bursaries. Of the 680 places in the School, 480 were funded by Greenwich Hospital, another 170 were recipients of Ministry of Defence support and only 30 or so pupils were full fee payers. Clearly a balance needed to be struck between the charitable objectives of the foundation and the establishment of a modern progressive independent school that would move forward with confidence and increasing independence.

Below: Headmaster Howard Blackett (2004–12) with his wife Susie. He steered the School through a major redevelopment and restructuring programme, with new state-of-the-art boarding houses, the establishment of junior houses and the introduction of day pupils and a day house.

Blackett, along with the new Bursar, David Charlton, rose to the challenge, and with the generous support of Greenwich Hospital the School embarked on an £18 million investment programme. The first initiative was an ambitious project to transform the boarding houses in order to make them acceptable and attractive to fee-paying parents and comparable to other boarding schools in the UK. By 2012 boarding houses had been substantially updated and modernised, and they now offer comfortable accommodation and facilities to both pupils and house staff. In addition, over £3 million was spent on the splendid Reade Music School with its excellent performance space – the Burns Recital Hall.

Since the millennium there have been other significant changes to boarding arrangements. A new sixth form extension, the Lady Hamilton Wing, was added to Nelson House to convert it into a mixed upper sixth house which also acted as a stepping stone to university. In their turn Blake and Drake were converted into junior houses for years 7 and 8, providing an environment ideally suited to children of that age. And perhaps the most far-reaching new initiative of Howard Blackett's headship was the decision to admit day pupils. September

The Pele legend and holiday lettings

There has been regular speculation among RHS boys that Pele spent some time at the School attending an intensive language course during the summer of 1956, allegedly sleeping in Hawke bed 25. This date does correspond to the establishment of the first Anglo-American language schools in the UK and Pele had just signed for the top Brazilian side Santos prior to making his league debut in a match against FC Corinthians on 7 September 1956, when he scored four goals. Might the RHS have hosted this football legend?

This may be the stuff of fantasy, but today offers a new and welcome income stream derived from the potential of the School's splendid buildings and grounds, and since 1998 the School has opened its doors and its facilities to rentals during the holidays. The largest lettings so far have been to international language schools, and the RHS has welcomed people from all over the world to the summer schools. Music and drama schools have also used the splendid facilities, along with minor counties cricket teams and a 'fathers and sons' rugby tour. These early introductions to the School have sometimes resulted in pupils signing up to attend full time. On a smaller scale, the swimming pool is in regular use by local clubs, and the chapel has been used for weddings, baptisms and the occasional funeral, to date mostly by those with a link to the School.

2006 saw the arrival of the first non-boarders since the Boreman boys had left Greenwich. While originally accommodated within the existing boarding house structure, the success of this initiative soon meant that a specialist day house was necessary and Raleigh House was duly converted into a mixed day house, to receive day pupils moving up from the junior houses or new arrivals from other schools.

There are two categories of day pupils: day boarders who have the option to stay on till supper and afterwards, and day pupils who attend between 8am and 6pm. Day boarders are each allocated to one of the boarding houses where they have access to desks and lockers (and beds), and are encouraged to take a full part in the life of the house and its activities and to become fully integrated into the community. Day pupils initially join the junior houses but from year 9 are all, boys and girls, part of Raleigh House, where again they take a full part in inter-house activities as well as normal school life. It is also possible for day pupils to stay overnight on occasions, which is popular with working families living busy lives.

The initial day intake was 15 pupils, but numbers rose rapidly and by 2012 there were around 170 day pupils. They have become an essential part of the School, contributing to its development

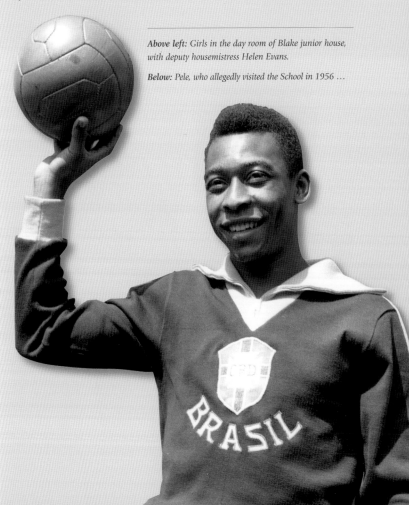

Above left: *Girls in the day room of Blake junior house, with deputy housemistress Helen Evans.*

Below: *Pele, who allegedly visited the School in 1956 …*

LOBS – Look Out Boy Sailor!

'Look out boy sailor', or 'Lobs', has been a part of school slang for decades, still used today to indicate the looming presence of someone in authority approaching. It was also the title of the satirical magazine – the RHS's *Private Eye* – which ran for 60 editions from 2005 to 2012. Edited by a member of staff, it consisted of contributions from pupils and staff, and took a refreshingly irreverent look into current school events, issues and concerns. As well as satirical articles, photographs taken by pupils, often captioned with speech and thought bubbles, it had a serious side in covering subjects as wide-ranging as Joseph Kony, the French election, the London Riots, the Occupy Wall Street demonstrations, National Feminism day and much more.

While the tone was light, it was recognised as providing the pupils with a voice – and in its time was a valuable educational tool for the international students who, as their English teachers affirmed, would always make time to read it. Perhaps most importantly, it was a tribute to the confident ethos of the School, that both staff and pupils could allow themselves to laugh and be laughed at in the pages of this invigorating magazine. It was an indication of a thoroughly healthy society and a school at ease with itself; and while Lobs ceased on departure of its talented editor, William Bowry (Bowza), the opportunities for the brightest pupils to hone their skills of expression and develop their creative sides continues in many forms, including a healthy debating society, entry to public speaking competitions and opportunities to make contributions to other school publications.

and evolution and helping it to integrate more fully with the local community and so to become a distinctive part of Holbrook and Suffolk. The fact that their parents live locally means that a stronger relationship has grown up between the School and the parents, who are now a regular feature at sporting matches, concerts and other events. Day pupils have contributed to a rapid spurt in academic achievement. While blending almost seamlessly into the day-to-day life of the School they have also developed a real fondness for the School's long-standing traditions and regularly participate in the large set piece parades, often with proud parents and relatives looking on.

Another major initiative was to tackle external perceptions of the Royal Hospital School. Despite the rapid changes of the previous 15 years or so, it was still mistakenly seen by some as a large military institution rather than a school. There were still many highly visible naval images: the cannon and the *Ganges* figurehead prominent at the entrance, large models of ships, ranks of photographs of men and boys in naval uniforms, paintings of naval battles and lots of naval memorabilia and relics. The prospectus, which started with six pages trumpeting the School's history, was not always seen as welcoming to non-seafarers – precisely the audience and the market who now had to be reached if this great school was to grow and flourish for all. The challenge was to preserve and cherish the long and distinguished naval heritage of the School while making it more accessible to a new community who did not necessarily share directly in that heritage.

Some of the items were removed: the cannon and some model ships went to Greenwich and the figurehead back to the HMS Ganges Museum. Old photographs were taken down and some memorabilia was moved into storage pending the establishment of a heritage centre. The School has softened its military connections and established itself in the marketplace as a leading independent school – but still one that is very proud of its history and the values associated with its heritage.

The best of the naval and seafaring traditions remain, with nine spectacular ceremonial divisions undertaken annually in full naval uniform (with all boarding and day pupils involved), the celebration of past sacrifice on Trafalgar Day and Remembrance Sunday, participation in the annual Seafarers' Service at St Paul's and the continued importance placed on sailing as a core activity. Marching to meals continued for a while, but with well drilled practices for parades this was not considered necessary, and today pupils have all the freedoms associated with any other major independent day boarding school. The new approach kept what was worth keeping, but removed the elements that were seen as less helpful to the updated and modernised ethos

of the School. Needless to say, some of this change met with opposition from some old boys and longer serving staff; but it was clear that it was a necessary forward step and today those returning to the School invariably embrace the change and recognise the positive atmosphere.

The 'noughties' saw a range of inventive productions win high acclaim. The first of these was 'Rewind Refocus', an artistic celebration of each decade in the 20th century offering glimpses of many different art forms from Picasso to Dali to Gershwin and the Beatles, from dance to poetry to prose. Then in 2005 a similarly innovative dance show was staged under the title 'Pure Dance'.

Alongside these creative ventures the School also participated in some high-profile formal events, including the introduction of the highly popular Burns night ceilidh with haggis piped in and addressed, Robbie Burns poetry recitals, highland dancing, best-dressed sporran and stripping the willow! And in 2007 a spectacular Trafalgar Night dinner was staged to celebrate 75 years at Holbrook, complete with a large-scale ice sculpture replica of HMS *Victory*.

Yet another decision was to create even greater flexibility to open up the School to a wider range of customers, and also to market it both to growing numbers of international students and to the children of members of the other armed services. Greenwich Hospital has gradually reduced the numbers of guaranteed bursaries and the focus has become one of promoting the School to a new and wider audience and on raising its profile generally within the independent sector. The School now has a healthy mix of pupils from backgrounds including forces families, overseas students and children from the local community, all striving for academic excellence and broadening horizons.

That all these changes have been effective is clear from the fact that by 2012 the most challenging of the targets set by the Admiralty for reducing the proportion of Greenwich's contribution to the School has been met. After eight years in post Howard Blackett felt he had achieved what he had set out to do, and confirmed that he would be leaving to explore fresh educational opportunities. He left a school which is now perceived as a mainstream public school, fit for purpose and much better placed to meet the new challenges posed by the 21st century. It offers its pupils an amazing campus environment within which they can both learn and be taught to the highest academic standards while also fulfilling their potential and becoming happy, secure and confident young people. The School's two core principles are on the one hand, its commitment to service, loyalty and discipline, and on the other to its Christian ethos – and it has achieved its recent transformation while not losing the features that make it so unique; its rich seafaring heritage and its strong and distinct values.

Howard Blackett's successor as Headmaster was James Lockwood, previously the Deputy Headmaster. He understood the School and had a clear vision that recognised the importance of its continually improving academic reputation placing it at the centre of a values-driven community which combined the best of past tradition with the best of future opportunity.

CEREMONIAL

Below: The School band led by the Drum Major at the final church parade held at Greenwich on 20 March 1933. On this occasion, the Lord Mayor of London, Sir Percy Greenaway recognised the School's long and interesting association with London, confirming how boys regularly marched with their band to St Paul's Cathedral to attend the Annual National Service for Seafarers. The School at Holbrook has continued to attend many other formal events in London; for example, the Lord Mayor's Show, 75th Anniversary of the National Maritime Museum, Royal Tournaments and Festivals of Remembrance.

The educational inspectors who visited the School in the 1930s were on record as being concerned about the 'striking orderliness' of the boys' lives as they saw them being herded from place to place at the double. But at that stage, and for several decades more, a naval life was the destiny of most of the pupils, and their school environment was designed to prepare them for that eventuality. In particular, they would regularly form up for divisions – the naval term for parades – and await inspection.

Naval uniform ceased to be everyday dress in the 1930s, but it has always been retained for these formal occasions, and when girls joined the School in 1991 WRNS dress uniform was adopted for them too. Divisions used to be part of every Sunday at the School, but now they take place on nine occasions including Harvest Festival, Remembrance Service, Founders' Day, Leavers' Songs of Praise and Speech Day. The pupils in their number one uniforms form up in their houses and march to the parade ground, each house led by its prefects.

All public schools have their history, their traditions, their own personalities… but the Royal Hospital School is unique in its naval heritage which has, from the beginning, ensured that ceremonial duties have always formed a major part of school life. That these continue today in all their glory is a celebration of the School's venerable beginnings and its adherence over three centuries to both the intentions of Greenwich Hospital's royal founders and its close affiliation with both the Royal and the Merchant Navies.

Involvement in ceremonial events have always been part of life at the School since the early days at Greenwich. Regular royal visits saw boys on parade as part of the welcoming formalities. After Nelson's coffin lay in state in the Painted Hall before his funeral, both Hospital Pensioners and the schoolboys lined the processional route as it was carried to St Paul's Cathedral. During the 19th century visits from dignitaries (from royalty down) required formal marches, displays and inspections. And daily life was ruled by marching to and from lessons and meals, sometimes accompanied by the drum.

Above: *Heads of School. Chloe Crismani and Monty Beaton (paired to the right) and Deputy Heads of School, Lucy Bailey and Luke Jones (paired to the left) just before leading a spectacular ceremonial divisions at Holbrook (2012). These unique student parades are always well received, as they are attended by many proud parents, friends and relatives.*

Distinctive blue ensign

When Major Arthur Buckley arrived in 1949 as Chief Naval Instructor, he petitioned the Admiralty for an ensign for the School, and was allowed to use the 'defaced blue ensign', ie the blue ensign with the Greenwich coat of arms superimposed. The RHS thus joined a number of other prestigious seagoing institutions which have the right to fly this ensign. The blue ensign itself had its origins as the flag of the Blue Squadron of the Royal Navy, but the rules changed in 1864 when the blue ensign became the ensign flown by ships in public service, with the red ensign allocated to the Merchant Navy and the white ensign to the Royal Navy. The defaced blue ensign has since then been allocated to a number of governmental and public bodies associated with the Navy, of which the Royal Hospital School is proud to be one.

Top: *The traditional raising and lowering of the flag conducted daily during term time (morning and evening). The flag party consists of two pupils from the duty house accompanied by a bugler, all dressed in No 1s.*

Above left: *The School band, very much in demand, playing playing before a rugby international at Twickenham.*

Above left inset: *Guard Commander – there is much competition to be a member of the School's ceremonial guard.*

Left: *The whole School on parade at a ceremonial divisions; with the Heads of School facing away and the impressive guard, beyond which is each house set out in marching ranks.*

Above: The rededication of the Queen's Banner in 2006. Pictured are HRH The Duke of York, Heads (Freya Reeve and Seun Azeez) and Deputy Head of School (Thomas Wood), Head of Ceremonial (John Snoddon), Equerry to The Duke of York and School Chaplain (Rev. Charles Stewart).

The 70-strong marching band is in attendance, along with the 36-strong guard of honour, selected in year 9 from volunteers who train in their own time. The guard and the band are the focus of attention at the front of the parade, and it is they who give the salute to the reviewing officer – usually a senior officer from one of the three main branches of the services – along with the Headmaster and the Deputy Headmaster. These are the only adults involved in divisions, apart from John Snoddon, who is there in his role as Head of Ceremonial, and Roger Jones, the Bandmaster. The Head Boy and Head Girl, their deputies and the prefects (CPOs) run the whole spectacle. After the inspection, there is the march past, and the ceremony ends with the National Anthem and then chapel. Part of the ceremonial display is the march 'Holbrook', composed in 1968 by Lieutenant Colonel Vivian Dunn, original member of the London Symphony Orchestra (and assistant choral conductor to Sir Henry Woods), founder of the Proms, who retired that year as Principal Director of Music of the Royal Marines. On Speech Day the Nelson pupils who are leaving the School march past to the theme tune from *The Great Escape*, eventually forming up on the steps before throwing their 'gidges' (caps) into the air as a symbol of departure.

John Snoddon – whose title 20 years ago would have been Chief Naval Instructor – came to the School in 2004 after 36 years in the Royal Navy, where his duties included the managing of ceremonial occasions. This is one of his roles at the RHS, where he also runs the Duke of Edinburgh's Award scheme and informs new entrants about the history and background of this unique and very special school.

In another piece of homage to the School's naval past, he manages the daily flag ceremonies when, at 8am and 5pm, the School's ensign is raised and lowered. Two pupils in naval uniform, attended by a bugler, perform the ceremony – normally year 9s from the house whose duty it is that week. On Saturday mornings the whole house are present for the occasion, in their normal uniforms. There are also ceremonial sunsets three times a year when the guard and the band turn out for precision arms drill, marching and music. On recognised national days a countries flag is raised if that nationality is represented in the school community. Furthermore special occasions are celebrated. And special occasions are celebrated by the raising of flags, sometimes bearing messages, just as the Navy would dress their ships; for example, the wedding of TRH The Duke and Duchess of Cambridge was marked by flags spelling out their names.

PART III

LIVING AT
GREENWICH
& HOLBROOK

Daily Life

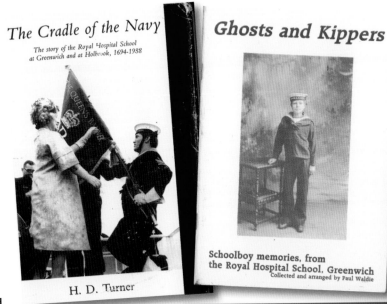

William Ravenscroft (1929–32) explained in *Ghosts and Kippers*, a collection of RHS old boys' memories, why his parents had chosen the Royal Hospital School for him – sending him away to board at the age of 11 and committing him to a naval career. It was, he said, 'a time of deep recession, most difficult for large families, with very little work about and exceedingly low wages. If I had not gone to GRHS, I would have had to leave school at 14 and then straight onto the scrap-heap, one of thousands of 14-year-olds. There were no handouts, no child allowances, and only when things got really desperate could one turn to the parish or local councils. Sending me away meant that there was one less mouth to feed.'

Over two hundred years after the School's foundation, as this account makes clear, the RHS was still fulfilling the purpose for which it was originally founded – offering an education, a home and a future to the children of naval families who might otherwise have fallen by the wayside. Herbert Marriott (1919–23) was typical: entry to the School followed the death of his father on HMS *Bulwark*, leaving six children fatherless. There was no alternative for the two older girls and Herbert himself, then aged nine, other than an orphanage after which, when he reached the age of 11, he was sent to the RHS. Life at the school was undoubtedly sparten; but the boys were housed, fed and taught, and they often recognised later in life that they had been considerably luckier than some of their contemporaries.

Far left: The Cradle of the Navy (1980) – *researched and written by former pupil Dan Turner (1926–30) – provided an insight into the story of the School at Greenwich and Holbrook.*

Left: Ghosts and Kippers (1993) – *collected and arranged by former pupil Paul Waldie (1967–72, Collingwood) – provided a compilation of Greenwich schoolboy memories. The Royal Hospital School Association (RHSA) and its members have through its various journals and publications helped to record and preserve the history of the School.*

It was unfortunate that I arrived a day in advance of the start of new term. I was cold, hungry, tired and very homesick, having lost my mother only seven months before. I had too much time for recollection, which didn't help. The company officer on duty at Trafalgar Quarters was Mr Searle (ex-Royal Navy and a naval Pensioner), known as Busty Searle. He seemed a mountain of a man to me. He took me to the dormitory where I was to be the only occupant for one night. Being February, it was very cold and there didn't seem to be any heating – if there was, it had no effect on me. I climbed into bed between cold sheets, feeling utterly miserable. I thought of home, the fire and the kitchen stove, which kept me warm during the winter months. After the events of that busy and life-changing day were over I was on my own, and I wondered what I had let myself in for.

Jack Judge (1924–28)

What was true of life at the School in the 1920s – the last decade of the School's occupation of the Greenwich site – was almost certainly broadly true of the previous two centuries. There are few directly personal reminiscences from schoolboys during that time, but records remain of the routine at the School, and it seems to have been remarkably similar to that experienced by the boys who were to form the last contingents at Greenwich. Lessons, drill, quite decent food, severe punishments. As a boy who was there during the 1870s wrote, 'It was different during Rev. Holme's time, he treated us like gentleman, but Burney – OH!!!' A strict disciplinarian, Superintendent Burney carried out public floggings nearly every day and stopped leave on Saturday afternoons; instead the boys were employed in scrubbing out the buildings. Burney may have been unusually harsh; but it was not until over 100 years after his regime that corporal punishment at the School formally stopped.

Top: A fond farewell for a boy off to Holbrook by train, probably from Portsmouth or Plymouth.

Right: Horatio Axup was just one of the boys who attended the ceremonial launch of HMS Royal Albert at Woolwich dockyard in 1854. The School provided an honour party for Queen Victoria who received the wine from the master shipwright to officially launch the vessel.

19th-century memories

The establishment in 1925 of the first old boys' association prompted visits to the School by several elderly gentlemen who had long memories of their time there. One of the most extraordinary was John Evans, aged 94, who had been present at the opening of the London and Greenwich Railway in 1836 and entered the School in 1840, the year of Queen Victoria's marriage to Prince Albert. He had remarkable memories of his days at the School 85 years previously: the girls leaving and the first block ship arriving; seeing the launching of Victorian warships and the School cheering Queen Victoria and Prince Albert at one such launch; the original drum and fife band being augmented by a brass band following a visit of the Duke of York's School brass band. He was in the choir when Mr Moy was both School organist and a vocal teacher, and won the silver medal and three book prizes on leaving, after which he stayed on for another year as a monitor.

Another visitor was Captain Stevens, a merchant seaman, who recounted how, every morning in springtime, brimstone and treacle (a mixture of sulphur and treacle that was thought to aid digestion) was served, and that the continuance of this habit accounted, he thought, for his longevity. He had led a very active life, taking part in many trading expeditions and gun-running during the American Civil War, before becoming a partner in the shipping company of Stephens, Suttons Ltd and director of a number of engineering firms and insurance companies.

Horatio Axup (1854–59) recalled marching to Woolwich to see the launch of the *Royal Albert*, perhaps the last of the wooden three-decker built in England. Queen Victoria, Prince Albert, the Queen's mother and the Prince of Wales were all present, and the boys formed a guard of honour. The ship first saw service in the Black Sea during the Crimean War. He visited the Painted Hall regularly, where he admired Nelson's waistcoat, worn at Trafalgar, and in 1855 remembered chatting with old naval veterans who claimed they were *Victory* men who had been present at Trafalgar; one stated that he had helped to carry Nelson's body to the cockpit after he was mortally wounded. This RHS boy was so proud that he may have grasped a hand that had touched the body of Nelson.

LAUNCH OF H. M. S. ROYAL ALBERT, SCREW STEAMER, 131 GUNS, AT WOOLWICH, MAY 13, 1854.

Uniform through the ages

In the 1730s the clothing of the boys was 'the same in quality as that of the Pensioners… each boy shall have an everyday jacket and serge waistcoat, made out of the Pensioners' old clothes, as often as needful; and an Irish ram skin pair of breeches once in two years'. They were issued with a clean shirt and pair of hose every week, a clean pillowcase once a month and a towel as often as necessary. In 1744 they had to wear a cap 'made out of old stuff', and in 1756 these caps were replaced by the leather cap that was to remain part of the School uniform for a century. 'Three strips of leather, stuck together, make a hospital boy's cap' was the taunt thrown at them by local Greenwich boys.

Mr Lawey (1869–72), who worked for 40 years for the Prudential Assurance Company and had retired in January 1924, remembered the uniform change introduced in 1870 by Captain Burney, the new Superintendent. The old coat, waistcoat with brass buttons, trousers and Glengarry cap were replaced by naval uniform with white straw hats; 'we thought we were all well on the way to being admirals'.

Archive drawings and photographs from the mid-19th century show a variety of uniforms. In the 1860s the Upper School wore 'a pea jacket, waistcoat trousers and glengarry cap, an ordinary white shirt with a soft turned-down collar fastened at the throat with a black ribbon tied in a bow knot'. Naval uniform was the norm in the 1870s, with white straw hats. Indeed by the 1920s, as Dan Turner records, the boys were issued on arrival with a blue serge suit and knitted jumper, a flannel vest and long pants, socks and heavy boots. They had to change into this clothing immediately and hand their 'civvies' back to the family who had accompanied them to their first day at the School. On day two they received their 'number ones': blue serge jumpers and bell-bottom trousers. 'In summer the only undergarment was a flannel shirt with the front, trimmed with blue braid, showing. In winter we had flannel underpants and over the flannel shirt a knitted blue jersey, with the sailor's collar and its white tapes. Caps were only worn with number ones, black in winter, white in summer.' Number ones were worn on Sundays, special occasions and when the boys went out of school. Number twos were worn at classes and parades, and the third suit was made of white canvas and called 'ducks'.

Today, both boys and girls wear naval uniform for divisions and other ceremonial occasions. But for most of the time normal School uniform is a tartan fitted skirt for girls and grey trousers for boys, topped by blue and white striped shirts with the School jumper and tie and, from year 9, Navy blazers with the School crest. Sixth formers wear the School's own design of suit, and prefects are allowed to choose a shirt of any colour.

Dan Turner (1926–30) wrote two books about his time at the RHS, one of which carried a foreword by Norman Worswick, the Headmaster at the time of publication, who said: 'The true bones of history are original sources, and this book is a rare miscellany of the life and times of an RHS boy in the 1920s. Just occasionally, the thread of history through to the present day appears – perhaps in a name long forgotten but still on a board here at the School, or in a piece of slang still used…'.

In 1926 a boy joining the School arrived, with his parent or guardian, at the School gate where there would be a company officer and two messenger boys. When a number of new boys had gathered, they were shepherded to the infirmary where two attendants went through the procedure of measuring, weighing and eye-testing, after which they were kitted out in their new uniform. The following day each new boy was allocated to a company and was given a number in that company freed up by a recent leaver; from now on, a boy allocated to, for example, company number 7, Howe, and given the number 73, was known as '7/73'. As Lawrence Jupp (1917–21) later said, 'Can't remember names… only numbers!'

Above centre and *left: Greenwich school boy c1850, with traditional 'glengarry' leather cap, coat and waistcoat with brass buttons.*

Above right: Greenwich uniform introduced by Captain Burney in 1870 with strong naval styling.

Every Tuesday and Friday we performed massed Swedish drill on the parade ground to music played by the School band. We had two bands; one brass and the other bugles and drums. While I was there a new chief officer instigated dancing the sailors' hornpipe instead of Swedish drill. Wednesday morning was a treat for us, as we left the School to march through Greenwich Park and around Blackheath, accompanied by both bands. On Sundays we had divisions and were inspected by the Superintendent, before going to church at the Royal Naval College. We also went to church on the Sunday afternoon, and if you were confirmed you went three times.

Jack Judge (1924–28)

The first three weeks for the 'New Jacks' were spent in isolation in Trafalgar Quarters, being issued with more items of uniform, visiting the infirmary for medical and dental examinations and vaccinations, being shown round the premises and learning how to march and drill satisfactorily. Then came the final march as a squad to the School where, by the bow of the ship, they were halted, dismissed and dispersed. They were suddenly now thrust in among hundreds of boys, some only a little older or bigger than themselves, others almost fully grown adults. There was a new language to be learnt, a new company to be part of, and they would find themselves addressed only by their new numbers in a kind of wail, like the undulating tone of a bo'sun's pipe.

There was also a new hierarchy to be absorbed into and they soon discovered that the School was mostly run by the boys themselves, though each company had its officer, an ex-Navy man who combined looking after his company with instructing the boys in all aspects of seamanship. Though the company officer was with his company from morning to night, he delegated most of the direct supervision to the Chief Petty Officer boy and his subordinates, the Petty Officers, also known as 'badge boys' or 'badgies'. The 'Chief' reigned supreme in the dormitory from his 'stand' where he presided surrounded by his sidekicks and served by a boy who was detailed to keep the stand clean

Opposite top: Pupils return to houses from morning lessons for 'standeasy' (morning break).

Top right: The 'muster yard' – before the colonnades were windowed in – complete with badminton court and boys preparing to march to mess. Most boarding houses have been transformed, with this area now roofed over to create an impressive multi-functional social area – kitchens, two TV rooms, two games rooms and a large day room.

Below: Girls walking to the main school block along Queen Mary's Avenue.

> *It was akin to suicide to let anyone know when your birthday was. After the appropriate number of bumps, we were tossed in the blanket. I remember hitting my head on the dorm ceiling on my 11th birthday. Maybe that is why I am not the brightest light on the Xmas tree.*
>
> 'Mac' (1945–50)

It is different today. The birthdays of pupils and staff are recognised by their names being called out in assembly or chapel each morning.

and act as an orderly. The Chief was in command when the company mustered, and drilled them into a smart unit. It was as well not to get on the wrong side of him and his Petty Officers, not least because they also supervised the distribution of food in the dining hall.

In the dormitories – where the floors were polished to a high shine and no boots were allowed to defile them – the beds were straightened each morning in line with the joints in the floorboards. Rolled nightshirts were placed in the centres of the pillows, all aligned with each other. Sheets were tightly tucked in and everything dusted. Those guilty of small lapses in discipline would be ordered by the petty officers to 'scrub the deck' in the dormitory in the evening when all the others were in bed reading or dozing off.

This was an onerous punishment, designed to cause the most discomfort to the polisher. One had to kneel on all fours with the back straight and the head up looking forward, with the cloth held under both hands on the floor. On the order 'scrub', the arms were swung across and back to the commands 'left, right, left, right' from the overseer, and one would shuffle back and forth across the floor, knees protected against the old knotty wood only by a thin pair of duck trousers.

Opposite: A Sunday morning 'lie in'. Girls bring their duvets down to the Hood House TV room.

Right: Photograph from 1920s showing the popular annual Fancy Dress Carnival. In 1926 entrants included 'Red Indian', 'Spotty Dick' and 'Sheik of Araby' and the report confirmed 'Every boy wore a carnival hat and a kaleidoscopic effect was the result. With a thousand boys wearing headgear comprising all the colours of the rainbow, dancing the Hornpipe was a sight that will long remain in the memory of those who were privileged to witness it'.

Punishing the whole company in the dormitory took the form of 'holding your boots out', where boys had to stand on their beds holding their heavy boots out at arms length until allowed to put them down. 'Doubling round the ship' was a common punishment outside the dormitory, and there were also beatings, ranging in the number of strokes, or 'cuts', according to the severity of the offence.

Although three evenings a week were taken up with classes, Wednesday and Saturday afternoons were free for sports or other diversions, and the evenings of those days offered films and dancing. There was an annual fancy dress ball, before which there was much secret picking through supplies for costumes which, when finally revealed, were often imaginative and effective; the prizes for the best costumes were well deserved, and the daughters of staff would generously brave the heavy-footed boys on the dance floor.

The move to Holbrook made little difference to this sort of life, which persisted through much of the 20th century. Derek Rowland, who was at the School in the 1970s, remembers the bed blocks well: 'These had to be squared every morning and the beds "dressed" so that they were all lined up on the same plank. No wonder my wife thinks I am OCD when it comes to the furniture in the house – she likes it at rakish and artistic angles!'

One of the boys who was at the School in the 1950s recalls that 'it would come as a surprise to modern youngsters to hear about the length of time we spent away from home then. From the age of 11 I was

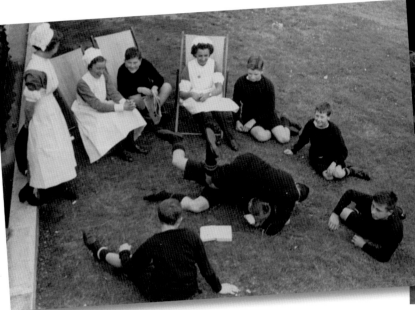

Above and bottom: Photos showing house matrons and infirmary staff interacting with the boys.

Above: Junior boys enjoying a hot drink in the newly established Drake junior boys house.

Opposite: Boys on rope ladders in the gymnasium (1960s). At this time the School had a gym display team which regularly performed in the local area.

My Bandmaster at RHS was Ernie Buckingham, a former Royal Marine – always immaculate, always puffing a fag! He was a multi-skilled instrumentalist but played the basses professionally. When I was asked to clean out his office once, I discovered, quite by accident, that the back of a small locked wooden cabinet was adrift. The back panel gave access to the cabinet, where I found a key. This key fitted the band room door, giving happy access to a room inside with a sink and without windows. It made an excellent smoking room, known to only a very select few. During a band trip to some local town I managed to get a duplicate key cut, having at once realised the potential of gaining access to the band room. The original was stowed back in its place.

I left School and joined the Royal Marines Band Service and never saw Mr Buckingham again. Until 1988(ish) that is. I was with an RM band at the Bath and West Show – a big three-day event – and during a stint on the bandstand saw the man himself sitting with his lovely little wife in the audience. At the end of the gig I went over and spoke to them both. Ernie put his head close to my ear and said, 'The best thing you ever did at RHS was to put that original key back in my locker.' We always thought we had them, didn't we?

Patrick Hill (1963–67)

despatched by train to Liverpool Street Station where I boarded the RHS special train to Manningtree. I was then at the RHS until the next school holiday (sometimes 16 weeks). There were no half term holidays and many of us could not receive parental visits for various reasons. I had just one visit during my first term, then no more at all. I suppose, in retrospect, it was a bit like a benevolent borstal, but I had a great time there.'

Another boy says that 'to this day my parents have never seen the place'. He also remembers that the only free time was Sunday afternoons and evenings when there was no prep. 'On Sunday afternoons you were allowed "leave out" which meant that you could leave the School and wander around, but only in uniform. I think I went out only once

during my time there.' School life in the 1950s, indeed, reflected life in the world outside, where post-war rationing and food shortages persisted till almost the middle of the decade and the standard diet was still untroubled by food imports and global marketing. Entertainment for many still centred on the 'wireless', though television existed for the few who could afford the sets. Films were an increasingly popular pastime, and rock music was beginning to make its mark on the new breed of 'teenager'. The rapid changes in society that were to characterise the 1960s were still in the future, and day-to-day existence for many was as it had been for decades, at the RHS no less than elsewhere.

Daily life at the School in the 1950s and 1960s, apart from time spent in lessons, drill and sport, very much centred on the houses, and the quality of one's experience depended to a large degree on the housemaster and the 'badge boys'. Some recall happy times and fair treatment, others bullying and victimisation. Most of those looking back today at the School in the middle of the 20th century talk about the 'hard times', though equally many of them say now that, though it was not a school for the faint-hearted, it taught them

everything they needed to get on well in life as adults: 'Apart from a good education, RHS gave me emotional strength and a fierce determination to face up to adversity and I have been eternally grateful for that. It might be hard for modern youngsters to understand what a good time we mostly had in what appear to be very harsh conditions, but in fact these were the same for most folk of that era, not just at RHS.'

There were the inevitable school rituals, as recalled by Alby Tuckett (1970–5): 'I think the funniest part of the Xmas shows was the "planking and submarine" for the "New Jacks", although they weren't very funny when on the receiving end. I remember being kept outside the dayroom as a group, not knowing what the hell to expect, and then being taken in one at a time to face our "New Jack" initiation

Through the ages:

Right: *1930s – boys at Greenwich with their bags, ready to move to Holbrook.*

Below Right: *1950s – a rare bus excursion for the pupils – it was a real privilege to leave the School site.*

Below left: *1960s – Holbrook staff relaxing with their mopeds – a close working community.*

1930s

1960s

1950s

Nelson House – full circle; 'New Jack' reception to university stepping stone

Although everyone at Greenwich was in a 'company', the 'New Jacks' (new boys) spent their first term in Trafalgar Quarters, where they prepared for life in the main school. On the move to Holbrook, a similar regime was planned for the boys, with each new intake spending their first term in Nelson House, before joining the main school in the junior houses on the east side. After two years or so they progressed to the senior houses on the west side.

In 1939, when war broke out, Nelson House was closed to boys, and half of it was converted into an emergency hospital. Later in the war the south side of Nelson was used for temporary accommodation for boys about to leave for the Royal Navy. In about 1947/8 it reopened as a regular house, just like all the others, being particularly successful under housemaster George Hardy, who went on to become Deputy Headmaster and was awarded the OBE on his retirement in 1985.

Nelson has reinvented itself on many occasions, becoming a sixth form house for boys in the 1980s, before the decision was taken in 2000 to turn it into a dedicated upper sixth (year 13) mixed house. Boys and girls are accommodated in separate wings, each boarder with their own room, and there are communal areas where everyone can mix. The aim is to provide an environment which stimulates both the need for concentrated study in the A Level year and independence in the transition to university and adult life outside school. The communal area includes a common room, kitchens and a bar, where a sensible approach to alcohol can be engendered. The arrangement has worked well; the young people enjoy being with their peers and appreciate the self-reliance and responsibility which being part of the house involves. Since this change the house has been run by a housemaster and housemistress, a married teaching couple, initially Marc and Sarah Godfrey followed by Chris and Catriona Herbert, and this has served to enhance the family feel and the friendly atmosphere of Nelson House.

Above: Since 2000 Nelson has been a mixed sixth form boarding house, providing a positive experience as pupils prepare to move on to further education.

Below: In 1968 the new 'Queen Elizabeth Room' became available outside class-hours, for all members of the sixth form to mix and study. This space was later converted to become the biology and physics laboratories.

ceremony in front of the rest of the house. I got the submarine, where I was laid on the floor on my back, covered with a raincoat with one sleeve held up so that I could see through the top like a periscope, whereupon I was told a story from above about a German submarine that was being hunted by the British Navy in the war and I was the captain. The story ended with my sub falling foul to a depth charge and being blown up, and at this point a bucket of water came flooding down the sleeve of the raincoat and soaked me head to foot. How the rest of the house laughed! I didn't realise how funny it looked until it was our turn the year after.'

The boys were undoubtedly badly behaved at times. Many of them now recall the boltholes they found where they could go to smoke – some of them more than a little hazardous. One boy ended

The junior houses – Blake and Drake

In 2009 the innovative decision was taken that all new entrants to the School in year 7, whether boarders or day pupils, should be placed in one of the two newly designated junior houses, Blake for girls and Drake for boys. Joining a senior school as a boarder or day pupil aged 11 can be a daunting prospect, and for some entry into a house where one's companions were of all ages up to near-adulthood could be especially challenging. In Blake and Drake new girls and boys have the blessing of knowing that their companions are their own age or only a year older and that the established year 8s were themselves new to the School a mere 12 months previously. All these pupils act as 'buddies' for the year 7s, and the supportive staff are there to boost their confidence and provide a home-like atmosphere.

Each house has a housemaster or housemistress, along with a matron, a resident tutor and another member of staff who runs house-based activities. The daily routine differs from that in the senior houses, reflecting the age of the children. Prep is part of the timetabled day, which means that all academic work is complete by 5pm, followed by after-school activities or opportunities to interact with each other in the houses. Parents of day pupils can pick them up in the knowledge that the evenings are their own, and boarders have plenty of time to relax or complete house duties before 'lights out'.

The boys' and girls' houses interact socially, for example with parties, discos and external trips, and they are all encouraged to make friends with each other and visit each other's house. In the three years since this new arrangement was introduced, it has demonstrably paid dividends in terms of classroom behaviour, social confidence and independence. The ability of the staff to interact with their young charges as children still, rather than having to balance their needs with those of much older pupils, has led to vast improvements in achievement and responsibility. As Joanna Hewitt, Blake's housemistress from 2009 to 2012 says, 'There is a different atmosphere now; the girls want to share more and have the chance to develop as individuals within a safe environment'.

Above: Boarding houses have a wide range of social facilities, which can include table football, televisions, tuck shops, pool tables, table tennis, pianos, gaming stations, libraries, board games and much more.

Right: Raleigh House became a mixed day house in 2010. It has retained the old muster yard, but now covered with AstroTurf and decking to provide a useful entertainment space with wooden garden furniture in the summer months.

up with his leg dangling into the classroom below after exploring a passage through the roof cavity and slipping off a joist. The tower was apparently an excellent hiding place for various nefarious activities because internal ladders gave access almost to the top.

Even into the 1980s, as teachers who are still at the School from that time recall, the regime deserved the word 'harsh'. The prefects were all-powerful and the School was very hierarchical. Parents rarely made an appearance; one housemaster of the time remembers opening the front door of his house to a new pupil to find the boy standing there alone; when asked where his father was, he said that he had just deposited him and driven away. That teacher never met that father. Once a boy was absorbed into his house it was the centre of all loyalty and friendship; classmates met in lessons but did not fraternise except in sporting teams.

Towards the end of the decade the system was softening; corporal punishment was formally outlawed in 1986. And then, inevitably, the arrival of girls in 1994 changed life at Holbrook forever. It was a considerable culture shock for both staff and pupils, and long-standing habits had to change quickly. Some of the boys resented what they saw as the favouritism offered to the girls in their newly refurbished houses, but were reconciled later on as the boys' houses

Left: Junior boys and girls socialising in Blake House.

Raleigh House – the day house

In September 2010, four years after day pupils were first admitted to the RHS, Raleigh House reopened as a mixed day house for boys and girls from year 9 onwards; day pupils in years 7 and 8 are members of the junior houses. Raleigh is very well equipped, with common rooms, study rooms and places to keep possessions, and is fully staffed with a housemistress, a deputy housemistress who lives on the premises, academic tutors to help with prep and other staff who visit to support and lead activities. It closes when the pupils go home at the end of the day and is open on Sundays when there are divisions. As a day house it does not have sleeping accommodation; day boarders who wish to stay over on occasion are given the opportunity to do so in senior boarding houses.

Raleigh operates in exactly the same way as the other houses and attracts just as strong a loyalty. The house competes on equal terms and takes part in every inter-house activity. The day pupils have become fully accepted and integrated, and indeed the increased presence of locally resident parents at matches, concerts and other School events has had a positive effect on the other houses too, with many more parents who can visit turning up more frequently to cheer on their teams.

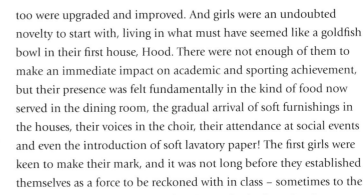

too were upgraded and improved. And girls were an undoubted novelty to start with, living in what must have seemed like a goldfish bowl in their first house, Hood. There were not enough of them to make an immediate impact on academic and sporting achievement, but their presence was felt fundamentally in the kind of food now served in the dining room, the gradual arrival of soft furnishings in the houses, their voices in the choir, their attendance at social events and even the introduction of soft lavatory paper! The first girls were keen to make their mark, and it was not long before they established themselves as a force to be reckoned with in class – sometimes to the resentment of the boys who had previously won the prizes; but the girls too felt intimidated when finding themselves the cynosure of a sea of male eyes at meal times or when summoned up to the dais at assembly.

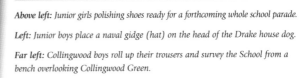

Above left: Junior girls polishing shoes ready for a forthcoming whole school parade.

Left: Junior boys place a naval gidge (hat) on the head of the Drake house dog.

Far left: Collingwood boys roll up their trousers and survey the School from a bench overlooking Collingwood Green.

It was not until girls were present in every year group, and until the last boys who had begun their RHS lives at an all-male school left, that co-education really settled down and bedded in. Fears that the boys' sport would suffer if their numbers were reduced to make way for more girls proved unfounded. Social events with nearby schools declined, but the range of activities on campus at Holbrook grew. More female staff arrived too, leavening the common room. A healthy co-educational atmosphere soon developed and both boys and girls benefited immensely.

Over the next two decades the houses went through several developments. The first upper sixth girls were originally housed in a separate section of Cornwallis, which meant that some of the boys had to be redistributed among the other houses, as had also happened to all the Hood boys when displaced by the first girls. This caused some unhappiness, since house loyalties were such a strong element of life at RHS. But the boys in Nelson House, which had for some time been a separate sixth form community, were asked to help with the integration, and their more mature approach proved invaluable in defusing the situation and pointing out all the undoubted advantages of a mixed education – though it was not until Drake, the last boys' house to be refurbished during that phase of improvement, was brought up to the standard enjoyed by all the other houses that the issue subsided.

The integration of girls was made considerably more straightforward by the appointment as Senior Mistress of Hazel Anthony, who joined the School a year before girls started. She recalls that the first girls all had connections with the School, whether through siblings or parents, which to some extent eased their acceptance; but it was also the case that in the early days Hood was surrounded in the evenings by boys deeply curious about these strange creatures who had arrived in their midst. The first girls had to be brave, and there were some who found the goldfish bowl atmosphere hard to take. There were, after all, very few of them, and they had to be their own role models; for the first few terms, as those who were there at the time recall, the new arrivals appeared to be 'in' the School but not 'of' it. However, it quickly became apparent that the girls were softening the edges, and making the lives of the boys in the rapidly changing RHS culture easier; the boys too had to learn quickly that attitudes needed to change and long-established givens questioned and challenged.

The refurbishment of boarding houses involved a multi-million pound investment and they now exceed the standards of most boarding schools in the country, providing a comfortable home and a caring environment. A boarding inspector visiting Hood House confirmed that it was one of the best boarding facilities she had seen in the country. The houses retain their 1930s fabric, but have been modernised to provide a comfortable 'home from home'

Below (top): Concentration – girls verses boys in a gaming encounter.

Below (centre): Preparation – back house pupils practice together for house singing and drama competitions.

Below (bottom): Contemplation – chess has always been a popular pastime.

Opposite: Pupils enjoy the large campus, with lots of fresh air, open space, shady walks and picnic spots. This photograph was taken from the south eastern field boundary, close to Callaghan's Copse, where trees had been planted on the suggestion of former Prime Minister, James Callaghan, a great supporter of the School, serving on the management committee 1947–51 and attending Speech Day in 1966.

The study bedrooms are furnished with individual beds with integral desks and cupboards, and in senior houses each room houses between one and four pupils, ensuite for most and with some single sixth form studies available. The old muster yards that formed a quad have been roofed over, and this has provided extra space for social areass with televisions and games, libraries, music facilities, study rooms with computers and kitchens where snacks and drinks can be prepared. Staff are on hand day and night; each housemaster or housemistress lives on site with his or her family, and there is also both a resident tutor and a resident matron in each house. Visiting tutors are there every evening to oversee prep, to help with problems and to run activities. In contrast to the past, when parents were not expected to visit the houses, they are now most welcome, with regular functions for them to attend. Resident staff are always available and their doors can always be knocked if something is needed or a problem arises – staff are very accessible and happy to support the pupils wherever and whenever they can.

The house staff clearly have a parental and pastoral role. Many of the pupils still come from service families who may be posted abroad,

and the growing numbers of international students are also far away from parents and siblings. The staff are well trained to deal with homesickness as well as disciplinary matters, and also to offer support for family issues such as divorce or bereavement. Bullying is now extremely rare, with a well trained team of sixth form Peer Supporters (formerly Anti Bullying Counsellers – ABCs), and the pupils themselves are very proactive in bringing any problems of that sort to the attention of house staff.

The changes to boarding arrangements – Nelson becoming a mixed upper sixth house, Raleigh now dedicated to day pupils, years 7 and 8 being placed in their own junior houses – have been successful. However, the older pupils in years 9 to 12 sometimes feel a little bereft of juniors who are now in Blake and Drake, and for the upper sixth, leaving the house to which they have been fiercely loyal during all their years at school can be a wrench, even though they are departing for the adult comforts of Nelson. It is without doubt that boarding at the RHS is now a very different experience from what it was a mere two decades ago.

Health and Welfare

Right: Off-duty infirmary nurses enjoy a well-earned cup of tea.

Below: The Hood matron, Lesley Wilson helping pupils get ready for a divisions parade. Matrons have always played an important role in the welfare of the pupils at both Greenwich and Holbrook.

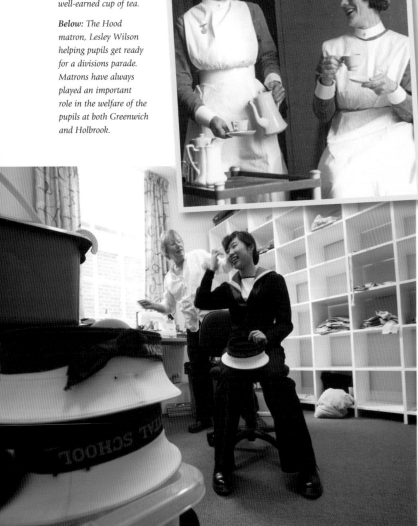

Old boys who remember the rigours of life at Holbrook in the years after the move recall with a shudder the chilblains and chapped legs caused by the bitter wind in winter and the rough serge of their shorts. Discomfort had to be endured, and the matrons had remedies, but real medical problems were more than adequately catered for in the new buildings. The large infirmary had its own operating theatre with X-ray equipment, and it was staffed with full-time resident nurses. There was even a mortuary, which had been a requirement at Greenwich for the Pensioners and was clearly regarded as necessary also at Holbrook, though fortunately it was used only once. Doctors and surgeons could be called on when needed, and there was also a regular school dentist; Jack Williams joined in 1945 and is said to have peered into over 6,000 mouths during his 45-year career at the School. The 1950s saw a major flu epidemic when one of the houses was used as an isolation unit, but on the whole the boys were fit and healthy, and when they were ill they received excellent care; their name for the infirmary was 'up home' since it was the place where they could expect to receive the sort of loving attention that their mothers would have lavished on them.

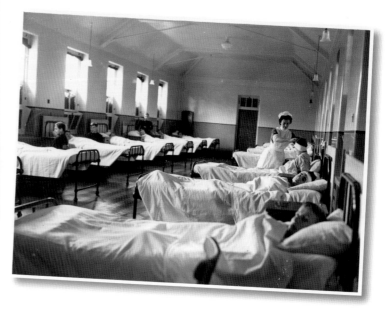

My wife was a nurse at the School infirmary from the mid-1950s until she retired, with a break to look after our children. The infirmary had its own X-ray machine and operating theatre, and she would act as the theatre nurse, removing boys' tonsils and sometimes their appendixes. On one of our evenings off, when we'd taken the bus into Ipswich, we returned to find that the surgeon had had to be summoned to remove a boy's appendix; Sister Thompson who was on duty had thoughtfully kept it to show us. I also remember the mortuary being used once, when a dead body was washed up on the river bank – the caretaker of a laid-up merchant ship downriver from Holbrook Bay, who had drowned.

Peter Page, gardener (1944–2010)

The war had only just finished when I went there, and everything was rationed, even the fuel. I think that my most abiding memory will be of chilblains and chaps. The chaps started in the very first week and I remember rubbing zinc ointment onto them and they would bleed. The chilblains that we had were just unbelievable and the fingers would split wide open either across or lengthways. The ones on the toes just itched. A Collingwood lad, Polly Purkiss, had them so badly on his hands that he was excused writing for a whole term and he had to wear gloves all the time. During my first year, POs would sit in on the junior classes for prep. They took great delight in giving cuts with the edge of a ruler on the back of your fingers and of course across the chilblains. Both my brother and I have housemaids' knee through polishing the floors with no kneelers, which was used as a punishment.

'Skinge' (1946–49)

I remember we had flannel underwear and blue serge shorts, and our wee chapped legs used to bleed, but matron, God bless her, had some wonderful pink cream that made it all better.

Chick Fowler (1950–53)

Opposite: *Hospital beds in the old infirmary. In the early days at Holbrook there were flu and diphtheria epidemics.*

At Greenwich in 1921 over 400 boys were sick with influenza and there was also a severe outbreak of diphtheria and scarlet fever. This perhaps explains why the School Surgeon Commander became actively involved in studying sickness in closed communities and the development of immunisation programmes. In fact a number of early medical publications refer to research undertaken at the School, including an interesting study on the incidence of myopia (short-sightedness) amongst the boys (1883).

Above: *Boys cleaning the floors in Neptune's Hall at Greenwich, 1909 – good practice for scrubbing the main deck!*

Below: *Surgeon Captain PM May and his infirmary staff at Greenwich, 1927, who had to treat bouts of influenza and diphtheria. An outbreak of the latter resulted in the sad loss of a boy in 1941, although the School mortuary was never actually used for a pupil. Thankfully this was the last record of a pupil death at the School.*

Today there are five nurses who offer 24 hour care. They run seven surgeries a week, which are supplemented by five GP surgeries run by local doctors. The School dentist and orthodontist make regular visits, a physiotherapist comes in once a week and a counsellor is also on hand. The pupils are medically assessed every September when the new school year starts so that potential problems can be identified and issues such as food allergies catered for. The staff deal with sports injuries, broken bones and illnesses such as chickenpox and mumps, and the wards in the Health Centre offer refuges where sick children or those recovering from hospitalisation can be nursed and monitored. All the staff, both teaching and support, as well as senior pupils, are aware of the need for pastoral care within the self-contained community of the School, and the high level of medical provision at the RHS is a great reassurance to parents and children alike.

Also part of the value the RHS places on pastoral issues is the position within the curriculum of PSHEE – personal, social, health and economic education. The subject has been taught at the School since the early 1990s, but with Howard Blackett's arrival it was given greater prominence and today it is taught by dedicated specialists and in an innovative and accessible form. The courses are taught from year 7 to 12 and cover sex education, substance abuse, body awareness, self-confidence and other issues of vital importance to young people beginning to feel their way in the world.

It would have taken an Act of Parliament for me to come to RHS, as my father, the Headmaster Norman York, was not a naval man. So I went to school elsewhere, but of course came home for the holidays and had the run of the place, which was magical for a young boy and his two siblings. But I did later have a much closer connection with the School, after training as a dentist and setting up in practice in Colchester.

When Jack Williams, who had done the job for decades, retired in the 1980s, he offered the contract to someone else, which surprised me as I had expressed an interest. 'You're not ready for that yet,' was his response. But in 1992 I eventually got the job and stayed until I retired. The work usually took three days a week, with pupils and staff opting to come to me for the dental work they needed, though many of the pupils also had their own dentists at home. I was able to have some influence on the diet, after I noticed the incidence of caries going up after sweet machines were installed, and got them removed.

My father, as Headmaster, was a forceful taskmaster, and the School was a tough place. I remember noticing the difference after girls came – I could see that the hard lads at the School were being challenged in a different way, and some of them had trouble dealing with it. Of course, the School is a totally different place today.

Patrick York (School Dentist 1992–2011)

Right: Two pupils being attended to by Sister Anne Thompson, in charge of the modern School Health Centre. The secured metal containers are for storage of prescription drugs destined for the boarding houses.

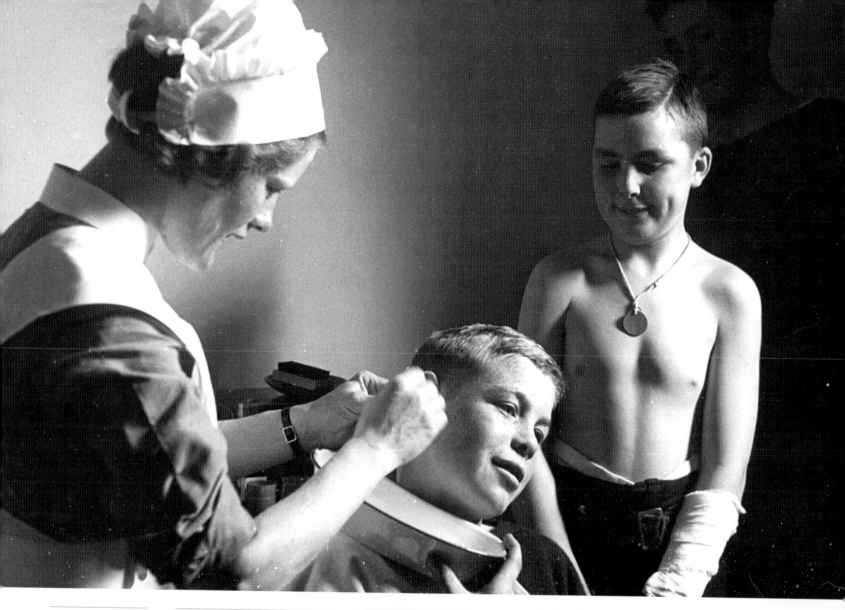

Below: The School dental service – 'Now, open wide and say ah!'

Above: Ears – Being syringed in the 1930s.

Right: The Health Centre team are on call 24 hours and are always available to deal with injuries and ailments.

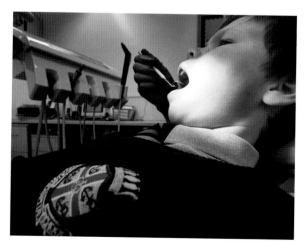

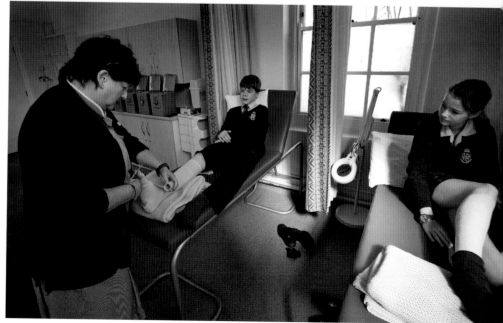

Food

In the first half of the 18th century, breakfast for the boys at the School consisted of five ounces of bread, an ounce of butter and half a pint of beer, supplemented by 'firmity with sugar sufficient' (frumenty, a cracked-wheat dish) on some days and 'water gruel with sugar and currants' on others. They had another half pint of beer at supper and a pint with their dinner at midday; 'small beer' – brewed on the premises – was then the standard drink with a meal, as it was much safer than water. Cheese was a daily menu item, beef or mutton were served five days a week, along with plum pudding on a Wednesday and either rice pudding or pea soup on the two meatless days each week.

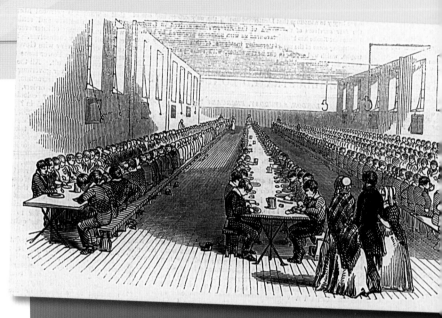

Above right: The 1811 dining hall at Greenwich from the Illustrated London News, 18 February 1848. 'The boys having entered the hall, take their places, silence is obtained, grace is said, and then silence until the boys are told to begin their dinner, during which they are allowed to converse'.

Left: The modern cafeteria-style server, with salad bar in the foreground and a variety of hot main courses served beyond.

Below: Postcard showing dining hall at Holbrook, before the Jellicoe room was partitioned out of the west end. Up until 1970 the whole School was served together – this continued for the Christmas meal until 2010.

The dining hall at Greenwich was large enough to seat 1,000 boys for a meal at the same time. The tables were similar to those found on Navy mess decks and fixed to the wall at the end of each table was a mess rack which contained the utensils. Seating was by seniority and a 'New Jacks' place was at the lower end. Two boys were detailed off to fetch food from the kitchen and the same boys were responsible for clearing the mess after the meal. When the food arrived at the table, two senior boys would serve it and they, of course, had the best pickings. Boys lower down the table did not fare so well; for instance most of the food was steam-cooked, and if the afters was apple pie, the corners of the pan where the steam had condensed produced what was known as sloppy duff which was considered good enough for 'New Jacks'. Sometimes the authorities would have a raid on these practices and reversed the roles. The food was good and wholesome, but boys being what they are, it was never completely to their satisfaction. A lot of food had slang names: 'wang', for example, was the general term for a meal, 'stungey' was a sandwich, bread was 'toke' and 'fat dobs' was bacon.

Jack Judge (1924–28)

Below: The original dining tables and benches remain, but now pupils use trays to collect their meals from various serving stations.

'Founders' duff'

In 1824 it was decided that 4 November – the date William of Orange was born in 1650 and also the date he married Mary in 1677 – would be celebrated as Founders' Day, and that plum pudding would be served. In the 1920s, as Dan Turner records, the boys called the pudding 'foundation pong' and by the 1950s it had become 'founders' duff'. Resembling Christmas pudding, which was also a highlight of the nutritional year, it was much appreciated. The tradition continues today.

Food in the 1950s

Our food was for the most part nutritious, healthy and, on the whole, adequate, though one was usually hungry – and the predominant feature of the menus at Holbrook in those years was one of unvarying routine. From the day I joined in September 1954 until my last term, six years later, I could predict with some certainty what was going to be served at any meal of any day of the week, in any year. There were no choices and the only slight variations in the weekly menus that I can recall occurred in the summer term, when cold meats and salad replaced some of the warm evening meals that were so essential to stave off hypothermia during the achingly cold Suffolk winter nights. And there was no reason to suppose – and the staff who were still there after making the move from Greenwich to Holbrook confirmed it – that these menus had changed much since the move from Greenwich.

Our meals followed an unvarying regimen, blessed always by an unforgettable grace, delivered by the godlike Head Boy from the balcony of the dining hall: 'Bless O Lord these gifts to our use, grant us thankful hearts and help us to remember the needs of others'. Every day bread, flops and marmalade or jam were served at breakfast with mugs of 'kai', and again with tea at supper. At stand-easy (1100 hours), and again in the evening after prep, there was a slice of currant bread or a rock bun or piece of fruitcake. Kai was made by grating up blocks of Pusser's cocoa, looking like giant bars of Cadbury's chocolate, and diluting it with as little boiling water and as much condensed milk as possible. It was close to heaven on cold winter mornings.

We were allowed to supplement our meals with items brought from home or purchased at the tuck shop. Marmite, ketchup and HP sauce were popular as were jars of jam and honey and some weird mixture of diced vegetables and salad cream that slightly resembled Russian salad. There was never enough butter. If one was at the bottom of a mess table, all the reasonably thick flops had been taken by the time the plate arrived. So a popular pastime was to save the cream from the top of one's daily milk bottles for three or four days and then shake it all about for hours with some salt in a small jar – Marmite jars were perfect – until it formed a satisfactory ball of butter.

Being a plate or mess boy was the first step on the ladder of promotion within the School. One was responsible for laying up and clearing the tables, and also collecting the food for each house and pushing the heavily laden trolleys out from the galley – which, as with all boys and wheeled vehicles, became something of a competitive race between the houses. On one memorable occasion I had reached what I regarded as terminal velocity on my trolley, and was happily coasting along standing on the bottom shelf. Suddenly, to my horror, the Headmaster stepped into my path. Though I tried to go full astern, we collided and plates and dixies of hot food slid inexorably off the shelves and cascaded all over him. To his eternal credit, after he had picked himself up, he muttered, 'My fault, Wilson, I wasn't looking where I was going.'

Howard MacKenzie-Wilson (1954–60)

The 'red light' system

An abiding memory of boys at the School in the 1940s and 1950s was the huge clatter and ruckus as plates, bowls and cutlery were collected. Until 1956 the dining hall was controlled by the duty master, and everyone was supposed to be silent when he stood up; the trouble was 'Nobby' Lumsden was so short that he had to stand on a platform or chair in order to be seen, and even then he could be seen only with great difficulty. In 1956 the newly appointed Headmaster, Norman York, clearly found the noise unbearable, so he installed a series of red light bulbs around the hall, controlled by a switch at the top table. At the flick of this switch 660 boys were supposed to remain silent. At the second and subsequent flicks, knives, forks, spoons and crockery were each passed in succession to the tops of the mess tables, where the PO boys and leading hands sat, who stacked them. At the final flick, the plate boys collected all the dirty cutlery and crockery on huge, heavy trolleys, to return them to the kitchen and collect the next course. This novel procedure attracted huge ribaldry from the School, but persisted until 1970 when a cafeteria system replaced table service.

A diet sheet from the Royal Naval Asylum in the early 1800s shows a similar spread of provisions, though Sunday dinner by then included greens. Potatoes had become a staple part of the menu, served at dinner every day, sometimes with broth and bread and sometimes with meat. The provision of bread and beer remained constant.

By the end of the 19th century beer had disappeared: bread with cocoa was the daily breakfast and bread with tea was supper. Dinner was much more varied, with meat on the menu every day along with daily variations on the theme of potatoes, onions, carrots, turnips, cabbage, barley, oatmeal and herbs. In the 1920s, as Dan Turner remembers, the food was remarkably good considering the generally poor living conditions in the country at the time, although the daily menus showed little variation – and the move to Holbrook made no difference, since the ex-naval catering staff travelled with the School to their new home. Old boys have varying memories of the food and the experience of eating in the Holbrook dining room, though most acknowledge that they did very well on the whole: 'When I went on leave and saw what my mum had to survive on I didn't think we were too badly off at all.' One boy remembers 'Nelson's squares (mincemeat

My introduction to School food came when, cold and hungry, after the first ever train journey alone for many of us, without our parents, we filed into the enormous, half darkened dining hall to two dimly lit tables, where our supper appeared through the glowing galley doors. None of us had ever eaten in such a huge space. The walls of this room seemed to reach up through the darkness to the heavens. That first meal consisted of strips of bright pink, flaccid streaky bacon swimming in a sea of unnaturally bright red tinned tomatoes. In my innocence, having never seen either of these delights in my life, I shyly enquired what they were. The petty officer boy at the head of the mess table curtly replied, 'It's called train smash! Eat it. It's good for you. It's all you're going to get.' Unable to swallow this unappetizing mess, I was glad to discover that there was plenty of white bread with little pats of butter, apparently called flops, and some bright red jam, washed down with huge mugs of sweet, weak tea that had a characteristic, never-to-be-forgotten taste after stewing for an hour or so in the urns.

Howard MacKenzie-Wilson (1954–60)

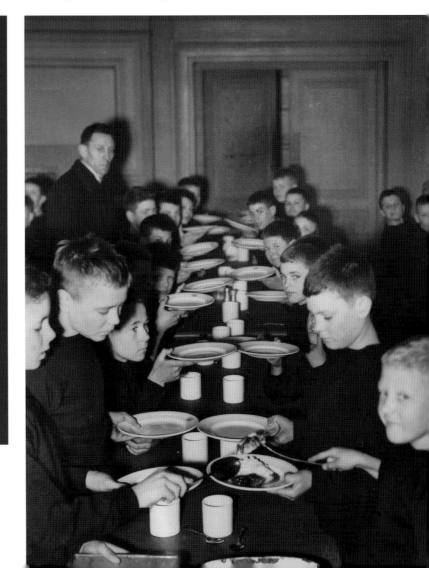

Opposite: *1960s – boys served at the tables when the 'red light' system was in operation.*

Above: *2000s – Christmas dinner is a colourful fancy dress affair with brass-accompanied carol singing and judging of the house Christmas cake competition.*

Right: *An early Holbrook drinking mug, c1938.*

between two layers of pastry), very tasty', and another 'pea doo, which looked awful, but it was the best lentil soup I have ever tasted!' though someone else discovered in his portion of pea doo 'two maggots, a beetle and a piece of glass; no kidding. They didn't put me off finishing it off though – I just hooked them out!'

Many boys from the 1950s remember the 'great bread riot', a protest aimed at getting better food. Bread was baked every day at the School apart from at weekends, so by Sunday it had got rather stale. Every boy could order as many extra slices of bread at each meal as he wished – the extras were known as 'sparies' – and one Friday, as a Nelson boy recalls, 'Our badge boys went down all the tables telling us to order as many sparies as possible, which we did. I can't remember how many I ordered but none was wasted, we ate the lot, mostly dry. After chapel George Hardy lined the whole house up and lectured us about our bad behaviour (the Headmaster had bent his ear and seemed to blame Nelson) and our matron was in tears because her boys had been so naughty. One of the outcomes was that Nelson lost its coveted place in the corner of the dining hall and was moved right under the dais.' As another Nelson boy, Bernard de Neumann, recalls, 'The Headmaster was right to blame us – we were the prime movers.'

The bakers had to come in over that weekend to bake extra bread, but it seemed that the protest had its due effect as the food improved. De Neumann has another memory of that era, when he was a senior boy in Nelson: 'Some of us spotted one of the kitchen staff regularly disappearing surreptitiously at the end of the day with a large piece of good-quality meat in the basket of his bicycle, at a time when the meat we were served was often both meagre and stringy. So we plucked up courage and reported what we'd seen. He disappeared and we had better food.' He also remembers, years later, talking to George Hardy about a picture conservator from the National Maritime Museum who had come to the School to inspect the paintings. In the dining hall he climbed up a ladder to get a close-up look at one of the paintings and came down with a puzzled look on his face. 'There seem to be a large number of fruit stones stuck all over the picture,' he said to Hardy, who was baffled and at a loss to explain. De Neumann enlightened Hardy later: 'Sitting in our fixed house blocks round the dining hall, we sometimes, for fun, launched "mortar" attacks on other houses by firing fruit stones at them. The great height of the ceiling helped in this endeavour, but sometimes the stones seemed to vanish – and it was the visit by the conservator that finally revealed where the misfiring missiles had ended up.'

Being seated 'down bolt' at the foot of the table, and therefore condemned to the thinnest flops, the bits left round the edges of

puddings and the smallest portions, all ceased when a cafeteria system was introduced in 1970, although as houses went into the dining room in rotation, those at the end of the queue had to wait much longer for their food. The catering staff were still, as they had been for centuries, ex-naval, until the mid-1980s when the contract for the food was awarded to the catering firm Compass (now Chartwells). There are 37 kitchen staff employed by the caterers, 11 of whom are chefs, under the catering manager, Gavin Yuill.

Today, meals are much more relaxed, and the food is awesomely good. The breakfast menus always include plenty of fresh fruit, cereals, muesli, croissants, toast and a variety of hot options. Lunch offers baked potatoes, pasta dishes, salads and three choices of a main course with a variety of vegetables, followed by a cooked dessert, fruit and cheeses. Supper consists of pizza, burgers, soup, sandwiches and again salads and a pudding; with additional healthy options being introduced all the time. Pupils are all encouraged to try new foods, think about nutrition and consider how they manage their own dietary needs.

The food is all cooked on the premises, including the bread and the biscuits, with separate options available for those with food allergies – and the breadth and variety of the menus are more than adequate to cater for those with religious prohibitions or food preferences. The kitchen supplies the houses with bread, milk and fruit, and also caters for the health centre and the café in the Trafalgar Rooms. Hospitality anywhere in the School is an additional task, whether it is drinks and biscuits for staff meetings, a Headmaster's lunch or a cricket tea. The catering staff run regular themed days, serve an outstanding whole school Christmas dinner, complete with award-winning Christmas pudding, and organise special events such as the 'Ready Steady Cook' demonstration. The quality of food produced for formal dinners and special events is second to none: CCF, sixth form, leavers, scholars, sports, Trafalgar Day, Burns night dinners have all been catered for, and are always memorable occasions thoroughly enjoyed by the pupils, staff and parents attending. There is also the need to cater during the holidays for visiting organisations. It is a year-round operation, with brief breaks at Christmas and Easter.

The whole complex enterprise is overseen by a food committee on which sit Gavin Yuill and Terry McCusker – a head chef who has been at the School since 1988 – along with Sarah Godfrey, Director of Pastoral Care, and a pupil representative from every house. They discuss menu options and listen to suggestions and criticisms – and are there also to feed back on possible eating disorders or other food-based problems.

Looking back on three centuries of food at the RHS indicates that, throughout the time, the pupils were probably, in general, luckier than many of their contemporaries in the nourishment with which they were provided. Campaigns to improve school food and outlaw 'junk' have highlighted the issues many schools face. But none of this applies to the RHS today; staff and pupils are fed nutritiously and copiously, and the food is delicious.

Support staff – serving the community

David Goodwin, the logistics manager, says that retirement, rather than moving on to another job, is the main reason why his staff leave – and this is more than borne out by the longevity of service demonstrated by many of the School's support staff. In the kitchen, Colleen Taylor and Michael Sealey can notch up 22 years each and Terry McCusker 24. Eileen Clover has been there even longer – and her 34 years are preceded by the many years her grandparents worked at the RHS after moving with the School from Greenwich to Holbrook. Her grandfather's occupation as a sail-maker allowed her father to attend the School in the 1930s, and her husband ran the water treatment plant for 32 years. She herself has had a variety of jobs but is now in charge of cleaning the swimming pool and the gym.

Gloria Smith, who is the cleaner at Howe House and also the early morning supervisor, has worked at the RHS for 30 years – and she too can claim an extra part in its history as her father helped to build it. Tracy Webb – 13 years in the stores department – remembers when the entire School uniform was supplied free. Moving with the times – pupils now order uniform online, direct from the supplier, however, she still issues the 'number ones' – the naval uniform worn for divisions – along with stationery, furniture, electrical equipment and anything else needed.

Along with the 37 staff employed by the estates department – who include ground staff and gardeners as well as maintenance people – there is a large team of support staff who work in the main School buildings and in the houses. They agree that the RHS is a happy place to work, despite early starts (before 6am in many cases) and the need to work through the School holidays to look after visiting organisations – and the years many of them stay clearly attest to this happiness.

Opposite: Naval portraits from the Greenwich Hospital Collection watch over the impressive dining hall, with arched entrance to the separate Jellicoe room, now a formal dining and special events venue.

Right: Meals are wholesome and healthy. Pupils and serving staff develop positive relationships – a smile is never far away. Sunday roast is always a favourite.

The RHSA, 'Old Boys' and Former Pupils

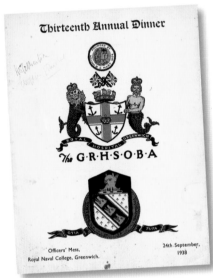

Left: Old boys regularly returned to their old School at Greenwich, as here in 1921 where boys studying at the RN College are photographed with the officers of the School. The Old Boys Association provided a formal structure enabling former pupils to stay in touch with each other and the School.

Above: An early membership card and menu from an early formal dinner. Many former pupils are very proud of their connection with the School.

The RHSA owes its origins to an old boy, FA Rendle, who wrote to Captain Oliphant in February 1923 suggesting that an old boys' association would be a good idea. Two years later, in July 1925, former pupils were invited back to the School for Prize Day and many turned up, ranging in ages from 16 to 94. After tea in Queen Henrietta Maria's drawing room in the Queen's House, the old boys unanimously agreed to set up an association, with a temporary committee under the chairmanship of the Captain Superintendent to steer its affairs until such time as a constitution could be drafted and democratic elections held. It was estimated at the time that at least 4,000 old boys under the age of 50 were still alive.

By January 1926 the Greenwich Royal Hospital School Old Boys' Association (GRHSOBA) was firmly established with the Superintendent (later the Headmaster) as President, an arrangement that continued until 2011. The first annual dinner was held in July 1926 with 'medals and decorations to be worn'. From the start there were branches in Portsmouth, Chatham and Plymouth, and soon, with so many old boys serving in the Royal Navy and the Royal Marines, there were branches onboard the larger warships too. The association grew in strength and influence throughout its time at Greenwich, and when the School moved to Holbrook it became the 'Royal Hospital School Old Boys' Association' and continued to thrive.

Extended families and continuing links

Herbert Marriot and his five brothers were orphaned when in 1914 their father was lost whilst serving on HMS *Bulwark*. After attending Swanley Orphanage they (as with so many others attending this home) went on to Greenwich Hospital School. Interestingly one day in 1922, whilst completing a station (job) for Admiral Oliphant he met with Nellie Brown, his kitchen maid. As a result he volunteered to continue this station on a regular basis – eventually they married each other in 1928. There are many examples of large seafaring families being educated at the School, for example the seven Pascoe brothers who attended the School 1904 to 1924 and in a co-educational context, the seven Bailey children educated in the period 1990 to 2010 (when the twin girls left). There are a significant number of former pupils now sending their own children to the School, with examples being the Cantelo, Todd, Beaton, Allan and Topley families. It is encouraging to note that in 2012 at least three other families extended their links with the School by a further generation.

Above: In 2012 two girls from the early 1990s have carried on the RHS tradition: Aimee Frankham (née Debenham, 1993–95, Cornwallis) with son Zaccary (2012– , Drake) and Abby Kilian (1991–93, Hood) with daughter Alice (2012– , Blake).

In 1939, on the eve of war, the dinner was held for the first time in the Painted Hall at Greenwich. By 1946 compulsory entry to the Navy ceased and the Association developed the original shore-based branch structure. After girls joined the School in 1991 the new title 'Royal Hospital School Association' was adopted and girls began to enrol, despite all members sometimes being collectively designated 'old boys'. Through the name changes caused by the move to Holbrook and then co-education the Association has, throughout its life, contributed greatly to the School.

The taking of the San Joseph was painted by Thomas Barker about 1850. It shows the surrender of this Spanish Ship to Nelson at the battle of Cape St Vincent, 14th February 1797. This picture forms part of a bequest to the School under the will of Mrs E.A. Hooper widow of F.J. Hooper, who was a boy at the Royal Hospital School, Greenwich from 1894–1898. The remainder of this bequest was used to provide Table Tennis Tables in the Boarding Houses.

Above: Many old boys have supported the School throughout the years. This inscription confirms the gift of a Nelson painting and some table tennis equipment for the boarding houses.

Right: On transfer to Suffolk the Association presented the School with a beautifully sculptured mural tablet inscribed with the history of the School from the date of its foundation, up to the eve of its departure for Holbrook. This gift is found at the east end of the reception hall designed to enable those who enter to read a concise historical record of the School and to connect the present with the past.

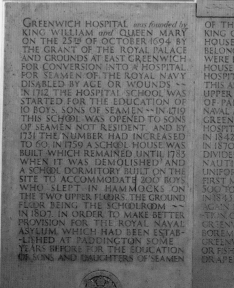

GREENWICH HOSPITAL *was founded by* KING WILLIAM *and* QUEEN MARY ON THE 25TH OF OCTOBER 1694 BY THE GRANT OF THE ROYAL PALACE AND GROUNDS AT EAST GREENWICH FOR CONVERSION INTO A HOSPITAL FOR SEAMEN OF THE ROYAL NAVY DISABLED BY AGE OR WOUNDS ~ IN 1712 THE HOSPITAL SCHOOL WAS STARTED FOR THE EDUCATION OF 10 BOYS, SONS OF SEAMEN ~ IN 1719 THIS SCHOOL WAS OPENED TO SONS OF SEAMEN NOT RESIDENT, AND BY 1731 THE NUMBER HAD INCREASED TO 60. IN 1759 A SCHOOL HOUSE WAS BUILT WHICH REMAINED UNTIL 1783 WHEN IT WAS DEMOLISHED AND A SCHOOL DORMITORY BUILT ON THE SITE TO ACCOMMODATE 200 BOYS WHO SLEPT IN HAMMOCKS ON THE TWO UPPER FLOORS. THE GROUND FLOOR BEING THE SCHOOLROOM ~ IN 1807 IN ORDER TO MAKE BETTER PROVISION FOR THE ROYAL NAVAL ASYLUM, WHICH HAD BEEN ESTAB-LISHED AT PADDINGTON SOME YEARS BEFORE FOR THE EDUCATION OF SONS AND DAUGHTERS OF SEAMEN

OF THE ROYAL NAVY & ROYAL MARINES KING GEORGE III GRANTED THE QUEEN'S HOUSE AT GREENWICH WITH LANDS BELONGING TO IT *and* SCHOOL BUILDINGS WERE ERECTED AND CONNECTED TO THE HOUSE BY COLONNADES ~~~ IN 1821 THE HOSPITAL SCHOOL WAS TRANSFERRED TO THIS ASYLUM & BECAME KNOWN AS THE UPPER SCHOOL OF THE ASYLUM ~ BY ACT OF PARLIAMENT IN 1825, THE ROYAL NAVAL ASYLUM WAS CONSOLIDATED WITH GREENWICH HOSPITAL AND THE ROYAL HOSPITAL SCHOOL WAS THEREBY FORMED. IN 1842 THE GIRLS' SCHOOL WAS CLOSED IN 1870 THE SCHOOL WAS RE-ORGANISED, DIVIDED INTO UPPER NAUTICAL AND ~ NAUTICAL SCHOOL, AND THE NAVAL UNIFORM AND REGIME ADOPTED ~ THE FIRST MODEL TRAINING CORVETTE "FAME" 500 TONS WAS ERECTED IN THE GROUNDS IN 1843. THIS WAS REPLACED IN 1862, AND AGAIN IN 1872 ❋ THE BOREMAN FOUNDA-TION, ORIGINALLY THE GREEN COAT SCHOOL GREENWICH, WAS ENDOWED BY SIR WILLIAM BOREMAN IN 1672 FOR 20 BOYS BORN IN GREENWICH, SONS OF SEAMEN WATERMEN OR FISHERMEN, & WAS GOVERNED BY THE DRAPERS COMPANY ~ IN 1887 ❋ WAS

INCREASED TO 100 BOYS WHO WERE ADMITTED AS DAY BOYS *to the* UPPER NAUTICAL SCHOOL FOR EDUCATION *and* WERE ALLOWED TO WEAR NAVAL UNIFORM ~ THE FOUNDATION FUNDS WERE INSUFFICIENT TO SUPPORT THEM AS BOARDERS ❋ ❋ ❋ ❋ WHEN THE ROYAL HOSPITAL SCHOOL WAS REMOVED TO HOLBROOK IN 1933, THIS ARRANGE-MENT CEASED AND THE BOREMAN FUNDS WERE APPLIED BY MEANS OF EXHIBITIONS *to the* HIGHER EDUCATION *of* SELECTED GREENWICH-BORN CHILD-REN OF SEAMEN WATERMEN *or* FISHER-MEN WITH PREFERENCE TO THOSE OF MEN WITH SERVICE *in the* ROYAL NAVY ROYAL MARINES *and* ROYAL AIR FORCE ❋ THIS TABLET WAS PRESENTED BY THE GREENWICH ROYAL HOSPITAL SCHOOL OLD BOYS' ASSOCIATION ~ (OLD BOREMAN'S BOYS INCLUDED) INAUGURATED 1925. FIRST PRESIDENT REAR ADMIRAL OLIPHANT SUPERINTENDENT *of the* SCHOOL TO RECORD THEIR GRATITUDE AND LOYAL AFFECTION FOR THE SCHOOL

The Heritage Centre

The venerable history of the Royal Hospital School aroused, as early as 1851, the desire that there should be a museum as part of the School. In that year George Fisher, the forward-looking Headmaster, wrote to Admiral Sir Charles Adam, Governor of Greenwich Hospital, requesting that instructions be given for fitting out a room for the museum. A museum was established only for a short while, however, over the years the School has continued to acquire an impressive collection of artefacts and memorabilia related to its heritage.

Above: King George VI speaking in Neptune's Hall (the former school gymnasium) during the formal opening of the National Maritime Museum on 27 April 1937. Seated, from the left, are HRH Princess Elizabeth (HM Queen Elizabeth II since 1952), HM Queen Elizabeth The Queen Mother (visited Holbrook 1968) and Queen Mary (widow of King George V – visited Holbrook 1938). The School Heritage Centre celebrates its royal connections and continues its links with the Museum.

In the 1920s, when the decision had been taken to move the School to Holbrook and consideration was being given to the future use of the Greenwich Hospital buildings, pressure was growing for the establishment of a national maritime museum. In 1934 this was finally achieved when an Act of Parliament transferred the use of the site and land formerly occupied by the Royal Hospital School (including the Queen's House) to the trustees of the nascent National Maritime Museum, which was formally opened by King George VI in 1937. The legal position is that, if the National Maritime Museum ever vacates its Greenwich site, freehold reverts to Greenwich Hospital to which ownership of the site was transferred forever by an Act of Parliament in the reign of George IV, 1825. Some items associated with the School remained at Greenwich but others moved with it to Holbrook.

The School has continued a close relationship with the Museum that occupies its former site. When HRH Princess Elizabeth opened its East wing in 1951 the School provided a guard of honour, and they were also there in 1999 when, now of course HM Queen Elizabeth II, she opened Neptune Court, the £15 million redevelopment of the old Neptune's Hall. On that occasion the chapel choir and band performed at the opening ceremony, and the choir also sang at a trustees' dinner held the previous evening. Back in 1962 Norman York, the Headmaster, unveiled a tablet in the Caird Galleries (entrance to the Museum), commemorating the School's occupancy of the Queen's House. Some of the historical paintings which hang in the Holbrook buildings are part of the Greenwich Hospital Collection, which is mainly on loan to the National Maritime Museum, and some of the icons, including the captured cannon, which still proclaims the School's close relationship with Lloyd's and the Navy, are now at Greenwich.

Royal occasions tend to encourage a resurgence of interest in the School's historical links. Exhibitions on its history were prepared in 1968 for the visit of HM Queen Elizabeth The Queen Mother, and again in 1977 to celebrate HM Queen Elizabeth II's Silver Jubilee. The centrepiece in this

The *Antiques Roadshow* – a day to remember

The School has a number of artefacts which are reputed to have an association with Nelson – a dirk, a pair of buckles, an eye glass, a pendant decorated with a letter N supposed to have been given to Neslon by to Emma Hamilton, a watch movement and a drawing of the great hero, which used to hang in one of the boarding houses. In 2010, Rob Mann took these pieces to a nearby *Antiques Roadshow* filming day in the hope of learning more about them and getting them authenticated and valued:

'I queued for the military expert, who told me that without provenance none of the items had any great value, including the drawing. I wasn't happy about this, so I queued again for Philip Mould, the art expert, but just as I got to him I was told that filming was over for the day. But he'd caught sight of the picture and was immediately interested, so I was asked whether I could return to a later venue. I settled for the day at the All England Club in Wimbledon.

'When I arrived – accompanied this time by the Head Boy, Sam Kester, and the Head Girl, Lynsey Choules – I'd done my queueing so was filmed straightaway. First stop was Graham Lay, the military man. He questioned the pendant having a direct Nelson connection, the style suggesting a later date. The dirk, the buckles and the eyeglass were certainly of the period, provenance would be the key and a proven Nelson link would increase their value tenfold. The watch movement was more interesting because of its inscription which reads "Lord Nelson, Lord of the Nile, August 1798". He said that if it could be proven to have belonged to Nelson,

it would be worth £30,000 to £40,000. Determined to prove the Nelson link, I responded "I'll be searching the School for provenances!"

'Then we met Philip Mould to discuss the drawing. He said that he believed it could be by an artist called Henry Edridge, who had started as a painter of miniatures. I told him that we believed the drawing had been given to the School in 1854 by Sir Everard Home, who had apparently acquired it from Earl of St Vincent in the 1820s. Philip asked Sam whether the pupils knew the picture, and was told that it hung in one the boarding houses and that ball games were sometimes played all around it!

'Philip went on to tell us that this was "a peculiarly potent image of the great man". He dated it to between 1798 and 1800, and went on to say that, because it used a particular form of cross-hatching "almost like velvet", he believed that it was indeed by Edridge and that it was highly collectable and worth about £100,000: "on one level you have the great hero, portrayed in front of the ships of his fleet, but on the other you have his soul". The programme finished with Fiona Bruce telling the audience that the School would be setting up a small museum and that the drawing would take pride of place within it.'

Below: The Nelson Relics held by the School are displayed in the Heritage Centre for the benefit of the School and the wider community. A small early 19th-century eyeglass in a frame on a pinchbeck chain purported to have been used by Nelson, a pendant supposedly given to Lord Nelson by Lady Hamilton and buckles and naval dirk which are of the right period and possibly belonged to Nelson.

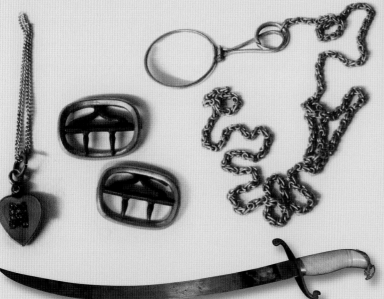

Above: On 25 August 2011 outgoing Heads of School Lynsey Choules and Samuel Kester (both 2003–10) attend the Antiques Roadshow *at Wimbledon with teacher Rob Mann. The show's art expert, Philip Mould, surveys an Indian pen and ink drawing of Lord Nelson (right) by Henry Edridge, dating it to about 1799, broadly corresponding to the start of his association with the School as Royal Naval Asylum.*

Below: *The historic Williamson skis – presented in 1929 and laid out here on an original 1933 boarding house bed spread with the traditional anchor motif.*

Right: *This Gale and Polden Souvenir Album of about 1900 includes a fabulous series of photographs illustrating life at the School.*

These Skis & Sticks were presented to the Royal Hospital School Greenwich in October 1929 by C.P.O. T. Williamson who wore them in November 1912 when with the search party which found the bodies of Captain Scott. R.N., & his companions who had perished on the return march from the South Pole in the previous Spring.

Jubilee exhibition was the original charter issued by William and Mary in 1694 setting up Greenwich Hospital, along with a print of the 'Destruction of the Soleil Royal' at the Battle of La Hogue in May 1692, which was the catalyst for Queen Mary's desire to establish a hospital for wounded and disabled sailors. The exhibition also included material representative of each of the admirals after whom the boarding houses are named.

As a major part of the School's celebration in 2012 of its foundation 300 years earlier, a new Heritage Centre has been established at the School, with some help and advice from the National Maritime Museum. This coincides both with the Queen's Diamond Jubilee year and with the 75th anniversary of the opening of the Museum. The Heritage Centre project has derived great strength from its connections with these two enduring institutions – monarch and Museum. It will include many treasures that have been presented to the School over the years, including the portrait of Nelson that featured in April 2012 on the *Antiques Roadshow*.

Also part of the display are items related to Admiral Lord Jellicoe, the skis and sticks used by Thomas Williamson when he participated in the expedition which discovered the bodies of Scott and his companions in the Antarctic, and many other iconic objects connected with the School's history. In the 1980s, after the location of a number of treasures 'bogeyed away' in the Bursar's safe, there was correspondence between the School and Philip Newell, visionary Director of Greenwich Hospital, who expressed a hope 'that one day these items would form the nucleus of a School Museum' further confirming that 'historical heritage… is vital to a school'. Thirty years later, this has become a reality – and one that will benefit both former and current pupils in equal measure.

Above: Another of the Nelson relics on display – purchased as the handles to Nelson's sea chest and presented to the School by the Misses Forbes of North Rhode, Cheshire, in 1934.

Below: The Heritage Centre was largely funded by donations from parents, staff, former pupils and friends of the School.

Below right: A number of items associated with Admiral Earl Jellicoe have been presented to the School: his full-dress belt and sword, his coat of arms, a bronze bust (below) and some of his early naval records including punishment book.

SEAMANSHIP AND SAILING

One of the original purposes of Greenwich Hospital's School was to enhance the teaching of navigation, and those early pupils – the orphan sons of seafarers who would almost certainly otherwise have received no education at all – were undoubtedly the recipients of a valuable start in life and an entry into an excellent career. But as the School grew and took in more pupils whose capacity to absorb the minutiae of mathematics, astronomy and navigational techniques was limited, the curriculum broadened to include other aspects of seamanship. The boys were all destined for a naval life, they would all – even those well trained in navigation – start on the lower decks and they all needed to know the skills and routines needed for life on board ship.

For the first 150 years of the school's existence, the boys learned seamanship and lived a life at School which echoed, with its drills, its language and the focus of its education, life at sea. And then in the early 1840s this training was considerably enhanced when it occurred to the fertile mind of Lieutenant John Wood Rouse, who was in charge of technical training, that the nautical education of the boys would benefit hugely from the provision of a land-based training ship in the grounds of the School. This was the origin of the large model ships that were, for the next 90 years, to be a well-known feature of the maritime scene at Greenwich. The first of these ships was *Victoria and Albert*, which was designed and built by Lt Rouse in 1843, with the

Above: The Swinging Model was used for seamanship training at Greenwich; featured here in the Illustrated London News, 6 April 1889.

Left: The Holbrook Creek Life Buoy where the four Cornish shrimpers (Blake, Collingwood, Hawke and Howe) are moored during the summer months. These vessels were presented to the School by Trinity House.

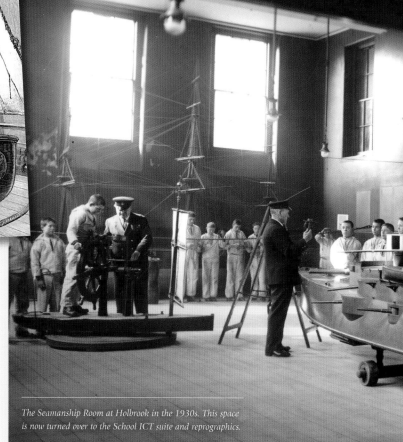

The Seamanship Room at Holbrook in the 1930s. This space is now turned over to the School ICT suite and reprographics.

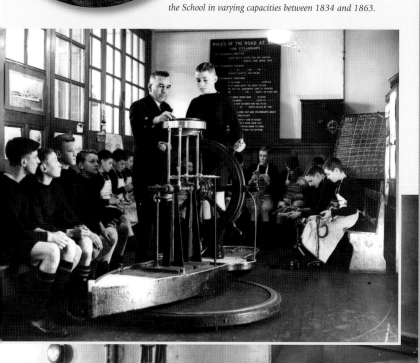

Left: Celestial miniature globe used to help teach navigation – one of the scientific instruments belonging to former Headmaster, Rev. George Fisher who worked at the School in varying capacities between 1834 and 1863.

John Wood Rouse – claim to *fame*

Born in 1785 into a family with a long seafaring history, John Wood Rouse joined the Navy at the age of 15 and had a successful career before both losing a leg and being promoted to Lieutenant during the campaign against the Ottoman Empire in the early years of the 19th century. He then joined the Coast Guard service and commanded a revenue cutter before being appointed senior Lieutenant at the Royal Naval College in Portsmouth; part of his salary was the right to free wooden legs from the dockyard's carpenters. The Portsmouth job ceased in 1837 and, as his wife had died, John Rouse became a Pensioner at Greenwich Hospital.

It was not long before he took an interest in the education of the boys at the School, and was appointed Lieutenant Superintendent with the job of supervising their industrial training, drill, gymnastics and nautical exercises. He carried out this job with energy and common sense for 17 more years, and his effectiveness was rewarded by considerable advances in the prowess of his pupils. He also changed their education fundamentally by building the precursors of *Fame*.

Lieutenant Rouse was very popular with the boys, certainly partly because he reduced corporal punishment to a minimum; instead the boys performed useful tasks around the School and what he called 'professional amusements', such as learning to play in the drum and fife band and doing rowing and sailing exercises on the Thames. For the Great Exhibition of 1851 he set his boys to work on a miniature corvette – the *Prince of Wales* – which was transported to Hyde Park, fired a 20-gun salute to proclaim to the world that the exhibition was open and was the focus of mimic warfare which raged on the Serpentine for some weeks with John Rouse as 'Admiral of the Fleet' and 20 of the boys as his crew. He lived to see his younger son John become Secretary of Greenwich Hospital, and died in 1857. His descendants record that at least one of his great grandsons and five great-great grandsons served in the Royal Navy during the Second World War.

Rouse had lost his leg during the landing on Kinaliada during Duckworth's expedition through the Dardanelles to threaten Constantinople and the Turkish Navy. He thus had a direct historical link with the School's cannon, which had been captured during that campaign and had stood in front of the Queen's House since 1807.

Above left: Learning to navigate – boys looking on in serge shorts and jumpers.

Inset: This colour lantern slide image shows the Prince of Wales *mini-corvette, which was manned by RHS boys on the Serpentine at the Great Exhibition, 1851.*

Fame and its predecessors – 'I saw three ships'

The first training ship, *Victoria and Albert,* was a sloop-of-war. The hull was built in sections in Chatham Royal Dockyard before being dismantled and removed to Greenwich for reassembly. Masts and rigging were salvaged from scrapped vessels, as no doubt were many of the structural timbers. She was judged to be unsafe during early 1860 and was put out of bounds to the boys. Her replacement, *Victoria and Albert II*, was constructed from the salvageable parts of her predecessor, but she lasted only ten years, probably because so much already rotten timber was reused.

But the usefulness of the training ship was clear, and Greenwich Hospital ordered an entirely new replacement to be built. *Fame* was constructed during 1872–73 by Green's of Blackwall, and was described as a three-masted corvette, but fully rigged as a ship (square rigged on all three masts) with a new figurehead of 'Fame' holding her long trumpet.

During the school year she was manned by two crews, respectively from the Upper School and the Nautical School, each of 100 boys. She was operated as a normal man-of-war of the period, watches being kept and time and watch changing indicated by the normal signals from the ship's bell. Entering and leaving harbour routines and depth sounding by heaving the lead were practised assiduously, and when in harbour it was 'hands to paint ship'. Action stations included gun drill and making and setting sail; in fact life was as nearly as practically possible the same as if the company were on active service at sea. As a concession to safety, nets were slung out from the sides and above the main deck to catch any unfortunate boy who might fall from aloft.

In 1914 the yards were taken down and the crews reduced to boys in their last six months of training. The masts and rigging were gradually reduced over the next ten years, until in August 1926 the three remaining stumps and rigging were removed. Access was forbidden to the boys, as *Fame's* dismasted hulk was now in a state of advanced deterioration and dangerous. The teaching of ship handling remained a requisite in the boys' training, and so a replica fully rigged ship with a miniature hull, rigging and sails was constructed in the Seamanship Room.

When the School moved to Holbrook in 1933, *Fame* was broken up, with only the bow section, with the figurehead and stump of the bowsprit, and the stern retained. The bow section was fitted to the south end of the small-bore rifle range of the new school overlooking the playing fields, and the stern, including the 'gingerbread' and coat-of-arms of Greenwich Hospital, was purchased for the Mariners' Museum in Newport News, Virginia, USA. Both may still be found at these final resting places and today, some say that *Fame* is the longest tall ship in the world, spanning the Atlantic.

Above: Early photograph of seamanship training on board the drill ship Fame.

Below: Early colour painting of Fame *with bronze cannon and flags – framed and part of the School collection.*

aid of the boys and using old materials; she cost a mere £256. She was followed in 1861 by *Victoria and Albert II*, which lasted ten years before being replaced by the most notable of the three, *Fame (see box above).*

The ships were used to train the boys in all aspects of seamanship as required by the Navy in the mid-19th century, including engaging an enemy. 'Action stations' required sailors and gunners to be stood to in readiness to ascend the masts, set and trim sails and handle heavy cannon and ammunition with great efficiency and speed. Drills familiarising the boys to life onboard a man-of-war were practised

including, when weather conditions permitted, hoisting, lowering and working sails. They were taught to handle cannon and to fight and repel boarders with pikes and cutlasses. They also practiced damage control and fire fighting, which were particularly important in wooden ships, impregnated as they were with tar and pitch and carrying well filled powder magazines.

The last term at the School was spent enhancing their knowledge of seamanship (signal flags, semaphore, Morse code, helmsmanship, knots and splices, blocks and tackles, boat handling, weather lore), learning the ropes, heaving the lead and sleeping in hammocks. Their geography lessons concerned places within 20 miles of the sea that could be shelled, or reasonably taken by landing parties. And as they always had, elite students learnt to shoot the sun, stars and planets, and how to relate these heavenly bodies' apparent positions to their own situation on the high seas.

Fame continued to be the focus of seamanship training until the School left Greenwich for Holbrook, by which time the ship had become dangerously decrepit; a relic of her figurehead went with the new School, but no drill ship was built there. Boat work continued using naval cutters, whalers and sailing dinghies on the River Stour. Two new masts were constructed at Holbrook – a signalling mast at the main entrance with gaff and crosstrees, and a fully rigged 125-foot (38-metre) ceremonial main mast. This mast was retained until 1953 when maintenance costs became prohibitive and it was removed.

Above left: Boys climbing the rigging on the ceremonial mast at Holbrook – note the safety net below.

Below: Original Holbrook life buoy attached to the balcony overlooking the swimming pool.

I, like many others, spent many hours at the boathouse and sailing, tides and weather permitting. The interesting thing about three types of boat – 14ft RNSA, 27ft whaler and 16ft GRP – was that they were designed with space and stowage considerations in mind; everything needed to be stowed within the boat (mast and all). The arrival of the Fireflies gave us a really good racing boat, and some of us were lucky to be allowed to sail them. How many people remember Ernie (I think his surname was Spickett)? Ernie used to make RNSAs at the boathouse – between one and two a year, I seem to remember – though when he was moved to the kitchen this activity gradually ceased. I had good reason to remember getting a ticking off from Ned Long for electing to sail rather than play cricket for the School (I seem to remember you got more banner points for the latter). Oh happy days!

John (1966–74)

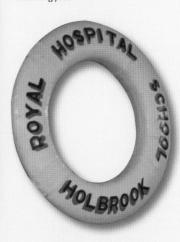

ROYAL HOSPITAL SCHOOL HOLBROOK

RHS Paralympian Sailor

The School has supported many sailors towards gaining national recognition. Hannah Stodel (1998–2004, Howe) started sailing at the age of three in a 'Mirror' dinghy, and quickly learned to adapt her sailing technique to counter her disability; she has no lower right arm. In 1999 she was the youngest ever winner of the BT-sponsored 'Young sailor of the year award', and was then fast-tracked as an Olympic hopeful. She won a series of national titles, participated in world championships from the age of 12 and became an ambassador for disabled sport, featuring in a TV promotional advert. At the age of 13 she sailed with Ellen MacArthur in the premier 'Round the Island Race', has participated in many national, European and world championship races and has taken part in the Admirals Cup. In 2004 she was picked for the British team at the Paralympic Games in Athens and was also part of the team four years later at Beijing. In 2012 she competed in the London Paralympic Games.

Above: Maintaining a Cornish shrimper on the slipway from the boathouse to the creek, spring 2012. The boathouse was opened on 2 May 1963 by Admiral Belloe. Since 1998 the School has acquired four Cornish shrimpers and a fleet of performance racing dinghies.

Below: On the left, Hannah Stodel (1998–2004, Howe), young sailor of the year in 1999, competed in the Paralympics in Athens, Beijing and London, finishing a close sixth on each occasion.

As the 20th century progressed, and as the School gradually moved towards a more academic curriculum and away from the automatic requirement that the boys would be heading for a naval career, sailing took over from seamanship as the School's main link with its naval heritage. It formed part, along with divisions and shooting, of the naval department of the School under the Chief Naval Instructor, until in 1998 the department was split up and sailing became an independent entity. The Director of Sailing at the time, Mike Hart, insisted on the acquisition of top quality equipment, and since then the sport has grown and flourished – and so it continues today, with sailing an essential part of the curriculum, and the only School sport that takes place throughout the year and in all weathers when possible.

The current Director of Sailing, Andy Nutton, joined in 2007. Together with Charles Boughton, who joined the School as a sailing instructor in 1994, he runs a highly successful and progressive sailing department. All new pupils joining in year 7 learn to sail, and after that sailing can be chosen as an activity or sports option particularly during the main April to October season, with the keenest and most competitive sailors on the water up to six days a week all year round.

There are over 46 single- and double-handed dinghies available for pupils to use on neighbouring Alton Water reservoir from RS Teras to high-performance 29ers. At a school level, the squad competes as a team in the British Schools Dinghy Racing Association programme of regional and national team-racing championships. An increasing numbers of elite sailors are put forward for regional and transitional development squads with a view to becoming national fleet sailors.

Talented young sailors

Oliver and Freddie Grogono, who live in Dubai, joined the Royal Hospital School in years 9 and 7 (2010–, Hawke) respectively as sailing scholars. At the age of 12, Freddie was ranked third in Britain after competing in the International Optimist Class (IOCA) UK event at Rutland Water, and his brother, Oliver, has two national championships to his name. In 2010, Oliver represented Great Britain in the Optimist World Championships in Malaysia finishing with two top ten results in a 230-strong competition.

The boys' parents have been the driving force in supporting their early top-flight sailing careers and, when the time came, they were looking for a school which offered them the opportunity to continue with their passion. Now that the boys are older they have stepped out of Optimists into double-handed sailing and, with the opportunity to sail almost every day, dedicated coaches and specialised training techniques such as video and GPS tracking technology on hand, they are in the best place to continue their sport and are playing a major part in the development of team racing at the School.

Above inset: Cornish shrimper cruises remain popular and qualify as a D of E expedition.

Above: Sailing scholar Joe Butterworth qualified in the GBR 420 squads for the 2012 World and Junior European Championships. He and his crew achieved consistent top ten places and in both regattas were the top under 18 boat. He earned a coveted place in the RYA Targeted Support Programme.

Top: Picking up speed on the trapeze at Alton Water, an excellent sailing facility on the School's doorstep.

Above right: International sailors Oliver (front right) and Freddie (front centre) Grogono celebrate with more sailing silverware.

The School also has four Cornish shrimpers for sailing on tidal waters and 46 dinghies mainly used on Alton Water, along with some motorised support vessels. Summer weekends can be spent meandering along the Suffolk coastal waterways and regular week-long sailing holidays are arranged. CCF activities include sailing, and the Duke of Edinburgh's Award can be gained on the water.

Sailing requires – and nurtures – a number of skills: dexterity, strength, perseverance and, in winter, fortitude. It also has a profoundly intellectual element, in the expertise needed to navigate effectively. Although navigation is no longer offered as a GCSE option, it is still taught as an after-school activity over a two-year course, and the School is recognised by the Royal Yachting Association as a fully fledged teaching establishment. Pupils who take the option of undertaking one or more of the courses on offer can go on to gain qualifications which can be used after school and lead to valuable careers.

The RHS is one of the few schools in the country to offer specific sailing scholarships recognising talent, and the sport is considered high profile within the school community. The availability at RHS of such a well supported activity is now a global marketing tool, with young people from all over the world choosing to come to the School precisely because it can offer such splendid sailing facilities and such high-quality training. The sailing department proudly boasts that it is continuing to maintain the RHS's traditional seamanship heritage in accordance with William's and Mary's founding charter.

PART IV

WORK & PLAY: THE SCHOOL TODAY

An Academic Core

The School was originally founded in response to the provision in William's and Mary's charter that their hospital at Greenwich should help the children of seafarers, however there was also mention of improving navigation. The teaching of mathematics at the time was rare in both schools and universities, and so the concentration on the subject offered great career opportunities to the pupils passing through the doors of, initially Weston's Academy and later of the Royal Hospital School. During the whole of the School's early history its pupils benefited from some extremely distinguished teachers not only of mathematics but also of astronomy and, as a development of both these subjects, navigation.

Thomas Weston was himself a distinguished astronomer and mathematician, and there were other later teachers at the School who were truly experts in their subjects. The Riddles, father and son, were both highly regarded in the first half of the 19th century, and the Upper School pupils continued to be well taught into the

Previous pages:
A physics lesson under the direction of teacher, Jonathan Allday.

Above: Taking and recording sextant observations – Illustrated London News, 19 February 1848.

Below: Various academic awards for reward for industry, application and general good conduct 1858; general attainment, 1924 and English award, 1941.

Scholarly boys carefully scribing at Greenwich, c1909

Above: The School has an excellent technology and design centre, incorporating art, textile and photography.

Right: In 1950 the Jellicoe Library was opened by partitioning off the west end of the dining hall. On 13 February 1987 the current Library, named in honour of HRH The Prince of Wales, was officially opened by Admiral of the Fleet Sir John Fieldhouse, who had played a prominent role in the Falklands campaign.

20th; but there remained tensions between the high levels of academic achievement available to the brighter boys and the more mundane teaching offered to the less academically able. The latter were often at the School only because they were the sons of seafarers and who were destined to enter naval service on leaving the School.

It is perhaps indicative of the approach towards academic teaching in the early 20th century that, when the School moved to its purpose-built new premises at Holbrook, the provision of a library was not considered a necessity! It was not until after the Second World War that the decision was made to reintroduce more academic streams, but the move even then was not without its difficulties, and the first headmaster appointed with academic improvement in mind resigned after less than a year.

However, the late 1940s saw the Jellicoe Room carved out of the dining room to create a library, and it was when Norman York arrived in the mid-1950s that the School moved firmly towards a more academic curriculum. Entrants were still usually the sons of

Academic achievement in the 19th century

Although most RHS boys progressed into maritime service, some moved on to achieve in other areas, for example as writers, scholars and journalists. William Parker Snow (1827–31), already mentioned as an explorer, wrote many books and most notably *The Southern Generals, Who they are? and What they have done?* which is still in print today.

James Runciman (1863–65) went on to become a pupil teacher at North Shields ragged school, and then attended a training college before entering the service of the London School Board, teaching at schools in Deptford and Blackheath. While still a schoolmaster, he educated himself at night and attempted journalism, soon writing regularly for the *Teacher*, the *Schoolmaster* and *Vanity Fair*, becoming the latter's sub-editor in 1874. In that year also he began a science degree at the University of London and passed the first BSc examination in 1876.

Journalism then became his sole career. He wrote on social and ethical topics and proved himself a vigorous and versatile writer. His best literary work described the lives of the fishermen of the North Sea, with whom he spent many of his vacations. A series of seafaring sketches which he contributed to the *St James's Gazette* was reprinted as *The Romance of the Coast*, and he dedicated his 'Dream of the North Sea', a vivid account of the fishermen's perils, to Queen Victoria, who accepted the dedication.

Henry Brewitt Taylor (1868–72) featured, decades after his death, in a 21st-century publication about foreign service which highlighted how boys from humble origins, even at the hierarchical height of imperial expansion, could reach high positions. He spent most of his life in the Far East where he was later caught up in the Boxer revolution in China and had a distinguished career in the Chinese customs service, working in cities like Shanghai, as well as in remote regions linking them with the outside world. He was also a scholar and translated the Chinese novel *Romance of the Three Kingdoms*.

Left: An illustration by Sukoku Toryuo depicting Zhao Yun from the 18th-century Chinese epic Romance of the Three Kingdoms, *which was translated by former pupil Henry Brewitt Taylor (1868–72).*

Professors – an academic focus

The first known RHS old boy to reach the top of the academic tree was William Calvert, who was a pupil teacher for two years before embarking on a world tour visiting New York, Ceylon, Egypt and Malta. In 1875 he arrived in Chile, where he stayed for 36 years and became a highly regarded professor of history, geography and the natural sciences in the Lyceum of Quillota, under General Cintral.

At the School from 1955 to 1961 was Bernard de Neumann who, after a degree at Birmingham, worked for Marconi Research Laboratories as a 'pure' applied mathematician, producing computable functions for use by other mathematicians and modelling many systems including the development of Concorde, to show it could land safely. He was an honorary visiting professor in the mathematics department at City University, London, before joining full time in 1988. In 1995 he was chief mathematician in the Ministry of Defence working on advanced modelling missile systems, and on retirement has devoted much of his time to researching naval history and collecting material to furnish the RHS archive. His contribution to understanding more about the School and its history is immense, and the archive facility within the School's new Heritage Centre is dedicated in his honour.

Professor Adrian Hyde Price (1969–76) gained a first in politics at Aberystwyth University and went on to work with a wide range of UK and European universities in senior research and lecturing positions, including Humboldt, Manchester and Southampton. He has worked with the British Council, NATO and the EU, and in 1989 after the fall of the Berlin Wall, he was called on by the British Government to update them on the security situation in Eastern Europe. He is an expert in international affairs and security matters, specialising in European politics, Eastern Europe, Russia and the Baltic States in particular, and has written a number of specialist publications within his area of expertise.

Chris Gaine (1961–68) went on to teach in Wiltshire and for many years ran the University of Chichester's MA (Education) programme. He is now Professor of Applied Social Policy at the university. His main academic focus is the educational experience of ethnic minorities outside larger urban areas, a subject on which he has written extensively. He has also written about social inequalities for teachers, has led professional development events in three-quarters of English education authorities, is a frequent keynote speaker at teachers' and other conferences and has been invited to speak in several European countries. He has a particular interest in making the complex social arguments about race and difference accessible to young people.

John Morrow (1962–69) went onto gain a PhD from York University, Toronto, and then became Professor of Political Theory in the School of History, Politics and Philosophy at Victoria University of Wellington, New Zealand. In 2002 he was appointed Professor of Political Studies at the University of Auckland, becoming Dean of Arts in 2003 and Deputy Vice-Chancellor (Academic) in 2009. His research has focused primarily on 19th-century British and European political thought, with an emphasis on the relationship between romanticism and political ideas, and he has published widely on this area and on aspects of 19th-century liberalism.

Professor John Studd (1951–57) is a leading Consultant Gynaecologist practicing on Harley Street. Previously he was a senior lecturer at the University of Nottingham and has worked at King's College Hospital and the new Chelsea & Westminster Hospital, London. He has written more than 500 scientific articles and written or edited more than 25 post-graduate books on gynaecology.

Below: Professor Bernard de Neumann (1955–61, Nelson) – Mathematics – City University, London. This portrait is by John Wonnacott and won top prize at the Royal Society Portrait Painters show, and the £10,000 Ondatje prize.

Above left: Professor Chris Gaine (1961–68, Nelson) – Applied Social Policy – University of Chichester.

Above right: Professor John Morrow (1962–69, Collingwood) – Political Theory – Deputy Vice-Chancellor – University of Auckland.

naval personnel whose educational potential was not a criterion for admission, but the gradual reduction of seamanship as a central focus and the arrival of CSEs in the 1960s meant that even the less academically inclined could study at their own pace. The first university places in the modern era had been gained in the early 1950s, and under Norman York the School continued to grow in academic standing.

The early 1960s saw the first A Levels in arts subjects being taken. John de Neumann was a member of the first arts sixth form and one of the first to take Latin at A Level. New subjects were gradually introduced – for example the decision by Norman York to ask Desmond Morris to teach German as well as French – and this inevitably led to greater achievement. The 1970s saw many more taking A Levels and university places increasingly significantly; both teachers and boys who were at the School at the time recall impressive academic achievement in what was still called the 'U' stream (evoking the Upper Nautical School). Colin Morgan, who arrived in 1972 to teach English, also recalls that a lot of encouragement was given to the less able boys who, once they had gained a CSE, were able to return for an extra year to take an O level and then go on to an A Level if they wished.

Above: Pupils keen to contribute in a geography lesson.

Far right: Richard Todd QC (1976–83, Drake and parent). His work includes an impressive international practice; he has acted in the courts of Australia, Belgium, the Cayman Islands, the Channel Islands, Cyprus, France, Germany, Gibraltar, India, Italy, New Zealand, South Africa, Spain and the USA. He has been admitted to the bar of Hong Kong and the bar of the Cayman Islands.

Right: Lissie Todd, a barrister, judge and parent governor married to former pupil, Richard Todd.

Richard Todd QC (1976–83)

As he himself admits, from an early age there were hints of his future career path; he indulged in a relentless questioning of the School rules and punishments many of which (*he* felt) had no place in the heady days of the last quarter of the 20th century. Those who remember him recall him being in a state of near perpetual conflict with many of those placed in authority over him; nowhere was this more evident than in his long-standing dispute with the history department. His final breach with that department came in the lower sixth when he elected to abandon their classes altogether and teach himself. The following summer he was awarded a grade A at A Level with a distinction in S Level. He went on to win a scholarship to read law at Trinity College, Oxford, having topped the entrance exam in economics. He did well in his finals at Oxford before going on with a scholarship to the Middle Temple; he was called to the Bar in 1988.

Away from academic studies at the RHS, he spent time playing chess (he played at national level at the age of 13 and captained the School team), fencing (sabre) and public speaking. He continued with these interests at university and – after having carefully concealed his cricketing abilities from the talent spotters at RHS – also represented his college at the sport.

At the age of just 23 and in his first year of practice as a barrister he published a practitioner's textbook on family law which is still in print 24 years later. He was the youngest family lawyer to take silk in 2009. He sits as a recorder in Chancery and the Queen's Bench Division, has written several other legal texts and has lectured extensively.

Richard Todd has both won and been short-listed for a number of major legal honours, including being *The Times* lawyer of the week in November 2010; when asked by the newspaper who had been the most influential people in his life, he replied, '*sine qua non*, my wife, Lissie, Matthew March who taught me economics and my politics teacher, Dr Anthony J Bennett'. The influence of the RHS clearly remains profound even after nearly three decades, as his three older children have also attended the School.

International students – multicultural RHS

The first known foreign pupils to attend RHS were the sons of Moyse Hulot in about 1820. Hulot was a prisoner of war from Martinique, who after his capture was offered his freedom in exchange for service in the Navy. He served for 23 years and his sons were almost certainly among the first black pupils to benefit from the excellent education that the School provided.

The numbers of pupils from overseas who now attend the Royal Hospital School have made the establishment of a department to teach English as a foreign language (EFL) essential, though not every international student needs it. They are required to have at least some basic English tuition when they arrive. Since the department was established in 2000 it has grown from a single part-time teacher to three full-time staff.

The pupils come from all over the globe and from every continent. Some have a military or a naval connection, some come because of the excellent sailing, all want to improve their English and get the benefit of the education on offer. While they inevitably find themselves drawn early on to others from their own countries, they also integrate easily, take happily to boarding and throw themselves into all the activities, particularly those special to the School such as the band and the guard. The School benefits from the work ethic and sporting skills that many of the international students possess, and the boarding houses enjoy the wealth of different cultures, as well as on occasion the cuisines that they cook up.

EFL teaching is geared to individual levels of linguistic skill, and focuses on the vocabulary required for other subjects, such as science and maths. The pupils are all encouraged to keep diaries so that their ability in the written language improves along with their spoken English, in which they tend to become fluent very quickly. The international perspective is an important part of the Royal Hospital School's forward strategy, and so the needs of overseas students, at whatever level, are a priority. The increased number of International pupils has added real value to the School with the extra dimension they add to the experience of living and learning at Holbrook, and the broadening of friendship and understanding that they foster.

Left: Anran Chen (left) pictured with Gemma Tauchauer (physics teacher) and Harriet Pope (right), just after performing at the Nelson Mandela birthday concert in Cape Town.

Bottom: Bunsen flames – chemistry experiment.

Sometimes a decision can change one's life. I feel really lucky that I chose RHS. The experiences I have gained and the opportunities available to me have been remarkable, such as playing with the School band, flying with the RAF CCF and meeting the Queen!

I came from the Guangdon region of China to RHS in January 2009 aged 13. I can still remember a Saturday morning when my year group searched the whole School for me just because I did not know what a tutor meeting was or where it was being held. It can be quite daunting at first for overseas students, but that's how we grow up and I have had the support of great friends and teachers.

One of my most incredible experiences at RHS has been taking part in the Devizes to Westminster International Canoe Marathon which involved canoeing for 125 miles and transporting my canoe over 77 portages in a four-day race. There were, of course, pain and tears, but the sense of achievement afterwards was amazing.

I believe that at a school like this you should make the most of every opportunity as you may not get the chance to do these things ever again. Sometimes, to regret doing something is better than to regret not doing it.

Anran Chen (2008–)

Science remained a major strengths, as Chris Chick, who came in 1974 to teach physics, remembers. The science block was new when he arrived, but classes were still very large and the relatively low numbers of teachers was partially remedied by the showing of educational films. His physics laboratory was designed to accommodate 30 pupils, but often had to cram many more in. But a typical father at the time, who was more than likely to be a Chief Petty Officer in the Navy, was aspirational for his sons, and so the sciences, which could lead on to a good naval engineering career, were in demand – in keeping, of course, with the School's history and traditions. Results were impressive.

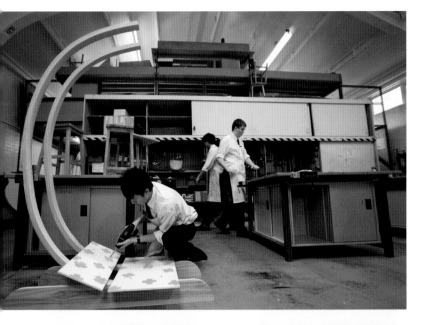

All the sciences were taught, as well as mathematics, and many of the boys went on to university as well as into the Navy, where entry at age 16 as an artificer was also a target. The School, in truth, did very well by its pupils at this time, when entry to university for working class boys, who made up the vast bulk of the intake, was still a challenge. The numbers who made it to Oxford, Cambridge and other top universities were a tribute to their teachers, who were happy to provide the extra tuition necessary to supplement the normal teaching programme. Indeed, brothers Michael Johnson in 1973 and Carl Johnson in 1978 are the first example at the RHS of two from the same family achieving Oxbridge entry.

From the 1990s onwards the School continued to develop its academic profile. The girls provided some excellent role models and the work of Simon Letman and Jonathan Allday in developing the curriculum, and of Paul Chapman, Sarah Godfrey and then Christian White in supporting sixth form study, was rewarded with improving academic results across the board and very high levels of university entry.

Under Dr Allday, the School focused more intently on academic standards. School routines were restructured, including the School day, the monitoring of academic progress and the number of GCSE subjects studied – all designed to create a greater degree of focucs. There was increased recruitment of experienced teachers from other independent schools, as well as young graduates with new, innovative ideas. The School sharpened its academic focus with new Heads of Lower School, Middle School and Sixth Form managing a team of tutors, empowered to support pupil progress. More subject related clubs and societies were introduced and a greater range of external speakers delivered talks to pupils. Academic results improved.

The arrival in 2011 of Matthew Christmas as Director of Teaching and Learning, and his promotion in 2012 to Assistant Head (Academic) has prompted the formulation of a new academic vision for the School. Its bones are threefold: through outstanding teaching to support and nurture every individual pupil so that each one achieves his or her full

Top: A garden chair in the making – design technology.

Above: Reading 'back house' in Blake old dayroom before its conversion.

Right: Goggles and white coat on – now you look like a scientist.

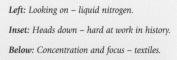

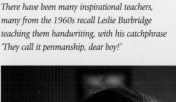

There have been many inspirational teachers, many from the 1960s recall Leslie Burbridge teaching them handwriting, with his catchphrase 'They call it penmanship, dear boy!'

Left: *Looking on – liquid nitrogen.*

Inset: *Heads down – hard at work in history.*

Below: *Concentration and focus – textiles.*

potential; the development of self-confidence and resilience among the pupils within a wide range of learning opportunities; and the provision of a strong infrastructure which will provide both teachers and pupils with all the tools they need.

The drive towards academic excellence is a key focus for the School, while losing neither the link with its naval traditions nor its well-deserved reputation for supporting the less academically able. The curriculum support department already offers help in areas such as dyslexia, dyspraxia and other difficulties from year 7 through to the sixth form. And while the RHS is fully committed to its multi-talented intake, it is also working rapidly towards being able to offer everything that the most able academic pupil could wish for, at all levels. At root, maximising every pupil's potential is the School's most important focus; and both highly academic pupils and those whose talents are elsewhere will, over the next few years, be supported by new ways of looking at both teaching and learning, including the provision of the most modern ICT based teaching and learning resources and a full commitment to all aspects of 'assessment for learning'.

Every aspect of teaching and learning is being scrutinised, from marking to reporting, as well as the nature of the curriculum, the relative performance of boys and girls and the different ways in which people learn. There are regular sessions sharing best practice among the teaching staff, as well as the increased use of value-added data to monitor the performance of individual pupils, year group cohorts and individual departments. The condition and nature of the School's academic and ICT facilities are being reviewed, as is the structure of the working week, academic enrichment activities, provision for the able, gifted and talented, the opportunities for independent learning throughout the School and the need to teach specific thinking skills and to instil within pupils the requisite habits of mind to succeed.

It goes without saying that the last two decades have witnessed dramatic cultural changes, both in the way information is accessed and in the approach society takes towards authority. The new technology has fundamentally affected previous educational givens; it is frequently now the case that pupils can teach their teachers as the digital age moves forward in leaps and bounds, and a much more interactive and interdependent approach towards the learning environment has become the norm.

The new academic vision will focus on 'mobile learning', with the provision of wireless technology in all the houses and the increased use of tablet technology very much on the agenda. Moreover, traditional structures are being challenged as the educational culture within the School grows and evolves. Working parties are looking at what the School does well and what less well, how barriers can be broken down between disciplines and departments and how both pupils and staff can benefit from new approaches to professional and educational development. The sharing of good practice at every level is the fundamental message.

Another aspect of the academic strategy and vision is the way in which international students are encouraged to come to the School, not only because it can provide them with an excellent education but also because they are there to play a vital role in its ethos. As a modern, forward-looking school, albeit founded on British naval traditions and never losing site of its unique heritage, the RHS seamlessly embraces all that is best in British and overseas cultures to produce truly international students with shared values of internationalism, democracy, leadership and service, and – whether they hail from the UK or overseas – wonderfully well equipped to work all over the world.

That all these aims are already being achieved is evident from the happy and confident learning environment that RHS already provides for both home-grown and international students. It is abundantly clear that moving forward into an even more effective academic and internationalist culture for the 21st century is a positive and easily achievable next step.

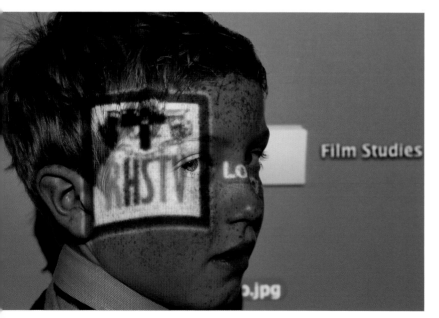

Above: Royal Hospital School TV – film studies.

PROMOTING ACADEMIC EXCELLENCE AND MAXIMISING FULL POTENTIAL

Pupils at the Royal Hospital School are not educated to simply pass exams, but to enjoy the adventure of learning and to develop a lifelong appetite for knowledge. For education to be a liberating experience, the School offers the widest possible range of opportunities, nurtures each individual and provides an exciting learning environment in which pupils are motivated to fulfil their academic potential and achieve their ambitions.

Emphasis is placed on strong subject-based teaching and with small class sizes every pupil receives close individual guidance along with class-based tuition supported by practical sessions, field trips and activities. The curriculum is broad and balanced, combining the best academic traditions with the latest technologies to provide pupils with a strong foundation for further education and to ensure that they leave school prepared for the increasingly complex challenges of tomorrow's word.

The School subscribes to the Durham University value-added measuring schemes, allowing academic tutors to map pupil progress at all levels and to help every individual to achieve his or her personal best. Rigorous tutorial support, under the direction of the Heads of Sixth Form, Middle School and Lower School, ensures that pupils are in a position to make informed choices and that they remain on track to reach their true potential.

The most able pupils are stretched through the scholars' programme and a rapidly developing scheme for able, gifted and talented pupils, with extended reading, visiting lecturers and discussion groups, aimed to open minds and extend learning. For those needing extra guidance and support, the curriculum support and english as a foreign language departments provide individually-tailored lessons.

Supported by high quality, enthusiastic teaching, excellent resources and dedicated tutorial guidance, pupils are encouraged to aim high, attain their personal best and – most importantly – to enjoy achieving it. RHS pupils are confident and proud of their academic achievements and believe that only the sky is the limit.

Below right: Engagement – geography.

Below left: Recording homework in 'planner' (academic planning diary) – mathematics.

The Christian Heritage

Attendance at chapel was, of course, a regular part of life at Greenwich right from the start, for a period using a dedicated School chapel and more often the Greenwich Hospital Chapel. However, budgetary constraints at the time of the move to Holbrook meant that a chapel could not initially be afforded at the new School site. But the will of Gifford Sherman Reade in 1929 allowed the use of some of the capital that would become available in due course, and so this enabled the planned building to go ahead. The splendid chapel was completed and dedicated in 1934 by the Archbishop of Canterbury, Cosmo Lang. The face of Arthur Smallwood, Director of Greenwich Hospital, who was such a prominent figure in the establishment of the new School at Holbrook, was immortalised in the statue of St Nicholas – patron saint of seafarers and children – which stands above the chapel's west door. The building is now listed Grade II*.

Top: 1960s choir boys singing enthusiastically. Regular favourites are the School hymn, 'Eternal father, strong to save' (sometimes known as the Navy hymn), 'Jerusalem', 'Guide me, O thou great redeemer' and 'I vow to thee my country.'

Above: Archbishop of Canterbury Cosmo Lang dedicating the Chapel of St Mary and St Nicholas in 1934. A plaque on the east wall of the apse records the event.

Left: The chapel, in the West wing at Greenwich Illustrated London News, 1848. The band sit in the organ-loft; the Lower School next to the organ; the Upper School under the Governor's Seat; and the nurses and cooks between the pulpit and reading desk. Service was performed on Sunday morning and afternoon.

Above: The mosaics were completed by Eric Newton CBE, who had a most distinguished career as an artist, art critic and author and died in 1964. He began a business making parquet and tile flooring which eventually turned to the designing and making of decorative mosaics.

Below: In 2006 sponsorship was secured to provide new candle holders in the choir stalls.

The chapel – a place of worship

The interior of the chapel is a mixture of very plain and very ornate. The walls and roof of the nave are painted white, with tall arched windows at clerestory level and small circular windows below, the surround of each of which is carved with a different pattern; the glazing bars also vary. The nave ceiling is a system of simple, white vaults. But the sanctuary is, by contrast, a blaze of colour, imagery and iconography. The main altar is covered by a baldachin or ciborium painted blue and decorated with a number of Christian symbols: the Chi-Rho (XP) for Christ; the pelican, or phoenix, feeding her young with her own blood, for the rebirth of the School at Holbrook; the letters IH, for Jehovah; the letters IHS, a cryptogram representing the first three letters of Jesus' name; and an anchor of the Admiralty pattern, also a Christian symbol of faith in Christ. There are also some symbolic oak leaves which probably represent the 'wooden walls' of England as embodied in the Royal Navy.

Behind the main altar in the semi-circular apse is the lady chapel with its own altar. The apse walls are decorated with highly coloured mosaics depicting the Nativity in the centre, attended by angels and with Moses' burning bush underneath and scenes from the life of Christ all around. The 14 Stations of the Cross on the side walls were donated to the School.

The chapel has two organs: a choir organ at the east end, which is a replacement for the original chamber organ which was destroyed in the chapel fire of 1983; and the magnificent great organ which occupies the gallery at the west end of the church.

This organ is one of the splendours of the Royal Hospital School. Built in 1933, it remains basically unaltered but is regularly refurbished and maintained. It has enormous power – though everyone who has experienced the grandeur of around a thousand voices singing in the chapel when it is full acknowledges that its power is necessary. The renowned international organist Carlo Curley visited the School to play the organ, and ranked it among the best in the country if not the world. As he said, 'I consider it to be one of the finest examples of the art of Romantic English organ building anywhere. The full organ quality is quite staggering (it is certainly not an organ for the timid) while the soft colours never fail to impress both listener and performer alike.' Young organ scholars also benefit from this magnificent instrument; expertly tutored by Peter Crompton, they often deliver virtuoso performances to the wider school community.

Left: *Peter Crompton (1975–), Director of Music and Ed Smitheram, former Deputy Headmaster, (1985–99) singing with the choir at the Royal Albert Hall Celebration of Christmas, under the direction of John Rutter CBE.*

Opposite: *The seventy-strong choir play an important role in the life of the chapel.*

Left: *Rev. Dr Charles Stewart (2000–10) surrounded by pupils all eager to stroke his beloved dog, Nelson.*

My ten years at RHS as Chaplain were some of the most enjoyable, memorable and fulfilling times of my ministry. The sweeping grandeur of the buildings and the beautiful setting of the surrounding grounds form a vista I shall forever remember. However, I suggest that the ethos of a school is more than the impressive buildings and surroundings, and more than merely passing examinations, vital though they are. During my tenure, I always believed that the essential purpose of the visually stunning school chapel, indeed the justification for its existence, is about what takes place within the building – namely to convey, share and explore with all who attend a vision of what the Christian faith is really all about. The essence of Christianity is not about religiosity but of loving relationships – 'you shall love the Lord your God and you shall love your neighbour as yourself'.

It is a vision that reminds ourselves that success, fame and the accumulation of wealth – the clarion calls of today's culture – are trivial in comparison with character, integrity, loyalty, commitment and compassion. It is one of the hallmarks of this fine school that it provides a community of staff and pupils in which these Christian virtues are cultivated, rehearsed and valued. These are the essential ingredients of an ethos that sets it apart from other educational institutions. In celebration of the 300th anniversary of its founding, Mairi and I raise a glass to toast this remarkable Royal Hospital School.

Charles Edward Stewart, Chaplain 2000–10

It was the case that all appointed Chaplains were naval men, and, modelled on the structure of the Navy, they ministered not just to Church of England worshippers within the school community but also to those adhering to the Church of Scotland and the free churches, as well as to Roman Catholics who, now that there is no longer a Roman Catholic chapel on site, have the opportunity to attend the church in nearby Brantham. The School today is predominantly Christian and mainly Anglican, but since Christianity transcends culture, chapel services are attended by the whole school regardless of background. There is a service on three mornings a week as well as Sunday, and the Chaplain also carries out the regular duties of a parish minister such as baptisms, weddings and funerals – though these tend to be for staff members, old pupils and parents.

There are major services for Founders' Day, Harvest Festival, when pupils bring food hampers to be distributed to local families in need, Commemoration Day and Remembrance Sunday, all a major occasions attended by the whole school (as well as many alumni).

The School Prayer

Almighty God, in whom we live and move and have our being; make this school as a field which the Lord has blessed: that whatsoever things are true and honest, pure and just, lovely and of good report, may here forever flourish and abound. Preserve in it an unblemished name; enlarge it with a wider usefulness, and exalt it in the love of all its members as an instrument of thy glory: through Jesus Christ Our Lord, Amen.

A chapel service also follows the nine days a year when the School has divisions, and there are Christmas and Easter celebrations before the School breaks up at the end of term. At the end of the school year, leavers have an opportunity to participate in a 'Leavers' Songs of Praise', when Nelson pupils are invited to select hymns for the penultimate service in the school year and relate their choice of hymn to their experience of their days at the RHS. And, in addition to all his other duties, the Chaplain also has an important role within the religious education department of the School.

The placing of the new music school next to the chapel was no accident, as the two buildings together are the focus of all music in the School, whether religious or secular. The Chapel Choir makes significant contribution to the sense of worship. To hear the whole school singing their hearts

Right: *Sixth formers departing chapel after the Easter Service 2012.*

Above inset: *School has chapel services on Tuesday, Wednesday and Thursday mornings, with congregational practice on a Saturday morning and regular Sunday services.*

Opposite inset: *List of Chaplains serving the chapel of St Mary and St Nicholas.*

Above: *The Chaplain since 2010, Rev. Philip McConnell briefs the choir in the vestry, with guest speaker and former pupil Rev. Nick Todd (1985–91, Drake) looking on.*

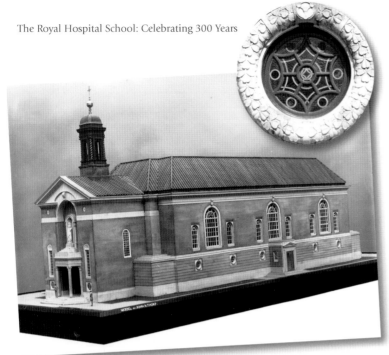

out in congregational practice on a Friday morning is uplifting indeed, and is entirely representative of the central place that the chapel and what goes on within it holds within the school community.

In truth, the chapel, the Chaplaincy and the Christian ethos of the School are at its heart. As Philip McConnell, who was ordained as a minister of the Presbyterian Church in Ireland and joined the School as Chaplain in September 2010, has said, 'Chapel is at the spiritual hub, ensuring that the ethos of the School is underpinned and pervaded by Christian values and helping young people plot their course in life guided by a moral compass'. His view of his role in the School echoes that of his predecessor: 'Chaplaincy is more than what takes place in a building. The Chaplains work proactively to build relationships with pupils as the basis for enhancing pupils' wellbeing, rather than simply responding to problems that arise. Chaplains are accessible and

Top left: The model of the chapel. You can see the six lunette windows on this side of the building that look rather like portholes from a distance. Closer inspection reveals that each of them is encircled by a carved wreath (inset), no two alike, and all 12 of them depict some aspect of Christian symbolism.

Above left: Prefects supervise the smooth running of morning chapel.

Above: The impressive chapel holds up to 1,000 people and when the grand organ accompanies the renowned Holbrook Sound the space fills with pride.

Opposite: Hymn books open to guide Howe House voices.

approachable and many pupils initiate consultation with Chaplains, seeing them perhaps as different from other school staff, as "neutral" and "non-aligned". As well as encouraging faith development, either by preparation for Confirmation, or providing opportunities for regular Christian fellowship, the Chaplains immerse themselves in school life through sport, music and a variety of other activities.

NURTURING PASTORAL EXCELLENCE AND A STRONG SENSE OF COMMUNITY

The foundation of the School was borne out of a Christian conviction to serve others and the Christian faith continues to underpin its philosophy.

Today the School comprises both day pupils and boarders, but the original boarding ethos still provides the foundation of school life. Close pastoral care is at the heart of the school community and every child feels nurtured, supported and encouraged. An established 'buddy' system ensures that new pupils settle in quickly and happily and great emphasis is placed on promoting open communication between pupils, their tutors, house-staff and parents.

Whilst the School's core values are based on Christianity, it welcomes and respects the needs and beliefs of all faiths and backgrounds. The whole school community gathers together most mornings for chapel – an important time for reflection, convergence and consideration.

Within the strong house system, each house has its own distinctive character and strong identity, engendering pride, loyalty and a sense of belonging. Every pupil feels valued without condition and within this framework of support and guidance, they visibly grow in confidence so that by the time they leave the RHS, they will have formed life-long friendships, experienced a wealth of challenges and achieved more than they had probably dreamed possible.

The Creative Arts

Despite the fact that the School was founded specifically to improve navigation, which inevitably meant that mathematics and science were the basis of the curriculum right from the start and that seamanship and sailing underpinned every activity, the more creative arts formed a part of the education on offer to the boys from very early on. The naval focus of the School inevitably led to the establishment of bands playing the sort of drum and fife music that was integral to seafarers' lives, and drawing skills were nurtured, not only as an important element in navigational

Left and below: Two early Greenwich photographs. The final church parade in 1933 and a formal photograph of the band taken on the steps of the Queen's House c1910.

Band memories

I joined the band during my first term at School and stayed with it until I left. The Bandmaster at the time was CT (Bandy) Ship, who lived with his wife and two small sons, Quentin and Pelham, in the cottage on the embankment opposite Drake House. While in the band I learned to play all of the valved brass instruments, starting off as third cornet and finishing as solo trumpet and band leader. Two of the highlights of my time at RHS occurred when, first, I played the 'Trumpet Voluntary' accompanied on the school chapel organ by the music master and, second, when I won the Silver Flute band prize just before leaving the School.

One of the perks of being in the band was the opportunity it presented to legitimately 'jump ship' when the band gave concerts at various locations all over the county. Given that we growing lads were still subject to food rationing and that the school meals at the time were consistently terrible, the biggest attraction of any band outing was the prospect of a decent feed being provided by the ladies of the local Women's Institute or the organisers of whatever function we were playing for. While the boys in the band were scoffing home-made cakes and thick slabs of fresh bread and jam laced with real butter (a rare treat in those days), Bandy Ship could usually be found behind the stage or the bandstand enjoying a quiet beer with members of the organising committee. On Friday and Saturday evenings, he exchanged his Bandmaster's uniform for a black tie and dinner suit before catching the bus into Ipswich, where he played trumpet and violin in the pit orchestra of the local variety theatre.

John Sherval (1945–49)

technique but also – as was shown by the prizes awarded at the end of the 18th century – for the aesthetic value they could add to even basic navigational artwork. But perhaps the earliest manifestation of a cultural element within the life of the School's pupils was the erection, within a decade of the School's foundation, of a small theatre which was the scene of plays performed in front of senior naval officers. Right from the beginning, therefore, the arts formed an important part of life at the Royal Hospital School – and over the years all manner of artistic and creative activities have grown and flourished within the rich educational culture that is now the fundamental norm here.

I remember great days in the band under Mr Buckingham, one of nature's gentlemen, and what he didn't know about brass band music wasn't worth knowing. I started as a cymbal basher, progressed to side drum, then became drum major (the youngest, up to then). I particularly remember summer fetes in sundry Suffolk and Norfolk towns and villages. Then there was the pièce de résistance, a trip to the Royal Tournament at Earl's Court, where we marched and played for the crowd as they were taking their seats for the tournament proper. There was a photo of this in the band room.

Mel Pearce (1958–65)

Ernie Buckingham was Bandy when I first joined the School. I never understood why the first thing he did was look at my teeth before deciding I should learn cornet. I'm glad he did though, as 30 years later I still play in a big band and in the concert and jazz bands at the School where I work. He gave me the opportunity to gain a great deal of pleasure in life.

Paul Stillman (1974–81)

MUSIC

Music today, of all kinds, is central to the School, both formally within the curriculum and informally as a major part of after-school activities. In 1828 a musical tradition was established at the School when the Captain Superintendent suggested music lessons and put forward an estimate for buying instruments and forming a drum and fife band, which later added a brass section. The band was formed and went from strength to strength over the next century and more, regularly parading round Greenwich, performing at school occasions and being part of ceremonials, often in front of royalty. The Royal Tournament at Earl's Court was one of its regular bookings; the School's last appearance there was in 1996. Throughout the 1990s and beyond, Bandmaster Roger Jones, has taken the band to another level, nurturing talent and building confidence in the now 70 strong marching unit. With an outstanding reputation there have been many opportunities for the band to perform at prestigious events throughout the UK and the band have toured the globe to wide acclaim.

The other major musical focus of the School was singing, whether as part of the chapel choir or as a member of the congregation. The splendid acoustics of the chapel, along with the huge power of the great organ, have always encouraged wonderful choral singing, which is one of the fondest memories for many of those who took part over the years. Frank Davies,

The Grand Organ and the experienced organ tutors attract young organ scholars to the School.

Left: *The School band play a concert in the Painted Hall at Greenwich.*

Far left: *John Rutter, the celebrated choral composer, invited the choir to perform at his famous Christmas Celebration concert at the Royal Albert Hall, where the choir were accompanied by the Royal Philharmonic Orchestra.*

RHS pupils and their musical achievements – rock, pop, stage and opera

1967 saw the launch of BBC Radio 1, and one of the first disc jockeys on air was RHS old boy Dave Cash (*right*) who was a Cornwallis boy in the early 1950s. His *Cash at Four* Sunday show attracted a guest list that included Peter Sellers, Spike Milligan, John Cleese and Rolf Harris, and he also worked with Sammy Davis Jr, Richard Harris and Terry Thomas. He joined Tommy Vance, Kenny Everett and Maurice Gardet to launch the first English-speaking station in France, Radio Monte Carlo International. He was a pioneer of pirate radio, star of the *Kenny and Cash Show*, had a top ten hit in 1968 with 'Groovy Baby', broadcast with Capital Radio for 21 years, starred as himself in the cult film *Quadrophenia* and in 1988 co-wrote and produced *At Last It's Hogmanay* with Billy Connolly and Robbie Coltrane for Channel 4. He has given generous praise to Leslie Burbridge, his RHS English teacher, who encouraged him to write and to use his voice in the 'Prose and Verse' competitions.

Baritone saxophone player Steve Farr (1959–65) was a member of rock and soul band Curly which won the Melody Maker Folk/Rock Contest at London's Roundhouse with a recording contract with EMI as the prize. They recorded the acclaimed 'High Flying Bird' and then Farr went on to be credited supporting Status Quo on the album *Hello*, also working on 'Rocking All Over the World' and 'On the Level'. In 1979 he joined Paul Young's band Q-Tips as part of the brass section; they appeared extensively on BBC television, including *The Old Grey Whistle Test*. Q-Tips opened for a number of major rock bands and The Who concert series in 1980 and Adam Ant' when playing to hundreds of thousands during tours of Britain and the USA later in the 1980s; Mickie Most described them on BBC Radio 1 as '…easily the best live band working at the moment'. Paul Young left the band and pursued a highly successful solo career before joining them for a reunion tour in 1993.

In April 2005 *The Far Pavilions* premiered at the Shaftsbury Theatre in London and ran for six months. Written by Michael Ward and RHS old boy Philip Henderson (*right*)

who arrived to teach music in the 1960s, particularly developed the choir into a major musical force. As Alan Moorhouse (1966–70) recalls, 'Frank Davies was able to take an ordinary cross section of boys and turn them into a choir so adept that they were occasionally hired out to cope with the bits of more complex works that some of the other local choirs and choral societies could not tackle. In my day I recall us going out to Bury Cathedral on one occasion to sing the more tricky parts of Britten's "Nine Lessons and Carols". We did other similar jobs too'

The arrival in 1975 of Peter Crompton as organist and assistant to Frank Davies consolidated the teaching and performance of music in the School; he went on to succeed Davies as Director of Music, and has appointed the talented William Saunders as Head of Academic Music to work alongside the experienced Bandmaster, Roger Jones (ex-Royal Marines) and a team of peripatetic instrumental and singing teachers. Around 300 pupils learn an instrument which can be as diverse as the harp, organ, snare drum or bagpipes.

The splendid music school, opened in 2008 by John Rutter and sitting next to the other musical focus within the School, the chapel, is a clear indication of the importance placed on music within the Royal Hospital School. Incorporating classrooms, practice rooms and a fully equipped recital hall, the music school is a visible and tangible inspiration to all those who wish to engage in music in any of its multiplicity of forms – and it is staffed in the evenings as well as all day, which allows considerable flexibility in both learning and practice times.

Music is taught to everyone in years 7 to 9, and after that is available for those who wish to continue with it as an academic subject to GCSE and A Level; there is usually a strong take-up, and the study of music is aided by an excellent music library. There are around 20 dedicated music scholars, who perform concerts each year and whose scope is swelled by newcomers to the School, such as Rion Shirayanagi, a splendid young pianist from Japan, whose individual talents serve to widen the possibilities for performance.

The choir and the band between them have carried the musical traditions of the School for most of its history, which meant that, although a School orchestra did perform as far back as the spring of 1950, there was not an established orchestra until the mid-1980s. Today, drawing on the talents and inclinations of many pupils joining from prep and primary schools, the orchestra has developed and built upon the traditional band instruments such as brass, woodwind and percussion to include capable string players.

(1959–63, Hood), it cost £7.5m to stage and was the first West End production by an RHS pupil. Philip has been composing for over 40 years, starting with 1960s pop songs (recorded on Pye and Parlaphone), then Radio Luxembourg jingles and going on to classical compositions, such as 'The Magic Wood' which he premiered with Genesis guitarist Steve Hackett.

Dave Zammit (1965–70, Hood) worked as a sound engineer for the 1970s progressive rock group the Gentle Giants, and invented and crafted for them a customised electric stringed instrument called the Shulberry. As he recalled, 'The only mandate was that it had three strings that could be tuned to the chord used at the beginning and within the song "Playing the Game", thus making it unnecessary to purchase a marimba as was used on the album.'

Michael Abbott (1968–72, St Vincent) began his music career in 1978 working with the Clash in London before moving to New York to work at the renowned Electric Lady Studios and legendary Hit Factory. In 1992 he co-founded Infamous Records in South Florida later selling it to Sony Music. Over the years he has worked on over a dozen gold and platinum albums with artists such as Bruce Springsteen, Paul Simon, David Bowie, Black Sabbath, Robert Palmer and Bryan Ferry.

Mick Taylor is widely acknowledged as a fine exponent of the difficult 'gayaki-ang' or vocal style of sitar playing. He is one of very few westerners to have seriously studied the history, theory and practice of the sitar developing his technique with tuition from some of the greatest Indian exponents. As a professional musician and solo concert artist he has performed extensively throughout Britain and Europe as well as regularly in India where the Indian musical press have saluted him as a 'sitar maestro'. He has also organised concerts in the UK for visiting artists and is regarded as a pioneering influence in developing the interest and awareness of Indian music and dance throughout Britain.

Alexander Robin Baker was a music scholar at the School before taking a BMus at the Guildhall School of Music and Drama, graduating in 2007 with first class honours. A baritone, he won the second prize in the 2008 Kathleen Ferrier Memorial Competition and has appeared both in Britain and in many other countries both as a soloist and as a member of a number of prestigious ensembles.

Right: Alex Baker (1996–2003, St Vincent) – *former pupil and young operatic star.*

Far left: In 2012 John Rutter accepted the position as Patron of Holbrook Music Society.

Below: Over the years, the RHS has spawned many rock and pop bands: the Volskys (*left, featuring Steve Farr, 1965*), the Hopeless Outsiders (1978) and the boy band Nelzone (2007), to name a few.

Meanwhile, the band remains integral to the School. It is a central part of divisions and other parades, it gives concerts locally and further afield, including tours overseas, and its individual musicians, such as the buglers, are there for occasions such as flag ceremonies. New pupils are encouraged to explore their potential as band members and, as they progress up the School, acquire formidable skills. There is an annual concert, and the band has performed at many international sporting fixtures (eg Lords and Twickenham) and at the reopening of the *Cutty Sark* in the presence of HM Queen Elizabeth II. The corps of drums plays annually in London at Trafalgar Night dinners and are in high demand for many prestigious events, for example participation in the 50th anniversary of the Army Air Corps at RAF Wattisham or perhaps a high profile function at the National Maritime Museum.

The choir is now mixed boys and girls and over 100 strong, including the full range of voices from trebles and sopranos through to basses. It sings at all the chapel services, and there are regular rehearsals; membership is a daily commitment as are the impressive programme of concerts every year. In addition to internal occasions, such as concerts on Speech Day, at Christmas and at charity events, the choir performs every year at the Seafarers' Service at St Paul's Cathedral in London, sings at other London venues such as the Guildhall, St Martin-in-the-Fields and the Royal Albert Hall at the Royal British Legion Festival of Remembrance and undertakes overseas tours every other year. They received a standing ovation at Notre Dame in Paris, sang before 2,000 people at the Vatican in Rome and have been acclaimed at events in Monaco, St Marks' in Venice, Salzburg, Barcelona and Nice.

John Rutter opened the new music school on the same day as that year's carol concert, which included two of his own compositions which he conducted himself. He was, in his own words, 'blown away' by the quality of the singing, and subsequently arranged for the choir to perform with the Royal Philharmonic Orchestra in two concerts under his direction, one at the Royal Albert Hall and the other at the

Top: *Members of the Sax Quartet performing at the annual band concert.*

Above: *Drum ceremony as part of the band concert on board The Star of India in San Diego harbour, California (2010).*

Left: *Monty Beaton playing the bagpipes in front of an Apache helicopter at RAF Wattisham.*

Ipswich Regent. As he then said, 'This must be one of the largest, finest and most committed choirs I have ever found in a school.'

Every Saturday morning the choir is joined by the rest of the School in the chapel for congregational practice, during which Peter Crompton rehearses the hymns due to be sung at forthcoming services (amidst banter with the pupils about whichever football team is due to play against his own favourites, Stoke City). This weekly practice (known invariably as 'congo') is one of the musical occasions which involve everyone in the School. Another is the House Shout which takes place every other November, alternately with a drama competition; it is a house singing competition for songs sung both in harmony and in unison, with cups and prizes on offer for the best. The first competition in 1989 included unisons – 'Sloop John B' and 'The Wall' by Pink Floyd – and harmonies – 'Scarborough Fair' and 'Swing Low Sweet Chariot' – with Cornwallis the inaugural winners.

And, of course, the pupils make their own music. In addition to the more formal arrangements such as the chapel choir, the band and the orchestra, there is a wide range of ensembles of various kinds operating at any one time. They include a brass ensemble, a string ensemble, a jazz band, rock and pop groups, a chamber choir for secular music, barbershop singers and small vocal groups. There is also a large choral society which has over 100 staff and local people as its members. Regular concerts are given in the chapel and rehearsals are held each Monday in the recital hall.

Clockwise from top: Bandmaster, Roger Jones, teaching keyboard skills, Mr Crompton conducts at the Remembrance Service, a pupil develops his rock guitar at the Love Live Music event and the band marching at a ceremonial parade.

Harry John Cornish

Born in 1839, Harry Cornish joined the Upper School in 1850 where he was educated by both Edward and John Riddle in navigation and nautical astronomy. He began his career as naval architect at Charles Langley's Deptford Green Shipyard, a yard which had in 1858 undertook the completion of fittings for Brunel's *Great Eastern*. In 1863 he was appointed ship surveyor by *Lloyd's Register*, an organisation he was to remain with for the rest of his working life. Soon after his appointment, his artistic expertise came to the fore when he illustrated the *Rules for Iron Ships*, the amendments for which were then under discussion. His artistic renditions of the principles of these rules were engraved and bound within the published volume when the research was complete. By this time he was working with Bernard Waymouth, principal surveyor to *Lloyd's Register,* and in 1868, when Waymouth was charged with formulating and preparing the *Rules for the Construction of Composite Ships,* it was Harry Cornish, with his beautifully executed artwork, technically correct but showing a lightness of touch, who among all the young surveyors won the competition to illustrate the rules. He produced 19 drawings which remain with *Lloyd's Register*. The Cornish drawings were exhibited at international exhibitions in Moscow and Paris where they were awarded gold and bronze medals respectively. They were displayed at the Science Museum, South Kensington, until returned to *Lloyd's Register* in 1925.

After Bernard Waymouth's promotion to Secretary of *Lloyd's Register*, Harry Cornish worked with his successor, Benjamin Martell, on the introduction of compulsory load-lines for ships, and when Martell retired in 1900, Cornish was appointed Chief Ship Surveyor, a position he held until his retirement in 1909. He died in 1928.

Above: Signed photographic portrait and artwork by former pupil Harry Cornish (1850–4).

Above: A pupil with a painting pallet – the Head of Art, Garry Ravenhall, looks on.

ART

During the first two centuries of the Royal Hospital School's existence drawing skills were highly valued since they were a vital part of the navigational techniques that were taught in the Upper School from the earliest days. In 1782 costly prizes were introduced for the best drawings, and the School regularly produced skilled draughtsmen who went on to influential positions within both the Navy and the naval architecture profession.

In the 20th century, when the emphasis on seamanship and navigation had declined, art played a very small part in the School curriculum, and by the early 1990s the subje ct was at a low ebb, with few pupils choosing to study it at GCSE. A more popular option was a 3D design course established by Don Hawkley and John Dugdale in which pupils were able to explore a sculptural dimension. A Level art was not even on the School timetable – any pupils who wished to study art at that level had to do so in their free periods. At key stage 3, art formed part of a carousel with design technology and in many ways it struggled to embrace its own identity.

When Garry Ravenhall joined the School in 1994 his first task was to establish just that, the identity of art at the RHS, and his first move was to drag the ceramics equipment out of the dusty, uninviting old art rooms in the main School block and set up a new studio in what was at the time a storage area attached to the new design block. It remains there to this day. Art was now physically united under one roof, and the next steps were to establish art as a subject in its own right and to introduce art A Level into the main School teaching timetable.

The School's philosophy for art is very simple: pretty well every child is creative in some way, and that creativity needs to be nurtured. Those who cannot draw to save their lives may be able to create sculpture, or vessels in clay, or paint pictures, or take photographs, or design garments or hats or jewellery or mobiles. They may be able to make screen prints or lino prints. The role of an art teacher is one of offering children the opportunity to discover whatever their own creative realm may be and then to allow them to follow their own creative journey within that.

Painting and drawing, with encouragement, quickly grew in popularity, along with ceramics, established by Don Hawkley, and an already successful and popular textiles course provided by Debbie Hitchen. Photography took a little longer to develop, though its value had been recognised as early as the 1840s by George Fisher. It now resides in the older part of the faculty, next to the ceramics studio, where the enthusiasm and technical expertise of its teachers have enabled it to become a very popular pupil choice. It has evolved from its chemical and darkroom origins to its more digital form today, although the

Talented artists – creativity

In 1998 Rory Dobner (1989–96, St Vincent) won the prestigious Burns Young Artist of the Year Award which brought his work to an international audience. He travelled abroad for several years, creating an underwater sculpture in Cancun, Mexico, and working in New York, Russia, Haiti, Hong Kong and South Africa. In 2005 he returned to the UK to set up his studio in Hampstead, London, where he specialises in unique, intricately detailed ink drawings often framed in specially sourced antique and vintage frames. He has completed a variety of impressive commissions including for Agent Provocateur, MTV, Christian Dior, British Telecom, Soho House, Robert Downey Jr, IBM, Meg Mathews and On Off London Fashion Week. His paintings, furniture and homeware ranges are on sale in the Liberty store on Regent Street, London.

One of the early pioneering intakes of girls was Alice Hawkins (1991–97, Hood), who went on to become an internationally acclaimed photographer, particularly for her representations of women. Her talent was recognised by Alexander McQueen, among many others, and she has photographed stories for a wide variety of magazines including *Harper's Bazaar* and *Vogue*. Famous faces such as Keith Richards, Donatella Versace, Marilyn Manson and Girls Aloud are in her portfolio, and she continues to extend her range and develop her critical talents.

Although Martyn Colbeck (1969–76, Hawke) is perhaps best known for his wildlife films, he is also a multiple award-winning wildlife still photographer. His dramatic photographs of elephants in Kenya and of bonobos in the Congo have won him many prizes, and he has had several exhibitions all over the world, as well as contributing his photographs to a number of wildlife books.

Other talented RHS artists include Sammi Knight, rapidly establishing himself as a hair stylist to the stars after developing his creativity at RHS, and Natasha Caruana who is a rising star in the world of art photography, teaching at the RCA.

Left: Rory Dobner (1989–96, St Vincent) a winner of the Burns Young Artist of the Year award.

Above: Self portrait of Alice Hawkins (1991–97, Hood) internationally acclaimed photographer.

traditional methods still help pupils to establish their fundamental understanding of the subject.

The latest element in the creative portfolio is art history. After several years of existing in club time and other available slots outside the regular timetable it has become a mainstream A Level and is growing in popularity. It offers children with a passion for art and architecture, but no wish to be an art practitioner, the opportunity to study the theoretical and stylistic side of the subject in essay form. Art A Level now exists on the main teaching timetable in two guises: the main art and design course and the fashion textiles course.

Over the years art has developed from being a poor relation at the RHS, with a confused identity, to being a subject with credibility and a strong identity and a large, dedicated team of enthusiastic and highly skilled professionals delivering a popular suite of subject specialisms to a large number of pupils. In 2012, around 70 per cent of the pupils in year 11 studied art as a GCSE option, a considerably higher proportion than at most comparable schools.

The success of the department has been reflected not only in consistently excellent examination results at all levels (year upon year), but in a growing number of pupils leaving school to make a name for themselves in the world of art and design. The art department can hold its head up in the confidence that nowadays the Royal Hospital School has possibly the best art department in Suffolk.

Above: *Pottery and textiles – pupils' art and design work is regularly on display in the impressive Jellicoe Design Centre opened by HRH The Duke of York in October 1992.*

Left: *In the art studio – applying the final touches with a hair drier. Pupils and teachers hold art exhibitions, sometimes open to the public and featuring paintings, drawings, textiles, ceramics, photography and many other media.*

DRAMA

The first recorded theatrical performance put on by the School was on 14 April 1722. A small theatre had been erected a year earlier and this provided the venue for a performance of Marlowe's tragedy *Tamburlaine* before the Lords of the Admiralty. During the late 19th and early 20th centuries the Neptune's Hall provided a performance stage for pageants, fancy dress parties and theatrical performances.

When the technology became available, cinema shows featured commonly in the boys' entertainment. In January 1926, a cinema projector was installed in the gymnasium at Greenwich, with the longest projection (170ft) in Europe and possibly the world at that time. The first films shown on the 16 x 12ft screen were *Galloping Hooves* and *Felix the Cat*, and from then on, Wednesday nights were movie nights. It took several years after the move to Holbrook for the cinema equipment in the hall to be ready for use, but once it was, many different comedies, thrillers, westerns and newsreels were shown over the years, along with educational films. Television took some time to arrive, but the filming of *Songs of Praise* in 1965, as well as Winston Churchill's funeral that same year, prompted the hiring in of televisions so that everyone could watch. The football world cup the following year made them a permanent fixture.

In the post-war years the houses each put on a pantomime or a Christmas play, while the others watched and judged the performances. Following the success of the Pageant of Empire at the School in 1953 to celebrate the coronation, regular plays were performed and the 1966 play, Thornton Wilder's *Our Town*, was notable in that a female lead was actually played by a girl, drafted in from outside School (Caroline Clack).

For many years, drama was not a major activity, however, now there is a drama department which teaches the subject from year 7 through to the sixth form, with a sizeable take-up of the subject both at GCSE and at A Level, as well as regular dramatic productions. Former Head of Drama, Melanie Bloor-Black, states: 'It is abundantly clear that there is a thriving group of aspiring actors, directors and designers just bubbling below the surface of the wider school community. The reach of the drama department is far and wide, as both a curriculum subject and

Above: Jekyll and Hyde *(2010).*

Below: Little Shop of Horrors *(2012).*

Above: Oliver *(2008).*

Right: Junior Production Winter Wonderland *(2011).*

Pupils hone their performing skills in junior productions and the house drama and singing competitions which have been running since 1978 and 1989 respectively, each rotating on a biennial basis.

a co-curricular option, contributing life skills as well as performance opportunities to the pupils' academic and pastoral experiences at the RHS. The annual senior production is a classic example of the phoenix of performance rising from the ashes of nightly rehearsals and the balancing of workloads by pupil and teacher alike. The quality of the shows is endlessly impressive in terms of the breadth of material undertaken and the selfless offering of time by all within the School. This community spirit has had a major impact on the general appreciation of what can be achieved with a few magic beans and a lot of good will. The introduction of a biennial junior production has been a further strengthening of all the department can offer to the wider school community in terms of performance and personal opportunities for years 7 and 8.'

The major Senior School production takes place in the spring term every year, with a musical one year and a drama production the next. The first School musical staged was *Tommy* in 1977 and this set off a rich tradition of spectacular musicals staged every two years including *Grease*, *Guys and Dolls*, *West Side Story*, *Oliver* and, in 2012,

Above: *The School's spectacular sets are built by staff and the 2012 production of* Little Shop of Horrors *featured a most impressive revolving stage.*

Above right: *Filming* Songs of Praise *in 1965.*

Below: *Pupils interested in drama are prepared for LAMDA examinations.*

RHS in film and television – moving images

In 1925 a Pathé film entitled *A Thousand as One!* showed RHS pupils doing massed drill; and this is one of earliest known filmed images of school pupils. The boys marched along followed by the band before a man who stood saluting. They did exercises in formation, and an aerial view showed them spread out slowly in lines with more stretching exercises and a final three cheers.

Four years later, in 1929, the School featured again in a Pathé film of Admiral Jellicoe presenting prizes to 'Nelson's cubs', the smart sailor boys of the Royal Hospital School, Greenwich. The film showed the Union Jack unfurled on a flagpole as the pupils stood outside the School and then marched along. Admiral Jellicoe saluted them and met some of them and shook their hands, followed by the pupils doing the hornpipe in formation on the parade ground.

In 1934 the School played its part in the formulation of copyright law after the band were filmed by Paramount playing 28 bars of the 'Colonel Bogey March'. After it played as a newsreel in cinemas all over the country, the owners of the copyright of this march, Hakes and Sons, sued Paramount for infringement of their rights, and it was established in law that there was indeed an offence when 'a substantial, a vital and an essential part' of a work was used without permission. In this case a mere 20 seconds of the four-minute piece constituted an infringement.

The magnificent buildings once occupied by and surrounding the School at Greenwich have also been frequently used as movie locations. Among the films shot there have been *Brideshead Revisited*, *The Mummy Returns*, *National Treasure: Book of Secrets*, *The Golden Compass* and *Pirates of the Caribbean*.

The first recorded involvement of the School with the (then) relatively uncommon medium of television was in March 1952 when a BBC Television film-maker visited the School to record various aspects of life at Holbrook (**above right**). Over ten years later, in July 1965, the BBC televised *Songs of Praise* from the chapel, with the choir singing three hymns, and the trumpeters, the congregation and Frank Davies, the Head of Music, all playing their part. As a commentary noted, 'Hymns of praise echo around the chapel, and boys sweat under the heat of the lights and with the effort put into the singing'. In the same month an RHS boy's poem 'The seaside resort in winter' was broadcast in BBC Schools' *Listening and Writing* series.

Shortly afterwards, an old boy who had left in 1961 featured on ITV's *Take Your Pick*, winning the star prize of an inflatable boat with an outboard motor; and the School was invited to take part in the BBC school quiz show *Top of the Form*. They were the only boys' team to reach the semi-final, which they lost against a school from Westcliff-on-Sea. *Songs of Praise* was again televised in the School chapel on Remembrance Sunday 1975, with representatives from all over the Shotley Peninsula. And in October 1989 Sir Harry Secombe visited the School with the TV programme *Highway*.

Numbers of pupils have gone on to work in the performing arts, for example acclaimed theatrical actor, Terence Booth who has also featured in *Eastenders* and *Casualty*. After featuring prominently in the hugely successful James Bond catwalk fashion extravaganza at the School in 1999, Kate Somerset Howe went on to perform at the London Palladium and became a finalist in *Grease is the Word*. She has also starred in the musical *The Assassination of Paris Hilton* and has been a lead performer on board the luxury cruise liner *Seaborne Sojourn*. Yet another prominent alumna is Bianca Hendrickse-Spendlove (2007–09, Hood), who made her debut in the soap *Hollyoaks* in May 2010 and joined the cast permanently three months later. Her character, Texas, is described as 'always causing trouble. She's very beautiful and always gets her own way with men.'

One of the most notable film-making talents to have come out of the RHS is that of Martyn Colbeck, an award-winning film-maker and photographer who has been filming wildlife worldwide for over 20 years. Working mainly in association with the BBC's world-renowned Natural History Unit in Bristol, Colbeck has filmed sequences for many of the best-known series produced by the BBC. He has also made many award-winning films on a variety of subjects including orangutans, gelada baboons, pygmy chimpanzees and the mountains of Africa. Of the five elephant films he has made, three have been in association with Cynthia Moss of the Amboseli Elephant Research Project in Kenya. Together they have uniquely chronicled the life of a matriarch known as 'Echo' and her family over a period of 15 years. He has also been involved in a collaboration with Disneynature filming a documentary about Oscar and Freddy, called *Chimpanzees*.

The sword master – Hollywood legend

Bob Anderson, who died on 1 January 2012, left RHS in 1937 and was serving on HMS *Coventry* when she went down off Tobruk. He survived and went on to win gold for team fencing at the British Empire Games in 1950, before coming fifth in the 1952 Helsinki Olympics.

He was a legend in Hollywood, recognised as the leading sword master, choreographer and stage manager of sword fight scenes in particular. His filmography is second to none, starting in 1953 when he was stunt double for Erroll Flynn in *The Master of Ballantrae*. He worked on *The Guns of Navarone*, *Casino Royale* with David Niven and other James Bond films, *Superman*, *The Three Musketeers*, the *Zorro* movies, *The Lord of the Rings* trilogy and the *Pirates of the Caribbean* movies. He is perhaps most famous as Darth Vader's stunt double in the light sabre combat sequences which he choreographed for the *Star Wars* trilogy, most notably in *Return of the Jedi* and *The Empire Strikes Back*. It is peculiarly fitting that a boy from the Royal Hospital School with its naval connections should be involved with coordinating swashbuckling scenes in blockbuster movies. As he himself humbly stated, 'We are all standing on the shoulders of those who went before us.'

Bob Anderson (1934–37) worked with many of the top names in Hollywood as the choreographer of sequences involving major sword fights. Pictured here with Johnny Depp, his filmography is stellar.

Right: Junior production Dandelion Time *(2010)*

Below: Kit Dobner (Jets) and Patrick O'Riordan (Sharks) promote the school musical West Side Story *(2003). The edgy mood was created by using the school tennis courts.*

Little Shop of Horrors. In 1987/88 there were a record three plays in one year, *Oh What a Lovely War*, *The Secret Diary of Adrian Mole* and *Charlie and the Chocolate Factory*, with later plays including *Tartuffe*, *Macbeth*, *The Importance of Being Earnest*, *Dracula*, *The Winslow Boy* and *Macbeth*, among others. Simon Warr, who otherwise teaches Latin and French, directs the plays with input from many other members of staff: Don Hawkley builds the sets, Peter Crompton directs the music and others do the lighting, choreography and anything else required. There is also a biennial junior play, with productions including *Bugsy Malone*, *Dandelion Time* – which used all of years 7 and 8 – and *Winter Wonderland* – the inaugural use of the recital hall for a dramatic event.

Music and drama take turns in the autumn term to stage the inter-house festival which, for drama, takes the form of a half-hour play which is entirely the work of the pupils. The first was held in 1978 and today there are prizes in a number of categories, including best play, best actor, best director, best set and so on. At the end of the festival, the upper sixth formers in Nelson House put on their own play which diverts the audience while the judging is taking place. In the autumn of 2011 Collingwood won most of the prizes with an outsanding (for a house play) condensed version of Shakespeare's *Henry V*.

The extremely high quality of the examination performance material at GCSE, AS and A Level has been commented on by visiting examiners.

Technological pioneers – visual effects wizards

After ten years spent designing sets, Robert Harris (1962–67, Howe) became Head of Computer Graphics at BBC East. His first major commission was the production of the computer graphics for *The Hitchhiker's Guide to the Galaxy*, and he then went on to found his own company and worked on all eight series of Anglia Television's *Knightmare*.

A pioneer of 3D in films and special visual effects is David Marsh (1962–67) who became Head of Computer Graphics at BBC East where he became fascinated by the potential for developing new technologies in film. He won an Emmy for the Outstanding Visual Effects category for the BBC series *Walking with Dinosaurs* and he now works for Academy Award-winning motion picture visual effects company, Industrial Light & Magic that was founded in May 1975 by George Lucas. He has worked as a sequence supervisor or technical director on many major Hollywood productions, for example work relating to *Star Wars*, *Pirates of the Caribbean*, *Men in Black*, *Harry Potter*, *The Mummy*, *Star Trek*, *Transformers* and *Avatar*.

Left: David Marsh (1979–84) created the visual effects for Davy Jones in Pirates of the Caribbean.

Below: Backstage practice. Costumes, makeup and props contribute to high-quality stage productions. The lighting and audio visual support is equally impressive and often controlled by highly professional pupil technicians.

By its very nature examination performance material should be more challenging as it is an opportunity to develop work for a smaller audience that stretches the individual actor, designer or director.

Pupils often perform classic works, such as William Shakespeare's *Measure for Measure* at the New Wolsey Theatre as part of the annual Shakespeare Schools Festival. The impact of this piece upon the audience was impressive, and the festival coordinator described the production as 'exciting, brave and committed! All in all it was a clever and accomplished piece of theatre,' illustrating the wider depth of theatrical talent at the School.

The School also employs a peripatetic speech and drama teacher who trains the pupils for LAMDA and English Speaking Board exams. And debating is a major activity within the School, keenly contested by all houses. Internally, there is a sixth form debating competition which takes place during the autumn and spring terms, with teams of three accruing points until the top four teams compete in a semi-final and the winning two go through to the final. Years 9 to 11 also have their own debating competition and there is a public speaking event for year 10. Externally, the School competes in the English Speaking Union (ESU) Mace Debating Competition which is contended for by schools nationwide, and also takes part in other national events run, for example, by the Rotary Club. In 2012 a speaker from year 11 won the regional award in the junior ESU competition, which the School regularly enters.

Below: The 1972 production of Billy Budd.   *Below: Tom Laurence showing off a spectacular costume.*

Top: *The extensive campus grounds are sometimes used as a setting for developing theatrical performances.*

Above: *Simon Warr, the irrepressible and energetic director of RHS School plays and musicals for more than 20 years. He is always supported by many other committed RHS staff.*

FOSTERING CREATIVITY AND IMAGINATION

Creativity is not just the realm of those with natural talents. Everyone has the potential to be creative and at the Royal Hospital School everyone is encouraged to try something new, discover unsuspected passions and use their imagination. Opportunities for experimentation are numerous – within the curriculum there is drama, music, art and design and outside the classroom dance, film club, photography and musical ensembles.

Music plays a particularly important part in school life, underlined by the substantial investment in a new Music School. As well as academic music, everyone can choose to play an instrument, sing in the choir, join the orchestra or band or simply develop a love and appreciation of music. There are regular school performances attracting audiences from far afield, as well as invitations to appear alongside the Royal Philharmonic Orchestra at the Royal Albert Hall and sing at the Annual Seafarers' Service at St Paul's Cathedral.

The art department is a hub of creativity and originality where pupils can experiment in a wide range of media, including photography, textiles and pottery, whilst the Jellicoe Design Centre combines practical skills with aesthetic values. Work from both is displayed all year round in an impressive atrium at the heart of the building.

There are many opportunities for pupils to take part in drama both in and outside the curriculum, whether through the inter-house drama competition, school plays and musicals or practical examination performances for the London Academy of Music and Dramatic Art. In addition to the drama studio, theatre takes place in a variety of venues, both inside and outside, and further afield the School also takes plays on tour and participates in national competitions.

Above: Band still life – music, gidge and trumpet.

Above right: Artists hard at work in the studio.

Right: Photography and creativity – lenses, mirrors and the real world.

Sport

The tradition of cricket at Greenwich Hospital, and later its School, was further encouraged by a famous match played in August 1796 between two teams, one consisting of one-legged Pensioners and the other of one-armed Pensioners. The match was held at Walworth and began at 10am, but was disrupted in the afternoon by a riotous crowd who broke in and demolished the gates and fences. Play was resumed in the early evening and then carried on to a second day, when the one-legged Pensioners won by 103 runs and were awarded the £1,000-guinea prize. Later matches featuring one-legged and one-armed players were played between Greenwich Hospital and Chelsea Hospital; the last on record was in 1841 when Chelsea lost by a wide margin because they had more one-legged players than their opponents.

The Royal Hospital School was also linked to the founding of rugby union. James Hill, the Upper School Headmaster in the 1840s, lived in the Queen's House and brought up his two sons there. In 1867 Rowland and Edward Hill established one of the 21 founding clubs of the Rugby Football Union and named it Queen's House Rugby Football Club after their birthplace. The club was regarded as one of the most formidable of the London teams and the most difficult to beat, and it included several noted players, including internationals, in its line-up; but after most of them had left in the early 1880s, it was disbanded. Rowland Hill went on to be knighted for his services to rugby and had a gate named after him at Twickenham.

Sport has always been enjoyed by boys at the School. It was decided in 1835 that '12 sets of cricket bats and balls be supplied annually to the boys'. The boys had played cricket previously with the aid of makeshift, stick-like bats, and better equipment was greatly welcomed. Early provision for gymnastics consisted of a long, three-foot deep trench filled with tan (the spent bark from tan pits) with arrangements

Left: Sir Rowland Hill was born in the Queen's House and was the son of the Upper School Headmaster, James Hill. He is regarded as one of the early pioneers in the development of the game of rugby union. It was not until the 1950s that rugby became a mainstream sport at the RHS.

Above and right: Cricket has been associated with the School for over 200 years and the early photographs of sports teams by F Sharp (Greenwich) include a number of excellent period images.

186

of bars, poles and ropes which were used for exercise in all weathers. Swimming was also encouraged and there was a swimming pool, of an unusual design, almost oval in shape with the shallow part in the middle, reached by a bridge where non-swimmers had to dodge the bullies determined to push them into the deeper part.

Archival photographs indicate that the School regularly fielded sporting teams against external opponents; there are many early images of football, cricket and boxing teams, some displaying trophies won. But in truth sporting facilities at Greenwich were rather limited and fixtures somewhat sporadic: George Hanes (1918–20) wrote later, 'I regret now that, in my time, we never had any sport such as football or cricket: all the types of sports a young lad would enjoy. We had to make our own. I and many others had a pair of roller skates. We used to go down the slope by the side of the Queen's House and around the *Fame*, and see who could do the run fastest.'

By the mid-1920s, however, as Jack Judge (1924–28) recalled, 'Football and cricket were played on the parade ground in our spare time during the week. On Wednesday afternoons the sports grounds at Blackheath were available to us and the inter-company matches were

Doggett's Coat and Badge

In 1913 RHS pupil GH Gobbett, who was a Boreman boy, won the oldest annual rowing race in the world, the Doggett's Coat and Badge. It is held over a 4 mile 5 furlong (7,200m) course on the River Thames between London Bridge and Cadogan Pier, Chelsea. Instituted by Thomas Doggett, an Irish actor and comedian, it is open to freemen and women of the Watermen's Company, and the prize is a traditional Watermen's red coat adorned with a silver badge displaying the horse of the House of Hanover and the word 'Liberty' in honour of George I's accession to the throne. It has been rowed every year since 1715 and winning is still regarded as a great achievement. The boats were originally those used by watermen on the river, which could take around two hours to complete the course, but the single sculls used today do it much more quickly.

The School also had some close second places including Harry Hardee, whose brothers George and Frank also competed. Harry became Waterman to George V in 1934 and as 'Chief Beggar to the Seamen's Hospital' raised significant funds for the Dreadnought Hospital in the 1930s. He became a master of the Watermen's Company in 1953, and was one of the most eminent London watermen.

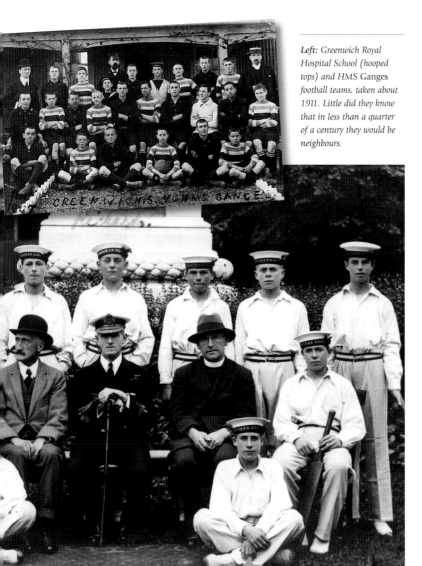

Left: Greenwich Royal Hospital School (hooped tops) and HMS Ganges football teams, taken about 1911. Little did they know that in less than a quarter of a century they would be neighbours.

Above: State Opening of Parliament 1947 with former RHS pupil and King's Waterman Harry Hardee on the left. The three Hardee brothers all competed in the oldest rowing race (some say sports event) in the world, Doggett's Coat and Badge, which has been held every year since 1715.

RHS Olympic gold medallists

In 1912 the first RHS pupil to win an Olympic gold medal was Gordon Rahere Hoare, who played for England in all three winning football matches in the Stockholm games, scoring two goals in the final against Denmark. He went on to feature in another ten amateur internationals and also played 34 games for Arsenal, scoring 13 goals. He served in the Great War as a member of the Footballers' Battalion and later played for Fulham, Queens Park Rangers and Manchester City before retiring in 1920.

1988 saw Malcolm Douglas Cooper, who left RHS in 1965, become the School's first double Olympic gold medallist, winning the shooting three-position event in Seoul, following on from success at Los Angeles four years previously. He held 15 world records and established his own rifle-making company, but his life was tragically cut short when he died from cancer aged 53 in June 2001.

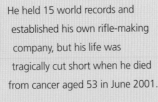

Above: Gordon Rahere Hoare (1896–99) won an Olympic gold medal in football for England at the Stockholm 1912 games.

Below: Malcolm Douglas Cooper (1959–61, Raleigh) won two Olympic gold medals (Shooting Three Positions) at the Los Angeles 1984 and Seoul 1988 games.

Left: Boys at Greenwich playing football, a parade ground tradition that continued through to departure in 1933. Gordon Hoare would have honed his skills and other boys like Jack Judge would have enjoyed the exercise, rough and tumble. This image was drawn for the Boy's Own Paper *in 1898 by J Prater.*

played there. Sports day was held on the parade ground and was thus very limited. There were school representative games, but the only one I remember was the annual match against the Duke of York's Royal Military School, affectionately known as the 'Dukies'. The main sports were boxing, football and cricket – no indoor sports such as volleyball, netball etc, yet the gymnasium had plenty of space for such games.'

The move to Holbrook offered vastly superior facilities, not just in the space available for proper sports pitches but also because every pupil now received his own sports equipment. As one old boy recalled, 'We now had proper cricket gear, including gloves, pads etc, in a posh zipped cricket bag'. And instead of 'three battered old cricket stumps set in a block of wood that had to be stood on the parade ground' there were several sets of new stumps and bails. The extensive grounds offered the opportunity to play many more sports, and there was also a gymnasium and a large covered swimming pool.

The war curtailed sporting activities, including sailing and rowing, and inter-school matches were also limited because of travel restrictions. But there was a great deal of inter-house rivalry in sports such as cricket, football, swimming, boxing, shooting, cross-country and athletics. Rugby had only just started so was not yet a strong school sport. But after the war and during the remaining decades of the 20th century, the range of sports and the facilities for them developed hugely. Bernard de Neumann remembers keenly fought encounters in a variety of sports in the 1950s particularly against arch-rivals the Duke of York's Military School near Dover; boxing was still at that time central to the sporting programme but was discontinued soon afterwards.

The arrival in 1948 of George Elsby revitalised cricket at the School. He was a fine professional cricketer, an all rounder who regularly completed 1,000 runs and 100 wickets in a season. In his time at the RHS he produced one of the finest wickets in the county, knew the cricket potential of every boy in the School and took an intense

The Devizes to Westminster International Canoe Marathon

Known as the Everest of canoe racing, the Devizes to Westminster course is 125 miles long and takes place, in the junior category, over the four days of the Easter weekend, with the three intervening nights spent camping. Each two-person kayak has to deal with 52 miles on the Kennet and Avon Canal, 55 miles on the River Thames and the final 18 miles on the tidal reaches of the Thames. There are 77 portages, where the competitors have to empty their canoes and carry them unaided to the next stretch of water.

Lee Menday and Les Thompson teach Kayaking at the RHS and train crews for the race. Training starts in the autumn term with about 50 hopeful competitors, some of them entering as part of their CCF commitment, and the entrants are whittled down until the final six or eight two-person crews are selected.

Interestingly Mike Farge (1958–63, St Vincent) was the first recorded RHS pupil to compete, finishing this gruelling canoe marathon in tenth place in 1965; but it was during the mid 1990s that the School became involved on a regular basis and have over the years achieved several highly creditable placings; in 2011 two girls' teams won the Junior Ladies Team Trophy, while three teams from the

School won the HMS Alacrity McKaig Cup awarded to the fastest combined CCF teams.

And then 2012 was a truly spectacular year for the School. The race took place in difficult conditions over the Easter weekend, with around a third of the competitors in the senior categories failing to finish. But all eight School crews completed the course and the winning RHS team scooped all three junior trophies – Best School, Best Juniors and Best CCF. This is believed to be a first in the history of the competition.

Right: *Pupils complete a rigorous training programme – Lee Menday and Les Thompson have supported over 150 pupil entries since 1996.*

In 1950 I was one of a boxing team representing RHS in the county championships. Four of our boys reached the finals and three won – a remarkable feat made even more interesting by the fact that all three winners were Cornwallis boys, namely Fred Gavin, Colin Robotham and yours truly. I have recently come across the programme, certificate and medal received on Friday 17 March 1950.

Brian Gunn (1946–50)

The football boots were actually made of stiff leather (which we dubbined), but it might as well have been wood. Each stud had three nails in it and these were hammered into the sole using a last which was kept in the cloakroom at the end of the boot room. The trouble was the nails were just a bit too long so they often protruded into the inside of the sole. The trick was then to blunt the ends of the nails to limit damage to the feet. A layer of cardboard was often used as an insole.

Ken Knott (1958–65)

interest in them. In 1966 the Groves Bat was presented to the School by the Captain of Britannia Royal Naval College to be awarded to the First XI batsman with the highest average. It was originally bought by Commander EM Groves from a charity auction in aid of prisoners of war funds during the First World War and was autographed by Lord Beatty and Flag Captain Lord Chatfield.

The sporting focus at the School has changed since 1997, when Paul Hardman took on the newly created role of Director of Sport. When he came, the School was strong in Rugby which was played in the autumn term, with football in the spring term and cricket and athletics in the summer. Football fixtures were becoming increasingly difficult to come by and soon after arriving, Howard Blackett made the decision to play hockey as the major spring term sport. Rugby remained a strong boys sport and in 2006 the 1st XV were unbeaten all season – and the School can boast international players among its alumni, including the versatile

An RHS boy teaches the US Navy to row

Rodney Pratt (1960–8), as he says himself, went to the RHS because he failed the 11+ miserably – but he had always loved science and when he actually got to do it at the School, he took off. After a degree in biochemistry at Manchester and a doctorate at Cambridge, where he took up rowing, he did a post-doctorate at Glasgow University and another at the University of Wisconsin, Madison, USA. While there he began coaching junior high school students in rowing. He then made a lateral move to full-time coaching when he was offered the post of the freshman heavyweight crew coach at the US Naval Academy, Annapolis, followed four years later by becoming head men's coach at Boston University, where he stayed for 18 years.

Above: In 2006 for the first time in the history of the School the 1st XV were unbeaten all season.

Below inset: After a successful first class cricket career, former pupil Don Topley (1975–81, Raleigh) returned to the RHS as cricket coach. He has led highly successful cricket tours to Sri Lanka and Barbados, seen here arriving at a match in a tuk-tuk.

Above: *Dr Rodney Pratt (1960–68, Blake), an inspirational rowing coach (right).*

Below: *Cricket – pace bowler Alex Cullen in mid-air.*

Peter Richards, who played for both Leicester Tigers and Harlequins as well as being capped for England, and Anders Mogensen, the promising England U18 and Northampton Saints winger.

Cricket is also very strong, under its Master in Charge, Don Topley, himself an old boy who went on to play professional cricket for Essex and later coached the Zimbabwe team. His son, Reece, was also educated at the School and went on to follow his father into a cricketing career. In the 1970s the School could field five cricket teams; now there are 12, who take full advantage of the five grass and two artificial wickets as well as the indoor nets and the bowling machines. Over the years cricketing tours abroad have been undertaken – to Sri Lanka in 2009 and Barbados in 2012.

For girls, under Catriona Herbert as Head of Girls' Sport, hockey is played in the autumn, followed by netball and rounders. In the 1990s there were too few girls to allow strong inter-school rivalries to develop, but by 2002/3 there were some formidable hockey and netball players who provided tough competition, and the girls now rival the boys in their success rates and sporting prowess. For example, the Anderson sisters, Josephine and Charlotte gained Great Britain hockey and England mixed hockey caps respectively.

Grass tennis courts were provided from the start at Holbrook with hard courts arriving in the 1950s, and in the 1970s the School developed a formidable reputation under Bill Curtis, who coached tennis as well as teaching what is now called design and technology; and today tennis continues to be a popular sport. Beyond the main sports there is a huge choice, with a large majority of members of staff also getting involved, whether in coaching the School or house teams at the various levels – there are 16 staff rugby coaches alone – or in organising minority sports such as squash and badminton. Lee Menday, for example, runs the kayaking programme, and also trains upper sixth formers as lifeguards for the swimming pool, running a lengthy and physically very demanding course which results in a full qualification.

There is a well-equipped gym and PE is compulsory for years 7 to 9. Swimming tuition is an important part of the PE programme with all abilities catered for and those who wish to train at a higher level able to do so in extra-curricular time with the School's own swim coach. There is a traditional swimming gala, though the junior houses also now have

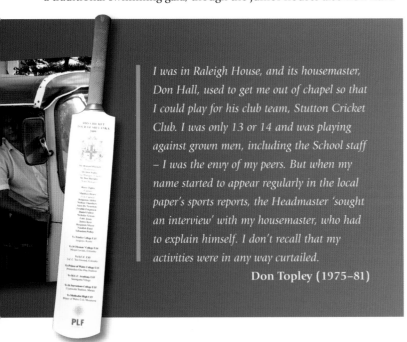

I was in Raleigh House, and its housemaster, Don Hall, used to get me out of chapel so that I could play for his club team, Stutton Cricket Club. I was only 13 or 14 and was playing against grown men, including the School staff – I was the envy of my peers. But when my name started to appear regularly in the local paper's sports reports, the Headmaster 'sought an interview' with my housemaster, who had to explain himself. I don't recall that my activities were in any way curtailed.

Don Topley (1975–81)

International sports – playing the game

In 1984, former pupil Don Topley took the field at Lord's in the test match against the West Indies. Whilst an MCC young cricketer, he became a substitute fieldsman and took a brilliant one-handed catch on the boundary off a Malcolm Marshall hook shot but put one foot over the rope over the rope – six runs!!! And then in 1994 he claimed that two matches in 1991 were, in effect, fixed, with Lancashire allowed to win a Sunday League match and Essex the accompanying Championship game. In his ten years as a seam bowler at Essex he took 367 first class wickets. He played in South Africa and went on to be Zimbabwe coach between 1990 and 1992. He is now the cricket coach upholding the cricketing traditions at the school he attended. His son Reece Topley was also educated at the RHS and is already surpassing his father's achievements at Essex and as a talented England U19 international.

Peter Richards is a former English rugby union player who played in three positions: scrum half (his preferred role), fly-half and centre. Richards retired in the summer of 2010 because of a back injury. His career began playing mini rugby at Farnham Rugby Club, before attending the RHS. He moved to Lord Wandsworth College, Hampshire for sixth form and played alongside Jonny Wilkinson reaching the Daily Mail Semi-Final in 1996. He has represented England at all levels from U16 through to full international. He took part in the 2007 Rugby World Cup in France, including the final. As an ex-Collingwood boy, his signed jerseys and photographs hang proudly on the walls of his former boarding house.

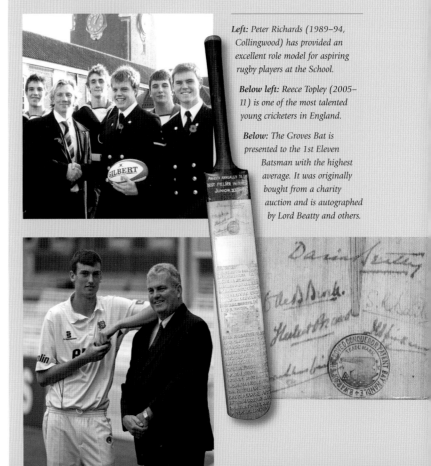

Left: *Peter Richards (1989–94, Collingwood) has provided an excellent role model for aspiring rugby players at the School.*

Below left: *Reece Topley (2005–11) is one of the most talented young cricketers in England.*

Below: *The Groves Bat is presented to the 1st Eleven Batsman with the highest average. It was originally bought from a charity auction and is autographed by Lord Beatty and others.*

their own event, and a large number of pupils and staff are in regular training for 'open water' swimming; the School runs a structured programme and enters pupils and staff in the Great East swim held annually at Alton Water. The pool is a busy place beyond lesson times too: water polo (Ipswich WPC), sub-aqua and swimming lessons for children in the local community all take place in the pool.

RHS enters a number of athletics events and regularly provides more athletes to the Suffolk team than any other local school. Many also go on to represent East Anglia at national level, and some go further still: Jonathan Ilori, who left the RHS in 2011 to study in the USA on a sports scholarship, is now ranked number one (for his age) in Europe for the triple jump and is part of the Olympic hopefuls. Both boys

Above left: *Parade ground start to the popular mini marathon.*

Left: *Royal Hospital School field a team in the dragon boat racing competition on Alton Water.*

Top: *Cross country – running along the sea wall embankment.*

Above: *The School has AstroTurf, hard and (in the summer) grass tennis courts. In season all 20 courts can be full of players.*

Above: Ben Allday (batting) and Matt Drury (wicket keeper) in action – the three main cricket pitches are named after English cricket grounds – Lords, The Oval and Canterbury (with a tree inside the boundary).

Left: Cross country – the final downhill straight.

Top: Basketball with the old original wooden gymnasium flooring, which after a flood was replaced with a modern synthetic surface.

Above: Athletics – Jonathan 'Jono' Ilori is a talented athlete specialising in the triple jump and now training in the United States.

Left: *Rugby scrum down – the School has a real strength in depth.*

Below: *Swimming has always been a popular sport and the School often wins local galas and regularly produces county swimmers. The junior and senior swimming galas are popular occasions with fierce house rivalry. The pool was built to Olympic size in the 1930s, with diving boards and trapeze over the pool, but now removed.*

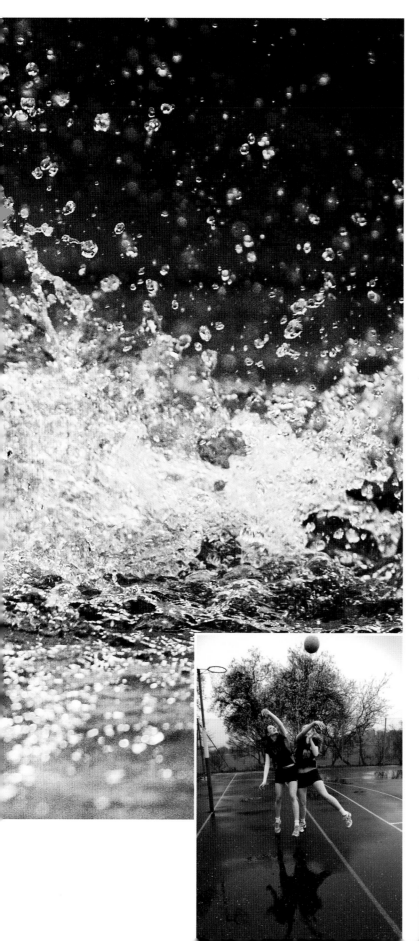

and girls compete in the annual cross country event held at the end of the spring term, and since 1984 there has been a fiercely contended mini-marathon. Indeed pupils at the RHS seem to relish the challenge presented by such events: in 1992 a biathlon event was held for the first time, with a three-mile run and 12 lengths of the pool; it was won by Chris Volley who went on to become British Triathlon Performance Development Coach.

For those pupils who do not quite make it into the Schools' representative teams there are league competitions, including football for both boys and girls in the autumn and spring terms. The boys also have fiercely competitive inter-house events in hockey, indoor hockey,

Top: Hockey dribbling skills – players are known to be fiercely competitive.

Left: Netball and rounders – two of the main competitive girls sports.

Traditionally school colours are orange commemorating the royal founder, King William III, green commemorating Greenwich, the original home of the School, and blue, the colour of the Royal Navy.

195

rugby 7s and cricket, while the girls compete in netball, hockey and rounders. Sports Day is the highlight of the summer term – RHS at its best, with the field filled with the whole School, staff and parents, and pupils competing in their houses after taking part in qualifying heats during the term.

Other sporting options include trampoline, dry skiing, table tennis and mountain biking, and the School even has a bowling green and a nine hole golf course. And there is an academic dimension too, with sports studies taught at GCSE and A Level for those who wish to take their sporting activities beyond participation and possibly into a career. Above all else, sports pupils have developed a competitive spirit, along with the ethos that it is 'the taking part and playing the game' that remain central.

Above left: In 2005 hockey replaced football as the main boys sport in the Lent term.

Above: Canoe instruction, water polo, lifesaving classes, swim aerobics, scuba diving and many other water based activities take place in the swimming pool (Big Pool, 'BP').

Inset top: Airborne – the new gymnasium sports surface provides bounce and lift.

Inset bottom: The School has its own bowling green, with majestic views down Queen Mary's Avenue towards Nelson House and across the River Stour. It is regularly used by pupils, staff and the local community.

DEVELOPING FITNESS, WELL-BEING AND HEALTHY COMPETITION

Fitness and well-being are promoted through the enjoyment of a wide range of team and individual sports played at all levels of ability. The School believes that physical fitness and competition helps young people to develop their self-esteem and confidence and, ultimately, a healthy body contributes significantly to a healthy mind.

It is recognised that children develop at different rates and therefore they are individually supported and nurtured so that they may develop in confidence and resilience through a wide range of opportunities. The coaching structure allows the more able performers to be pushed to maximise their potential, whilst also allowing pupils of any ability to extend their skills.

Team sports are at the heart of the sports programme promoting both physical health and social interaction and providing every

pupil with the opportunity to represent their School, whilst teaching important values for life.

- *To listen to and respect different opinions*
- *To cooperate and communicate effectively*
- *To decide upon and follow rules and understand how they promote teamwork*
- *To create team spirit and a collective identity*
- *To support and encourage team members working towards a common goal*
- *To take personal responsibility*

The overarching aim is to inspire a life-long interest in sport and, with so much on offer, everyone can find something they enjoy whatever their level of ability. This positive approach generates an atmosphere of excitement and healthy competition and many find themselves not only involved, but excelling in a sport they might not have considered trying before joining the School.

Various

As well as mainstream team sports like rugby, there are diverse sporting opportunities, ranging from keep fit sessions and weights in the gym through to scuba diving in the pool or even further afield (the Red Sea was a scuba destination).

Activity, Adventure and Leadership

COMBINED CADET FORCE

The balance that had to be struck in the late 1950s and early 1960s between the naval traditions of the School and its new academic focus inevitably involved a move away from the concentration on seamanship training that had previously been the norm. This was partly countered by the establishment of a new CCF contingent, a move that was initiated by George Hardy in the early 1960s. The School became the first in the country to have a naval section as the basis of its training programme. Membership of the CCF rapidly became popular, and the contingent was soon one of the largest in the country.

Today the CCF is compulsory for years 9 and 10. In year 9 the pupils all receive basic training before choosing their section in year 10; there are Royal Navy, Royal Marine, Army and Royal Air Force sections. In year 11 membership becomes voluntary, but well over half the pupils stay on, and many of them go on into the sixth form and become non-commissioned officers, helping to train the juniors.

Lieutenant Colonel Marc Godfrey combines his teaching role as Head of Politics with his position as Contingent Commander, assisted by Karl Weaver who is the full-time School Staff Instructor (SSI). There are also 20 other commissioned staff members who take on roles as officers within the four detachments of the CCF.

The contingent currently benefits from affiliations with HMS *Dauntless*, the Royal Marine Reserve (London), 4 Regiment Army

Adventure training weekend is an opportunity for year 7 pupils to settle in and get to know each other through participation in a wide range of outdoor activities.

When the CCF was formed some of the masters were appointed as officers with naval ranks, with the exception of George Hardy and Des Horne who assumed Army titles; the naval instructors were given non-commissioned ranks. I remember the Duke of Edinburgh visiting Ipswich to be shown the progress of his Award scheme, and some of us were sent as part of the RHS contingent. Part of the Bronze Award was a route march and three of us had to walk round the running track at the School where the inspection took place to simulate training for that event; we wore number ones, which has always struck me as odd since the actual route march would have taken place in full Army kit with backpacks.

Bob Collins (1963–65)

Serving in the Forces – Medicine, Marines and Sandhurst

Many former Royal Hospital School pupils still progress into the Armed Forces. Col Dr Richard Cantelo (1976–83, Collingwood) is a Consultant Anaesthetist at the Ministry of Defence Hospital Unit, Frimley Park. Similarly Col Dr Kevin Beaton OBE, served as Officer Commanding, Royal Centre for Defence Medicine at Queen Elizabeth Hospital Birmingham.

Former pupil and School Governor, Andrew Polson can boast two successes, his step-son Roland Brading became the youngest Major in the Royal Marines and his daughter Elizabeth Polson, a Captain specialising in Army Logistics. The Finn brothers all entered the services, Ivan became a Royal Navy Commander. Stuart a Royal Navy Senior Observer flying the Merlin helicopter and Tristan a Captain in the Royal Marines working with the UK Amphibious Battle Staff.

The School has also provided many high quality entrants to the Royal Military Academy Sandhurst. Matt Hall was commissioned into the Royal Military Police in 2000 and has served in many theatres of conflict, including charge of the British Ambassadors bodyguard team in Iraq. In 2009 Captain Rupert Anderson of the 1st Battalion the Royal Ghurkha Rifles, was awarded a special Mention in Despatches after he fended off more than a dozen attacks in four days to allow supplies to reach frontline troops. Claire Westerman served as an education officer in Afghanistan training British troops in the local Dari language, forging relationships with local villages and tribal elders and providing simple English lessons for the Afghan National Army. Finally 2nd Lt John Snoddon became the youngest serving commissioned Officer in the British Army, graduating just after his 20th birthday and then posted to the Royal Anglian Regiment.

Left: Matt Hall (1986–93, Howe). Commissioned into the Royal Military Police in 2000.

Below: Claire Westerman (1997–2004, Blake) passed out of Sandhurst in 2008 and trained to become an education officer in Afghanistan.

Air Corps and RAF Honington. These contacts, along with those with numerous serving parents, are critical in providing a direct link with the services, and of course the contingent also benefits from assistance provided by countless former pupils currently serving across the world.

2012 saw six officers being recognised for long service and commitment by the award of the Cadet Force Medal (for 12 years' service) and seven being awarded Clasps (for a further six years' service). Furthermore, 15 officers were delighted to receive a Queen's Diamond Jubilee Medal, in recognition of their continued service during Her Majesty's Diamond Jubilee year.

The training is designed to develop powers of leadership and participation, and although it is basically military in nature, there is a strong 'adventure' component to the wide range of activities on offer. These include map reading, orienteering, field craft, climbing, abseiling, flying and gliding, along with shooting and sailing.

Camps are a regular part of the annual programme, including adventure training camps in Wales, the West Country, Yorkshire and the Lake District. There is an annual central camp where cadets can join in activities with other schools and in 2012 cadets were hosted by the Royal Signals Regiment at Elmpt (formerly RAF Bruggen) in Germany. Serving former pupils often assist with opportunities and this visit was partly facilitated by Lt Col AR Thorne, HQ Rhine Garrison Station Commander, who is a former pupil in Cornwallis House.

The contingent regularly competes in the various section competitions on offer, the CCF Royal Navy National Regatta, the Sir Steuart Pringle Trophy competition, the Combat Cadet competition and the RAF Cranwell Ground Training competition. The School also participates avidly in the gruelling Devizes to Westminster Canoe Marathon entering teams that have won the School's Team, Junior Team and CCF Team Trophy.

Right: The CCF provides opportunities for pupils to gain flight experience and training.

Below left: Cadets 'coasteering' on the Cornish coast during CCF summer camp.

Below right: Silver Duke of Edinburgh's Award group take a well-earned break during an expedition on the Suffolk heathlands.

Bottom: Sparks flying with an angle grinder. The small REME section of the CCF help to maintain the contingent vehicles.

200

DUKE OF EDINBURGH'S AWARD SCHEME

In 1970 HRH The Duke of Edinburgh flew into the School piloting his own Wessex helicopter of the Queen's Flight. By this time the RHS was already heavily involved in his Award scheme and in January 1992 the School obtained its own operating license. It became a leading participant in East Anglia, with Nicholas Ward serving on the Duke of Edinburgh Advisory Panel and the School hosting regional events.

Today, the scheme is designed to offer opportunities to take on personal challenges, and entrants must complete four sections, which include volunteering for service, acquiring specific skills and participating in expeditions and physical activities; the latter, at Gold level, involves a residential course. The aim is for pupils to begin the Bronze Award as part of year 9 CCF training, after which participation becomes voluntary, with pupils completing Bronze in year 10, Silver in year 11 and Gold by the time they leave the School.

For many years Bronze expeditions have taken place in areas of Suffolk forest, coast and heathland, while Silver explorations were undertaken in Guernsey and, since 1968, the Greenwich Hospital's northern estates have hosted Gold expeditions on a regular basis. Orienteering is often part of the scheme. Originally introduced in September 1971, it now helps pupils to develop the map and compass skills that underpin expedition route planning and execution.

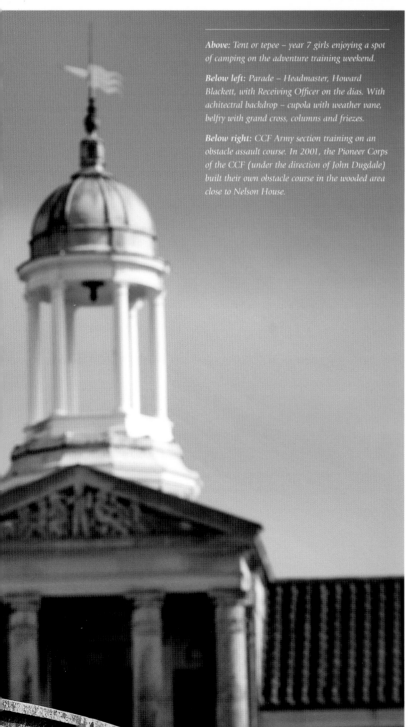

Above: Tent or tepee – year 7 girls enjoying a spot of camping on the adventure training weekend.

Below left: Parade – Headmaster, Howard Blackett, with Receiving Officer on the dias. With achitectral backdrop – cupola with weather vane, belfry with grand cross, columns and friezes.

Below right: CCF Army section training on an obstacle assault course. In 2001, the Pioneer Corps of the CCF (under the direction of John Dugdale) built their own obstacle course in the wooded area close to Nelson House.

Below: Extra-curricular – fashion show. Making the costumes or modelling – there are opportunities for all.

Above: Pupils rehearse for a School dance production.

Right: Nelson's famous couples night is won by 'Postman Pat and his Black and White Cat'. The upper sixth form boarding house provides a bridge between school and university.

THE CO-CURRICULUM

RHS boys and girls are never short of something to occupy their time beyond lessons. There are large numbers of after-school and weekend activities open to them, besides those regular boarding school stalwarts, the CCF and the Duke of Edinburgh's Award. All these co-curricular possibilities are coordinated by Clive Rennison who, as well as teaching mathematics and coaching rugby and cricket, manages the co-curricular timetable so that clashes are kept to the minimum. The regular staff are supplemented by external experts in offering these additional activities. Extra sports available are badminton, basketball, table tennis, golf and karate, with ice skating and roller skating trips arranged externally. Ballet and trampoline can be tackled, and less

strenuous pursuits include jewellery making, airfix modelling, extra art tuition and anything else a pupil wants to have a go at with or which a teacher can help, provided time can be found for it. Baking is a very popular activity as the pupils can consume their own creations and the car club, where pupils strip down old vehicles and maintain the CCF Land Rovers, is always oversubscribed.

There are several other clubs, often led by the pupils, for example Warhammer has gained in popularity, to supplement the more conventional societies such as the chess club, and there is a Green Team who are committed to monitoring the School's sustainability. Televisions and DVDs have put an end to the use of the hall as a cinema, but there are trips to Ipswich to see major new releases,

for example *Warhorse*. School discos are held in the assembly hall, as well as year group discos, ceilidhs and glamorous themed balls where young men escort the young ladies from their houses to the decorated Jellicoe Room. Nelson House holds Trafalgar Night dinners and Burns night suppers with much Scottish dancing, as well as fancy dress themed evenings into which the pupils throw themselves inventively.

Whole School Saturday evening entertainment has included hosting pop and rock groups, barbecues, inter-house five-a-side football competitions and basketball nights. Blake and Drake hold their own junior discos as well as hosting beach parties and fancy dress nights. The RHS talent shows provide an opportunity to entertain, with pupils performing acts, singing, dancing and playing instruments. Fireworks night is always celebrated with a spectacular display provided by hard-working members of staff led by Les Thompson. The inter-house general knowledge competition with buzzers and *University Challenge* style format is hotly contested. Staff compete against the School team in the first debate of the year and hold 'Just a Minute' style events against the sixth form too.

The School has a vibrant Medsoc, a group of pupils who have shown an interest in pursuing a career in medicine or something closely related. This group has a pupil President and is led by staff member Katherine Stevens. As well as organising visiting speakers,

Increasing numbers of pupils are part of the School Equestrian Team. Lessons and livery are provided at local stables and there is the opportunity to represent the School in inter-school competition and most notably, at the Royal Windsor Horse Show each year.

Right: Table tennis in Collingwood day room, located where the old muster yard used to be. The glass roof provides a natural light source, enabling a full range of house-based activities to take place in this multi-purpose space.

Below: Sparks fly at tech club – using an angle grinder.

Bottom right: The Model United Nations – encourages a global perspective.

including ex-pupils who are doctors and vets, the pupils themselves have addressed the society on matters related to health. Colin Morgan and Ruth Gitsham maintain a healthy Literary Society at the RHS, which has reviewed and discussed a wide variety of books over the years, with the occasional film version of the chosen book attracting a larger audience than usual.

The RHS has always been good at coming together to celebrate an occasion. Christmas dinner is a popular affair where the pupils are served by the staff and the houses enter a Christmas cake-decorating competition with some outstanding and imaginative designs to match the fancy dress atmosphere. In 2012, a jubilee tea was held on the terrace, with staff providing the entertainment, and the house Christmas parties are the stuff of legend.

A major new co-curricular activity, introduced by Matthew Christmas, is the Model United Nations, a worldwide initiative in which pupils take part in academic simulations of the United Nations, allowing them to develop their understanding of the international body and its work. As he has said, 'Involvement in the MUN will help pupils become informed global citizens as they learn about civics, world current affairs, effective communication, globalisation and multi-lateral diplomacy. With our boarding pupils coming from countries as diverse as Ukraine, Japan, Germany, Fiji and Tanzania, this is central to the international ethos that permeates all areas of school life here. Most importantly, the programme at RHS has quickly become pupil-led, with enormous enthusiasm and creativity from an executive group of year 12 pupils.'

ENCOURAGING LEADERSHIP, ADVENTURE AND SELF-DISCOVERY

Pupils are encouraged to pursue a huge range of interests, shared experiences and activities and, through them, develop the life-long qualities of self-discipline, enthusiasm and commitment. Having perspective, seeing what needs to be done and possessing the courage to serve the greatest good describes authentic leadership. It

arises naturally, without effort, in any person who is fully engaged in what they are doing. True leaders are honest and genuine and able to adapt to the needs of the moment without seeking for recognition for their efforts.

Learning skills for life starts from their earliest days at the School with adventure training and team-building events, as well as learning to sail, in the first term. Sailing is a unique opportunity born from the School's seafaring heritage and, as well as being great fun, it also teaches teamwork, develops confidence and generates a great sense of adventure and satisfaction.

In the Senior School, the combined cadet force promotes the benefits of responsibility, teamwork, leadership and endurance through a whole range of opportunities. Cadets can take part in activities as diverse as rock climbing, coasteering, power-boating and flying while learning safety skills and self-reliance on expeditions and in camp.

Older pupils understand that privilege is not automatic and they are expected to put something back through taking on positions of responsibility. They can demonstrate leadership skills through the prefect and peer support system, running clubs and societies and becoming role models for younger years.

Divisions – the most important legacy of the School's maritime history – teach pupils to have a pride in their appearance, to respect authority and to work together towards a common goal. The result is a spectacular occasion that generates tremendous pride in pupils and parents alike.

Above left: *An Army cadet on exercise.*

Left: *The Combined Cadet Force biennial inspection. The School can boast one of the largest contingents in the country and all those involved benefit from the experience, acquiring new specialist and life skills.*

Right: *The thrill of a successful abseil for Emily Nutt. There are many opportunities to participate in a range of adventure activities.*

Widening Horizons

The School's first overseas band and cultural tour at the end of June 1928 was five days in Deauville, France. Southern Railway provided cheap fares for the 100 pupils and accompanying staff. The band played, some boys boxed in the casino, there were parades and luncheons, Swedish drill, cutlass drill, club swinging, dancing the hornpipe and even a Harold Lloyd movie. It was confirmed that the pupils had behaved as gentlemen and that everyone was a credit to the School. About a month later, when HRH The Prince of Wales visited the School to distribute prizes, it was remarked that, during the overseas band tour, Greenwich schoolboys 'did more to strengthen the *entente cordiale* in one corner of France than an Army of astute politicians could have done in a multitude of conferences'.

For many years after the move to Holbrook, the School remained isolated and largely cut off from the world around and beyond, but by the 1960s opportunities to travel and learn were starting to evolve. In 1966 the School participated in a school cruise for the first time, and a year later 128 boys cruised round Italy. Over the following years the School went on to cruise with British India liners SS *Devonia*, SS *Nevasa*

and SS *Uganda*, the latter taking them to Venice, Dubrovnik, Istanbul, Rhodes, Santorini, Malta and Naples. These educational tours were popular and are fondly remembered by those who attended.

July 1980 saw the first long-haul tour to the USA, visiting New York, Philadelphia, the Shenandoah Valley, Washington, D.C. and Williamsburg. This trip included a specially arranged visit on board a nuclear powered aircraft carrier, the USS *Nimitz*. Nine years later pupils visited the east and west coasts of the USA, and in 2008 a band and cultural tour included Boston, New York, Washington, D.C. and Williamsburg – the latter home to the College of William and Mary which for many years supplied a regular flow of gap-year graduates who assisted with teaching history and sport in particular. A 2010 USA tour to

Left: RHS boys boarding SS Nevassa 1972. The East Anglian Daily Times reported 'The Royal Hospital School was not only a credit to itself, to East Anglia, to the ship, but to Britain as well' as they were adjudged the smartest young students out of the 1,100 onboard the ship, wearing 'neat blazers and grey trousers, with their hair properly trimmed, doing things and learning in an orderly style.'

Right: Stanley Good, Hawke housemaster and geography teacher from 1937–60, pictured with his teaching globe. Today the School champions global citizenship, with many opportunities to travel overseas.

Las Vegas, the Grand Canyon and California saw the School visit another historic aircraft carrier, performing a concert on board USS *Midway*.

Also in 1980 Peter Hall and Peter Wilkinson took 16 pupils to Italy on the first annual ski trip. Today ski trips can cater for anything up to 100 pupils, with nearly 40 participating in a tour to the USA in 2012. All those going on ski trips are supported by a comprehensive package of training and tuition prior to the tours. Over the years the languages departments have run a range of exchanges and cultural tours, with students of Spanish visiting Cuenca, German tours to Leipzig and Berlin and a French trip to Boulogne. The art and business studies departments have visited Paris, sailors have gone to Egypt, the history department visit the First World War battlefields and there is a regular sixth form geography tour to Iceland. The latter incorporating glacier jeeps, ice hikes with crampons, an amphibious boat tour of the ice lagoon, whale watching, rib boating, geothermal energy, geysers, volcanoes, waterfalls and northern lights. International sports tours have also been very well supported and have included rugby to Canada and New Zealand and cricket to Sri Lanka

Left: *Beach volleyball match with pupils from St Servatius College in Matara, Sri Lanka (2006). The RHS bought a minibus to help this school compete in island-wide cricket tournaments. International cricketer Sanath Jayasuriya was a former pupil of this school and supported our subsequent cricket tour to the island in 2010.*

Various top left: *Statue of Liberty in New York and The Capitol in Washington, D.C. – band tour to eastern USA (2008); The Colosseum in Rome – choir tour to Italy (2011); Berlin – MFL tour to Germany (2010); Las Vegas – cultural tour to south western USA (2010).*

Above: *Scottish country dancing with pupils of St Mary's Convent in Matara, Sri Lanka (2006). The RHS raised over £25,000 to support two schools affected by the tsunami.*

and Barbados. The pupils compete against overseas schools, receive expert coaching, visit international sporting venues and are introduced to international players. The choir have also travelled extensively, for example performing in major venues such as Notre Dame in Paris and St Peter's in Rome. All of these travel experiences present opportunities to learn and develop new skills and, importantly, encourage pupils to develop greater self-confidence and to grow as individuals.

In July 2006, perhaps the largest and most ambitious overseas venture yet saw 120 pupils and teachers travel to Sri Lanka. Their itinerary included seven concerts performed across the island by the band, and as well as a unique cultural experience it was an opportunity to visit the two schools for whom the RHS had raised significant funds following the 2004 tsunami disaster. The pupils attended lessons, provided some basic relief and participated in a sports tournament with the schools. During this venture seeing almost a fifth of the School riding elephant back along a trail created a lasting and impressive image, and the tour was recognised by all as an outstanding experience.

This was the first of a series of popular collaborative band and cultural trips. It was followed by the east coast of the USA in 2008, the west coast in 2010 and a spectacular adventure in South Africa, 2012. The latter included a visit to Soweto in Johannesburg, going on safari in the Kruger National Park, experiencing the Zulu battlefields, travelling to Durban and then onto the Garden Route before ending in Cape Town, the birthplace of Gifford Sherman Reade which was – as this was badged the RHS Tercentenary Tour – a highly appropriate final destination. Indeed the school band performed a concert on board their affiliated Royal Navy vessel, HMS *Dauntless*, with the impressive backdrop of Table Mountain and a number of parents and former

pupils in attendance. This was a warm-up for a full day of high-profile concerts performed in celebration of Nelson Mandela's birthday. As tour leader Rob Mann states, 'There is no better way to learn and to understand than to travel and experience for oneself', further reinforcing his catchphrase 'the world is your classroom'.

As the RHS has become increasingly multicultural it has embraced a forward-looking global perspective. Overseas pupils are all seamlessly integrated, with many of them participating in overseas work experience and environmental initiatives, and the School involvement in the Model United Nations is further evidence of its international outlook. The School recognises that there are many benefits to be derived from development of the global dimension both within the curriculum and, importantly, beyond it. The RHS pupils are increasingly respectful of others, and the last 20 years have seen the School transform itself in this respect.

Left: The annual ski trips are very popular and supported by ski training programmes prior to, and during, the tours. The School have travelled to the USA, France, Austria, Switzerland and Andorra.

Above: The sixth form geography study tours have been led by Rob Mann (inset) since 2003. Highlights have included a trip to Iceland, visiting the Blue Lagoon thermal pools (top) and the 'James Bond' glacial lagoon at Jokulsarla (bottom), which featured extensively in the car chase scene in Die Another Day.

GLOBAL OUTLOOK AND ENVIRONMENTAL RESPONSIBILITY

Although its history is British and rich with naval traditions, the School is not in any sense parochial. The most powerful force in advocating and promoting international understanding is exposure to different cultures and at the Royal Hospital School pupils are encouraged to see themselves as global citizens and to appreciate value and respect all cultures, religions and languages. Pupils of all nationalities are welcomed and, with 18 per cent of the boarding population coming from some thirty different countries as diverse as Ukraine, Japan, Thailand, Germany and Bulgaria, an international ethos increasingly permeates all areas of school life.

Model United Nations – a worldwide initiative in which pupils take part in academic simulations of the United Nations – helps to develop a knowledge and understanding of the world; learning about civics, current affairs, effective communications, globalization and multi-lateral diplomacy. Pupils attend conferences, both in the UK and abroad, discussing international issues from the perspective of countries other than their own. With increased awareness of the plight of those fighting for democracy and freedom around the world, a growing number of pupils have also become actively involved with Amnesty International.

Intrinsically linked with this global awareness is a whole school commitment to environmental responsibility. Pupils are expected

to demonstrate an active interest and concern for all natural environments, to be aware of proven problems and to play a practical role in tackling environmental issues. As a result, teachers and pupils together with the staff looking after our 200-acre estate are working to achieve the Gold Standard Carbon Charter by 2014. To help drive this carbon reduction initiative, a pupil-led Green Team works closely with the estates team to canvass support from the whole school.

Above: Fair Trade stall. The School tuck shop, located in the Trafalgar Rooms, stocks a range of Fair Trade items.

Left: The choir relax at a water park on their highly successful tour of Italy (2011).

Below: Sri Lanka – elephant back safari (2006).

Service and Charity

As a charity themselves, Greenwich Hospital and its School were ready all through their history to support fundraising efforts. In July 1852, for example, a grand bazaar was held at Greenwich Hospital to raise money for the Queen Adelaide Naval Fund. The band of the Royal Hospital School entertained the crowds.

A century later, in 1966, the School introduced a social services scheme, which involved pupils visiting old people in the neighbourhood and, together with the Women's Institute, helping to entertain residents at a nearby Cheshire Care Home. Twenty years later a St Johns Ambulance Section was formed, with 23 candidates passing their initial 'essentials of first aid' examination. They received the title 'Centenary (Suffolk) Combined Cadet Division', and the first big event at which the squad participated was the great tea party in Hyde Park.

In 1984 a charity run raised over £1,000 for the British Olympia Fund and March 1989 saw the School taking part in the first Red Nose Day for Comic Relief. £480 was raised through a number of events from marathon table tennis to sponsored parachute jumps. In June 1990 four boys staged a monumental world record attempt for non-stop doubles table tennis, attempting to beat the record which stood at 101 hours 1 minute and 11 seconds. They trained hard and started at 8.00am, but after 42 hours' play one boy collapsed with physical exhaustion and the attempt was aborted; nevertheless £700 was raised for Great Ormond Street Hospital.

A junior pupil embraces her gran – all generations are warmly welcomed at the RHS.

Above: Pupils working on a recycling project.

Over a century later, a charity cricket match in June 1997 saw Griff Rhys Jones captaining a cricket team of celebrities against the RHS First XI captained by Don Topley. Others playing included Samantha Janus, Richard E Grant, Clive Anderson, Jeff Banks, Rory McGrath and Hugh Laurie. The event raised over £8,000 for local charities. Perhaps the most successful single fundraising event was a sponsored fancy dress walk round Alton Water in June 2005 which raised approaching £25,000 to support two schools in Sri Lanka affected by the Boxing Day 2004 tsunami. Members of the School expedition returned to Sri Lanka just over a year later visited the Schools and were able to see for themselves how the money they had raised was being spent.

In 2000 it was decided that the School would nominate one or more charities each year for which coordinated fundraising activities would be undertaken – the first year saw the adoption of the National Asthma Campaign and the NSPCC. Charity fundraising is now coordinated under an umbrella body, RHS Community Action, which organises each year's activities and is run by the pupils themselves under two appointed Nelson House leaders. The policy is to benefit a local charity where financial contributions can be complemented by practical support. The first year, Jane Ward (the Headmaster's wife) did much to formally organise and promote community service activities at the School.

The regular annual fundraising events which support the charity – the Christmas fancy dress day, the February gala concert, the summer fete, collections at the carol and commemoration services – are supplemented by one-off events organised by individual houses, and for the year in question raised over £8,000. This was used to purchase equipment and support users in the music therapy suite. Involvement will continue into the future, with plans to visit residents and to help with music therapy and entertainment.

The School has a close involvement with Oak House, a home for the elderly in Stutton where a computer suite has been installed, funded by the School. RHS pupils, for whom computers are second nature, now regularly visit the home to help the residents learn to use the equipment. It is a salutary lesson for young people to understand that elderly folk, who are

Service to others – commitment

The emphasis placed today at the RHS on helping others finds echoes in the lives of many former pupils, including Ernest Britten (1935–38), who was a submariner in the Second World War, surviving depth charges off Capri and acting as a beacon for the landings at Anzio. He led a colourful life with a short spell as a deckhand in an unsuccessful expedition (with Commander Buster Crabbe) to recover Armada gold from Tobermory Bay, as well as working as a barman and a bouncer in a Soho pub, spending ten years as a teacher in a French convent and being one of the pioneering redcoats at Butlins (for 19 years from 1947). He was a qualified parachutist, diving instructor and Navy record-holding swimmer – at age 65, swimming the Solent to the Isle of Wight and back in five hours and at aged 70, completing a parachute jump into the Solent. He raised money for charities linked to the Submariners Museum, Gosport, where he served as an archivist for many years and his award of an MBE in 1996 delighted submariners worldwide. He is just one example of a pupil from the School who has received such an honour.

Just a few examples illustrate the many and valued contributions that former RHS pupils have made. Many have served in the fire and police services and others have joined the clergy; where some have been elected to General Synod of the Church of England and others have served as Chaplain to the Queen. Commander William Willis, who left the School in 1909, was appointed HM Inspector of Police after serving as a Chief Constable. He served with distinction in the First World War and received the Medaille Militaire. On 21 January 1941 he helped resuscitate a boy after a bomb landed close to a School and in 1953 he received a CBE. Edward 'Ted' Pearn joined the Fire Service in 1958 rising through the ranks to Assistant Chief Officer of Hampshire Fire Brigade before serving as HM Inspector of Fire Services, with wide ranging national responsibilities. Since 1993 Ted has been an active member of the United Nations Disaster Assessment and Coordination Team; advising peoples and governments all around the world. His services were recognised when he received the OBE.

Mike Freeney was a powerful force working to help public and private sector organisations transform their approach to disability and diversity. He had been diagnosed with spina bifida occulta and had suffered years of pain and immobility, however, he used his outstanding communication skills to persuade others to improve opportunity and equality. When he died in 2005 his lengthy obituary in the *Guardian* recognised his far reaching contribution – raising disability awareness, breaking down barriers and promoting diversity.

The Polar Challenge supports charity

In 2006 RHS brothers Alex and Jeremy Hinton joined up with Andrew Vinson to form the Breaking Trail team taking part in that year's Polar Challenge, one of the most gruelling tests of will and stamina possible. Both the Hintons are keen and highly motivated sportsmen and sailors, and since leaving school have taken part in a variety of sporting adventures all over the world. Jeremy even managed to row the Atlantic – by accident, after one of the two members of a French crew dropped out and he took over, with no previous rowing experience. They came last in the race but he, aged 23, became the youngest person ever to row the Atlantic. They have supported a number of charitable causes.

The Polar Challenge is a 350-nautical mile race in the Arctic finishing at the magnetic North Pole. Teams of three undertake a week's training so that they can combat one of the world's most extreme and hostile environments – the territory of polar bears, moreover – before embarking on the race proper. They race on skis, pulling their own supplies, and are on the journey for three weeks or so. Breaking Trail finished a highly creditable third, and in doing so raised large sums of money for their charity, the British Heart Foundation.

Above: *The Optua Games, held at the School each year, provides an opportunity to help disabled people participate in sport.*

Right: *Griff Rhys Jones arrives on a trailer full of celebrity cricketers, raising money for good causes at a charity match held at the School.*

Left: *The Hinton brothers (Alex and Jeremy) keeping warm as they raise funds for the British Heart Foundation.*

hampered by arthritic hands, fading memory and bewildering technology, need a slow and steady approach towards using applications which are foreign to them but which, once mastered, are a source of great satisfaction.

The relationship between the RHS and Oak House is a long-standing one. The residents visit the School for concerts, dramatic productions, chapel services, parades and displays, and are entertained in their turn at home by the band and choir, and by small parties of pupils who have tea with them, talk to them and learn to assist them.

Another partnership is with the Woolverstone Project, recognised nationally as one of the foremost providers of sailing for the disabled. The project has a tidal base on the River Orwell and its main training

centre is at Alton Water, which was able to extend and improve its facilities through funds donated by the School. Support teams of RHS pupils regularly attend its sessions, assisting with the preparation of the dinghies and with taking newcomers out on to the water. The School's work is enhanced by contributions made by members of the teaching and support staff who, together with local day pupils, continue to work for the project all year round.

Yet another annual project is with Optua (Be Your Best), who provide a wide range of services for disabled people across Suffolk and beyond. The School hosts an annual games day at the end of the summer term, staffed and run by the RHS Community Action and year 11 and sixth form pupils. The games are always fully subscribed and teams come from far and wide; the 2012 event appropriately had the Olympics as its theme.

As Barry Hocking, who runs community action in the School, has written, 'An education at the RHS aims to provide our pupils with an awareness of the responsibilities of citizenship and to prepare them for a life of service to others. For those who have participated regularly in weekly events and those who have joined in annual events, the RHS Community Action has been an education while serving the wider community locally, regionally and nationally.'

Education for life is about more than just passing exams and pupils learn that privilege and opportunity go hand in hand with responsibility. The School places great emphasis on the values of kindness, service, generosity of spirit and integrity and through the community action team, pupils have the opportunity to serve others, discover the value of self-improvement and support the wider community.

In school, they might fundraise for local charities and participate in recycling and conservation projects, while further afield they may opt to work in local schools, homes for the elderly or with a sailing for the disabled project. Other schemes include disability-awareness training and the Duke of Edinburgh's Award scheme and through these programmes of community service, social responsibility and self-improvement, pupils are well-equipped by the time they leave school to take responsibility for their own lives, to show initiative and approach life with an open and receptive mind.

Collaboration as a community is far superior to that of any as individuals. At the Royal Hospital School, the impact of a unified team and the power of hearts and minds united for the common good are recognised. In this open yet inclusive environment, every member of the school community is valued and encouraged to share perspective, play a part in decision making and take the lead without fear of judgement or failure.

Above: Flag waving at the Jubilee Tea, held to celebrate the 60 year reign of HM Queen Elizabeth II. Decorated tables lined the flag adorned terrace and activities included face painting, street entertainers, patriotic singing and a drive past of royal lookalikes. This event typifies the strength of the school community – on this occasion, all coming together to honour Her Majesty.

Left: Hood girls relaxing in the Coca-Cola themed retro bar.

213

List of Subscribers

This book has been made possible through the generosity of the following subscribers.

Georgina M Abbott	*RHS Community*	Charlotte Baldwin-Cole	*Howe, 2011–*	Lucy Bradley	*Hood, 2008–12*
Laura Ablett	*Raleigh, 2011–*	Zhangir Balgimbaev	*Collingwood, 2011–*	Dominic Branch	*Anson, 2008–10*
Jeff Adams	*Howe, 1974–79*	Benjamin Banks	*St Vincent, 2010–*	Richard Branch	*Anson, 2008–*
Matthew Adams	*Anson, 2009–*	Elisabeth Banks	*Cornwallis, 2007–*	Jana Bratusa	*Cornwallis, 2010–12*
Nigel Adams	*Raleigh, 1969–75*	Laura Banks	*Cornwallis, 2005–09*	Freddie Braybrooke	*Collingwood, 2010–*
Oluwaseyitan Agbaje	*Cornwallis, 2010–12*	Richard J Barker	*Blake, 1954–61*	Toby Braybrooke	*Drake, 2012–*
Henry Ager	*Collingwood, 2009–*	Greg Barr	*Drake, 1975–80*	Albert Breame	*Anson, 1932–34*
Matilda Ager	*Blake, 2011–*	Isabella Bartlett	*Blake, 2011–*	Freddie Brett	*St Vincent, 2007–*
Ransford Agyemang	*St Vincent, 2011–*	Willem Bartlett	*St Vincent, 2006–*	Charles Brice	*St Vincent, 2009–*
Alice Aindow	*Cornwallis, 2010–12*	John Bartrum	*Staff, 1991–*	William Brice	*St Vincent, 2007–12*
Camilla Ainsworth	*Blake, 2010–*	Aimee Batchelor	*Howe, 2010–12*	Charlotte Broomer	*Howe, 2010–12*
Oliver Ainsworth	*Collingwood, 2006–*	Matthew Batchelor	*Drake, 2010–*	Elizabeth Brown	*Howe, 2010–*
Sophie Ainsworth	*Raleigh, 2008–*	Jack Baverstock	*Hawke, 2007–*	Katherine Brown	*Howe, 2010–*
Alexander Alderton	*Hawke, 2008–*	Mike Beard	*Staff, 2010–*	Laura Brown	*Cornwallis, 2006–*
Connor Alkin	*St Vincent, 2011–*	Thomas Beasley	*Raleigh, 1996–2001*	Matthew Brown	*St Vincent, 2008–*
Cameron Allan	*Collingwood, 2004–11*	Angus Beaton	*Collingwood, 2007–*	Molly Brown	*Cornwallis, 2010–12*
Eloise Allan	*Raleigh, 2011–*	Cameron Beaton	*Collingwood, 2006–10*	Serena Brown	*Blake, 2011–*
Fraser Allan	*Collingwood, 2009–*	Martha Beaton	*Hood, 2009–*	Steve Brown (Buster)	*Collingwood, 1967–74*
Sean Allcock	*Staff, 1995–*	Monty Beaton	*Collingwood, 2007–12*	Lewis Browning	*Drake, 2011–*
Ben Allday	*Collingwood, 2006–*	Guy R Beattie	*Howe, 1965–71*	Maisie Bruffell	*Hood, 2005–12*
Josh Allday	*Collingwood, 2008–*	Yury Belevskiy	*Hawke, 2010–12*	Robyn Brunning	*Cornwallis, 1997–2003*
Toby Allday	*Collingwood, 2010–*	Lea Benk	*Howe, 2011–12*	RJ Bruno	*Anson, 1960–64*
Stanley Allison	*Drake, 1961–65*	Herbie Bennett	*Raleigh, 2010–*	Daniela Buck Bernat	*Howe, 2011–*
Eric Allsop	*Nelson, 1981–88*	Maximilian Berger	*Anson, 2012–*	James Buckland	*St Vincent, 2010–11*
Bill Andrews	*Hood, 1938–40*	Luke Berry	*St Vincent, 2007–12*	Lucy Buckland	*Howe, 2009–*
Dennis Andrews MBE	*Cornwallis, 1959–64*	Eloise Best	*Blake, 2011–*	Toby Buckland	*Hawke, 2010–*
Toby Anscombe	*Hawke, 1984–89*	Tara Biles	*Raleigh, 2011–*	Harriet Bull	*Raleigh, 2011–*
Daniel Anstey	*St Vincent, 2004–11*	Harrison Bilner-King	*Hawke, 2008–*	HD Bunney	*Raleigh, 1954–58*
Rebecca Anstey	*Howe, 2006–*	Oliver Bilner-King	*Hawke, 2007–12*	Dominick Burke	*Hawke, 2008–*
William Anstey	*St Vincent, 2008–*	Holly Bird	*Hood, 2007–*	Commodore Bryan Burns CBE RN	*Former Governor*
Alan Aplin	*Nelson, 1964–70*	Joshua Blackburn	*Hawke, 2011–*	Alan E Burrow	*Blake, 1952–59*
John Aplin	*Nelson, 1959–64*	Alice Blackett	*Howe, 2004–11*	Lewis Burrows	*Hawke, 2008–*
Ernest Appleby	*Raleigh, 2005–12*	Elizabeth Blackett	*Howe, 2007–*	Roger Burton	*Drake, 1962–66*
Emily Arbuthnot	*Raleigh, 2008–*	Mr and Mrs Howard Blackett	*Headmaster, 2004–12*	Andrew Buss	*Raleigh, 2009–*
Rose Arbuthnot	*Raleigh, 2010–*	Thomas Blackett	*Drake, 2003–08*	Rebecca Butcher	*Hood, 2008–*
Amy Arthur	*Hood, 1996–2003*	Graham Blackwell	*Raleigh, 1963–69*	George Butt	*Raleigh, 2008–*
Molly Arthur	*Hood, 2006–*	Annabelle Blair	*Hood, 2005–12*	Joshua Butt	*Anson, 2006–*
Benjamin Arulampalam	*Drake, 2011–*	Suzanna Blair	*Howe, 2009–*	Joseph Butterworth	*Collingwood, 2011–*
Matilda Arulampalam	*Blake, 2012–*	Charlie Boci	*Anson, 2007–*	Sefanaia Cakacakavakalotu	*Anson, 2011–*
Peter Ash	*St Vincent, 2008–*	Alan Bonwick	*Staff, 1994–*	Roy Campbell	*Nelson, 1955–60*
Robert Ash	*St Vincent, 2009–*	Acey Boocock	*Cornwallis, 2009–*	Gemma Campbell-Gray	*Howe, 2006–*
Lou-Lou Ashton	*Hood, 2010–*	Megan Boocock	*Hood, 2009–12*	Jack Cantelo	*Collingwood, 2005–12*
Andy Ashworth	*St Vincent, 1974–77*	Arthur Booty	*Anson, 1962–68*	Matt Cantelo	*Collingwood, 2007–*
Barrie Audus	*Blake, 1978–85*	Diana Booty	*Howe, 1994–97*	Colonel Richard Cantelo	*Collingwood, 1976–83*
Matthew Ayling	*Anson, 2007–12*	Natasha Booty	*Nelson, 1996–2002*	Sam Cantelo	*Collingwood, 2010–*
Lucy Bailey	*Howe, 2005–12*	Edward Bourne	*Collingwood, 2010–*	Ray Cappi	*Hood, 1947–52*
Luke Bailey	*Anson, 2009–*	Oliver Bourne	*Collingwood, 2010–12*	Nathaniel Carroll	*St Vincent, 2005–12*
CA Baker	*Hawke, 1959–64*	Natalie Bowles	*Cornwallis, 2005–12*	Paul Anthony Carry	*Blake, 1981–86*
Dexter Baker	*Anson, 2007–12*	Alex Bradley	*Anson, 2010–*	Richard Carson	*Blake, 1952–59*

Helena Carter	*Raleigh, 2010–*	
Igor Cerevka	*Hawke, 2011–12*	
Brian J Challis	*Howe, 1953–57*	
Nathan Chambers	*Anson, 2005–12*	
Ross Chambers	*Anson, 2007–12*	
Wai Yin Christy Chan	*Cornwallis, 2009–*	
Tommy Chang	*Anson, 2011–*	
Commander Chris Charlton RN (Retd)	*Drake, 1966–73*	
David Charlton	*Bursar, 2004–*	
Harry Charlton	*Hawke, 2006–*	
Kongphoom Charoenwan	*Hawke, 2010–12*	
John Chatterley	*Hood, 1949–54*	
Wing Sze Vincy Chau	*Hood, 2011–*	
Anran Chen	*Howe, 2009–*	
Callum Chesterman	*Raleigh, 2010–*	
Hamish Chesterman	*Raleigh, 2011–*	
Ho Quan Georgina Cheung	*Howe, 2009–*	
Lee Maggie Cheung	*Cornwallis, 2011–*	
Duncan Chilvers	*St Vincent, 1977–84*	
Elliot Chilvers	*Drake, 2012–*	
Philip Robin Chisholm	*Hood, 1968–70*	
Sammi Sum Yin Chiu	*Cornwallis, 2010–*	
Chi Sum Victor Chong	*Anson, 2009–*	
Andrew Choules	*Hawke, 2009–*	
David Choules	*Anson, 2004–11*	
Lynsey Choules	*Cornwallis, 2004–11*	
Rebekah Choules	*Hawke, 2006–*	
Matthew Christmas	*Teaching Staff, 2011–*	
Anton Chumel	*Collingwood, 2011–12*	
Yin-long Wilfred Chung	*St Vincent, 2009–*	
Manuel Cifrian	*St Vincent, 2011–12*	
David J Clark	*Drake, 1962–67*	
Emily-Jane Clark	*Cornwallis, 2005–12*	
Christian Clausen	*St Vincent, 2011–12*	
Raymond Peter Claydon	*Staff, 1995–*	
Raquel Clemente	*Cornwallis, 2011–12*	
Marcus Clinton	*Cornwallis, 1981–86*	
Adam Clough	*Raleigh, 2010–*	
Molly Clyne	*Howe, 2011–*	
Christopher Norman Cobbett	*Hood, 1955–58*	
Bob Collins	*Nelson, 1958–63*	
Benjamin Conner	*St Vincent, 2010–*	
Samuel Conner	*St Vincent, 2008–*	
Imogen Cooke	*Howe, 2011–*	
Fred Coombs	*Teaching Staff, 1960–85*	
Sophia Cooper	*Cornwallis, 2008–*	
Freya Coote	*Howe, 2011–*	
Charles Copping	*Hawke, 1992–99*	
Felix Corbett	*Hawke, 2009–11*	
Hugo Corbett	*Collingwood, 2005–12*	
Kitty Corbett	*Hood, 2007–*	
Laetitia Corbett	*Cornwallis, 2009–11*	
Benjamin Cottrell	*Collingwood, 2011–*	
Harry Court	*Anson, 2007–12*	
Robert Cowper-Coles	*St Vincent, 2009–*	
Philip J Cox		
Hayden Craft	*Drake, 2012–*	
Joseph Craggs-Ward	*Collingwood, 2009–*	
Thomas Craggs-Ward	*Collingwood, 2009–*	
Peter Crick	*Anson, 1946–54*	
Chloe Crismani	*Cornwallis, 2005–12*	
Liam Crismani	*Anson, 2008–*	
Peter Crockett	*Anson, 2010–*	
James Croser	*Collingwood, 2011–*	
Claire Cuddihy	*Hood, 2008–*	
Jack Cuddihy	*Collingwood, 2010–*	
Sean Cuddihy	*Collingwood, 2008–*	
Alexander Wilson Cullen	*Anson, 2002–07*	
Cameron Cullen	*Anson, 2006–*	
Lindsay Freya Cullen	*Hood, 2003–10*	
Morton James Cullen	*Anson, 1998–05*	
Dominic Curtis	*Drake, 2012–*	
Joseph Curtis	*Anson, 2010–*	
Kenneth and Marie Curtis		
Patrick Curtis	*Drake, 2011–*	
Ruth Curtis	*Howe, 2010–*	
WE Curtis (Bill)	*Teaching Staff, 1953–82*	
Brian I Cutler	*Howe, 1964–68*	
Diana Cutler	*Blake, 2012–*	
Mel Cutler	*Howe, 1962–67*	
Jack Dakin	*Raleigh, 2009–*	
Joseph Dakin	*Anson, 2007–*	
Hannah Dale	*Raleigh, 2011–*	
Ann Daniel	*Staff, 2005–*	
Toby Daniel	*Hawke, 1979–87*	
George Darlington	*Raleigh, 2011–*	
Chloe Daulby	*Hood, 2012–*	
Elliott Davey	*Hawke, 2009–*	
Emily Davidson-Brett	*Hood, 2007–*	
Benjamin Davies	*Hawke, 2004–12*	
Bethan Davies	*Cornwallis, 2007–*	
Conor Davies	*Drake, 2012–*	
Roman Davymuka	*Nelson, 2011–*	
Alex J Dawson	*Hawke, 1995–2002*	
Hylton Dawson	*Anson, 1939–42*	
Amani Day	*Hood, 2012–*	
Barry David Day	*Howe, 1960–68*	
Keith Day	*Nelson, 1974–79*	
Bernard de Neumann	*Nelson, 1955–61*	
John de Neumann	*Nelson, 1957–65*	
Captain and Mrs Peter de Neumann GM		
Andrias De Nysschen	*Hawke, 2007–12*	
Cornelius De Nysschen	*Hawke, 2010–*	
Marco de Nysschen	*Drake, 2012–*	
David De Rosa	*Nelson, 1961–64*	
Edward Derrick	*Hawke, 2009–12*	
William Devenish	*Howe, 1944–47*	
Christopher R Dimmock	*Hood, 1973–76*	
Max Dixey	*Collingwood, 2009–*	
Benjamin Dixon	*Raleigh, 2012–*	
Isobel Dixon	*Howe, 2009–*	
Polly Dodds	*Howe, 2009–*	
William Dodds	*St Vincent, 2008–*	
Abigail Donald	*Howe, 2008–*	
Jamie Donald	*St Vincent, 2007–12*	
Siana Douglas-Hamilton	*Howe, 2011–*	
William Douglas-Hamilton	*St Vincent, 2012–*	
Errol Drummond	*Anson, 2007–12*	
Petrus Du Toit	*Drake, 2011–*	
Sam Durling	*St Vincent, 2008–*	
Isabella Durrant	*Blake, 2011–*	
Oliver Durrant	*Drake, 2011–*	
Alice Eaden	*Howe, 2004–11*	
Charles Eaden	*Collingwood, 2007–12*	
James Eaden	*Collingwood, 2009–*	
Toby Eaton	*Collingwood, 2009–*	
Nadine JF Edwards	*Cornwallis, 2006–*	
Shannon AF Edwards	*Cornwallis, 2002–09*	
Victoria Edwards	*Cornwallis, 2011–*	
William Eels	*St Vincent, 2008–12*	
Andrew Egan	*Hawke, 2009–*	
Robert John Elms	*St Vincent, 2010–*	
Stewart Anthony Elms	*Blake, 1959–62*	
Siiri Elsasser	*Howe, 2011–12*	
Jake Embleton	*Anson, 2011–*	
Liam Emerson	*Anson, 2006–*	
Samuel Eminson	*Hawke, 2008–12*	
Samuel Engelmann	*St Vincent, 2009–*	
Sebastian Engelmann	*St Vincent, 2005–10*	
Stephanie Engelmann	*Cornwallis, 2008–09*	
Marc Erneke	*St Vincent, 2011–*	
Alexey Esaulov	*Hawke, 2012–*	
Hannah Evans	*Howe, 2009–12*	
Rhys Evans	*Anson, 2007–12*	
Verity Evans	*Howe, 2009–*	
Matthew Everest	*Collingwood, 2009–*	
Charles Ewen	*Collingwood, 2011–*	
Jan-Frederik Ewers	*Anson, 2011–12*	
Josephine Falk	*Hood, 2010–*	
William Falk	*Collingwood, 2009–*	
Daniel Farmer	*Anson, 2012–*	
Graham Farrar	*Blake, 1949–54*	
Kieran Farrer	*Drake, 2011–*	
Russell Farrer	*Hawke, 2008–*	
Kay Farrow	*Staff, 2003–*	
Callum Farry	*Anson, 2009–*	
Hannah Farry	*Blake, 2011–*	
Henrik Fassmer	*St Vincent, 2011–12*	
Torge Fassmer	*St Vincent, 2012–*	
Riley Faulkner	*Raleigh, 2010–*	
Cavan Fawcett	*Drake, 2012–*	
Ian Fawcett	*St Vincent, 1968–72*	
Alexander Fellingham	*St Vincent, 2009–12*	
Helena Fellingham	*Raleigh, 2009–*	
Drew Felstead	*Raleigh, 2008–*	
Annie Fenton	*Howe, 2007–*	
Bradley Fenton	*St Vincent, 2005–12*	
Freddie Fergusson	*Collingwood, 2007–12*	
Ella Finch	*Blake, 2011–*	
Alexander Finding	*Hawke, 2010–*	
Daniel Finding	*Anson, 2008–*	
Keith Fletcher	*RHS Community*	
Drew Florence	*Raleigh, 2010–*	
Georgia Folkard-Smith	*Blake, 2011–*	
Holly Folkard-Smith	*Blake, 2012–*	
Jessie Fong	*Howe, 2011–*	
Bethany Ford	*Hood, 2008–12*	
India-Rose Ford	*Hood, 2005–12*	
Yasmin Ford	*Howe, 2004–11*	
Robin Fordham	*Hood, 1962–66*	
Alice Foreman	*Howe, 2006–*	
Daniel Foreman	*Hawke, 2010–*	
Victoria Foreman	*Howe, 2008–*	

Harry Fosker	*Drake, 2012–*	
Jamie Fosker	*Raleigh, 2010–*	
David Fowler	*Cornwallis, 1950–53*	
Joshua James Frame	*Drake, 2012–*	
Captain William Frampton	*Collingwood, 1957–62*	
James Francis	*Hawke, 2005–12*	
Charlotte Freeman	*Cornwallis, 2003–10*	
Hannah Freeman	*Cornwallis, 2007–*	
Molly Freeman	*Blake, 2011–*	
Sam Freeman	*St Vincent, 2002–09*	
Alexander Freeney	*Hawke, 2006–10*	
Mike Freeney	*Anson, 1971–74*	
Nigel Freeney	*Anson, 1973–78*	
Vanessa French	*Staff, 1986–*	
Ashley Fretwell	*Raleigh, 2010–*	
Emily Fretwell	*Blake, 2012–*	
Professor Chris Gaine	*Nelson, 1961–68*	
James Gallington	*Staff, 1990–*	
Hannah Galsworthy	*Howe, 2009–*	
Phil Gander	*St Vincent, 1960–67*	
Pelayo Martinez Garcia-Maurino	*St Vincent, 2010–*	
Hannah Garlick	*Howe, 2009–*	
Rachel Garlick	*Howe, 2008–*	
Oliver Gerard-Pearse	*Collingwood, 2006–*	
Rebecca Gerard-Pearse	*Cornwallis, 2001–08*	
Matthew Gibb	*Collingwood, 1999–2003*	
Philippa Gibb	*Howe, 1996–2004*	
Commander Roger Gibb RN (Retd)		
	Collingwood, 1966–73	
Bob Gibbs	*Nelson, 1960–67*	
John E Giblett RVM	*Hood, 1946–51*	
Chris Gilbert-Wood	*Drake, 1970–77*	
Jack Gilbey	*Hawke, 2011–*	
Ruth Gitsham	*Staff, 1985–*	
The Gladwell Family	*Drake, 1990–*	
Mr and Mrs M Godfrey	*Teaching Staff, 1996–*	
Taylor Godfrey	*Raleigh, 2010–*	
Claire Gold	*Blake, 1992–98*	
Ian Golding		
John Goldsmith	*Anson, 1947–51*	
Bob and Maggie Good	*Teaching Staff, 1977–2001*	
Tony Goodburn	*Cornwallis, 1942–45*	
James Gooderham	*Staff, 1989–*	
Emily Gouge	*Howe, 2005–12*	
Florence Gould	*Cornwallis, 2008–*	
Conrad Graham-Ambrossi	*Drake, 2011–*	
Sebastian Grandon-White	*Raleigh, 2012–*	
Alistair Green	*St Vincent, 2007–*	
Joshua Green	*St Vincent, 2002–07*	
Natasha Green	*Howe, 2004–11*	
Nicholas R Green	*Raleigh, 1988–93*	
Robert FD Green	*Collingwood, 1942–46*	
Sebastian Green	*St Vincent, 2003–10*	
Elizabeth Greer-Read	*Cornwallis, 2007–*	
Gordon Grimsted	*Raleigh, 1945–49*	
Frederic Grogono	*Hawke, 2010–*	
Oliver Grogono	*Hawke, 2010–*	
Nicholas Groves	*St Vincent, 2005–12*	
Nikola Grujic	*Anson, 2010–12*	
Sam Gubbey	*Collingwood, 2005–12*	
Kaan Guenal	*Anson, 2011–12*	

Raymond Ian Gunn	*Cornwallis, 1947–51*
Dan Guy	*Hawke, 2007–12*
Lauren Guy	*Howe, 2009–*
Benjamin Hackett	*Hawke, 2008–*
Bradley Hackett	*Collingwood, 2005–12*
Joshua Hackett	*Hawke, 2008–*
Florence Hales	*Hood, 2007–*
Xavier Hales	*St Vincent, 2010–*
Matthew Hall	*Howe, 1987–93*
Dominic Hallam	*Anson, 2011–*
Curtis Hambly	*Hawke, 2009–12*
Alex Hancock	*Hawke, 2008–*
Mick Hancock	*Collingwood, 1972–79*
Nicholas Guy Hancock	*Cornwallis, 1958–63*
Nina Handt	*Hood, 2011–12*
Felicity Hanshaw-Green	*Howe, 2010–12*
Charles Hardern	*Hawke, 2010–*
Adam Hare	*Collingwood, 2009–*
Dr MJ Harley	*Howe, 1951–56*
Georgie Harmer	*Hood, 2011–*
Kate Harmer	*Hood, 2009–11*
Tom Harmer	*Collingwood, 2012–*
Beth Harris	*Howe, 2007–12*
Ciara Harris	*Howe, 2007–12*
Eleanor Harris	*Howe, 2009–12*
Ben Harrison	*Hawke, 2009–*
Connor Harvey-Ward	*St Vincent, 2010–*
Emily Harwood	*Cornwallis, 2010–*
Thomas Harwood	*St Vincent, 2010–*
Emily Hassall	*Cornwallis, 2006–*
William Hassall	*Collingwood, 2008–*
Barry Hawes (Mini)	*Hood, 1951–56*
Brian Hawkins	*Teaching Staff, 1962–96*
Stephen Hayes	*Staff, 1986–*
Behn Hayhoe	*Drake, 2012–*
Jessica Hazelton	*Cornwallis, 2006–*
David Head	*Raleigh, 2010–*
Howard Head	*Raleigh, 2010–*
Charlotte Heley	*Hood, 2010–*
Tom Heley	*St Vincent, 2010–*
Philip Henderson	*Hood, 1959–63*
Elle Henley	*Hood, 2007–*
Saffron Henley	*Blake, 2011–*
Callum Hensby	*Drake, 2011–*
Barry Herbert	*Collingwood, 1962–65*
Caitlin Herbert	*Cornwallis, 2001–09*
Catriona Herbert	*Teaching Staff, 1989–*
Chris Herbert	*Teaching Staff, 1989–*
Laura Herbert	*Cornwallis, 2003–11*
Owen Herbert	*Collingwood, 2005–11*
Hannah Hesling	*Howe, 2006–*
Anna Hewitt	*Hood, 2009–11*
Olivia Hewitt	*Hood, 2009–12*
Lewis Hickson	*St Vincent, 2011–12*
David Hide	*Raleigh, 1955–60*
Dr John Higgs	*Hood, 1973–78*
The Hill Family	*Nelson, 2010–12*
Michael John Hill	*Hawke, 1958–63*
Harry Hindley	*Drake, 2012–*
Sam Hindley	*St Vincent, 2010–*
Adonia Hirst	*Howe, 2008–*

Charles Hirst	*Hawke, 2007–12*
Callum Hobbs	*Raleigh, 2010–*
Barry Hocking	*Teaching Staff, 1998–*
George Hockley	*Hawke, 2007–12*
Maximilian Hoertnagl	*Anson, 2011–*
Stephen Hogden	*Cornwallis, 1961–65*
Shannon Holdway	*Hood, 2010–*
Barny Horsfield	*Raleigh, 2010–*
Arthur Howard	*St Vincent, 2005–12*
Malcolm Howard	*St Vincent, 2009–*
Kai Howells	*Drake, 2011–*
Tamsyn Howells	*Hood, 2008–*
Ian Howes	*St Vincent, 1963–69*
Leslie Howes	*St Vincent, 1959–64*
Robert Hoyland MBE	*Drake, 1965–69*
Jamie Hudson	*Hawke, 2005–11*
Adam Hunkin	*Collingwood, 2008–*
Charlotte Hunkin	*Hood, 2008–*
John Hunter	*Hood, 1974–81*
Hannah Ilori	*Hood, 2006–*
Ann January	*Staff, 2008–*
Harrison Jeffries	*Collingwood, 2010–12*
Callum Jenkins	*Collingwood, 2009–*
Charlie Jenkins	*Drake, 2012–*
Sophie Jenkins	*Cornwallis, 2011–*
William Jenner	*Drake, 2011–*
Zhesu Crystal Jin	*Howe, 2011–*
AD Johnson	*St Vincent, 1980–86*
Lauren Johnson	*Cornwallis, 2009–*
Luis Johnson	*Raleigh, 2011–*
Mark Johnson	*Drake, 2011–*
Bryony Jones	*Cornwallis, 2010–12*
Daniel Jones	*St Vincent, 2007–*
Edward Jones	*Collingwood, 2011–*
Harry Jones	*Drake, 2011–*
Lauren Jones	*Howe, 2006–*
Luke AL Jones	*Collingwood, 2005–12*
Matthew O Jones	*Drake, 2003–08*
Natasha Jones	*Cornwallis, 2009–*
Olivia Jones	*Hood, 2012–*
Paul Jones	*Collingwood, 1980–87*
Roger Jones	*Bandmaster, 1991–*
Tori Jones	*Cornwallis, 2009–*
William JS Jones	*Raleigh, 2003–10*
Cameron Jordan	*Drake, 2012–*

Charlotte Jordan	*Blake, 2011–*
Malte Junge	*Collingwood, 2011–12*
Manish Kala	*Anson, 2009–*
Lucinda Kay	*Howe, 2006–*
Peter J Kay	*Hawke, 1947–51*
The Kelland Family	*St Vincent, 2009–*
Francesca Kelley	*Blake, 2011–*
Lauren Kelly	*Hood, 2011–*
Steven Kemp	*Cornwallis, 1968–75*
Elfreda Kenneison	*Raleigh, 2010–*
Cameron Kerr	*Collingwood, 2009–*
Charles Kerr	*Collingwood, 2012–*
Imogen Kerr	*Blake, 2012–*
James Kerr	*Collingwood, 2007–12*
The Kester Family	*Hood/Anson, 2001–11*
Matthew Khan	*Anson, 2010–*
Max Khan	*Anson, 2007–*
Hong Jordan Ki	*St Vincent, 2008–12*
Theodore Kilham	*Raleigh, 2009–*
Yeung Jae Arnold Kim	*Anson, 2009–*
Yeung Ung Lucas Kim	*Anson, 2010–*
Michael Kirk	*Former Headmaster, 1983–95*
Bernard A Knight	*Cornwallis, 1940–44*
Annabel Knott	*Raleigh, 2011–*
Ken Kocking	*Howe, 1949–55*
Sara Kortenray	Greenwich Hospital
Andrew Kwok	*Collingwood, 2009–*
Alice Lambert	*Hood, 2001–08*
Charles Lambert	*Collingwood, 2003–10*
Claire Lambert	*Hood, 2006–*
Charles Lambourn	*St Vincent, 2008–12*
Jessica Langford	*Cornwallis, 2007–12*
Megan Langford	*Cornwallis, 2007–*
Ron Lansley	*Hawke, 1956–61*
PW Last	*Staff, 2001–*
Sarah Laurie	*Hood, 2006–*
Hao Yuan Brian Law	*Anson, 2007–12*
The Lawrence Family	
George Richard Lawson	*Nelson, 1965–70*
Adrian Layton	*Hawke, 1957–62*
Samuel Le Roy	*Raleigh, 2010–*
Jim Leadbetter	*Hood, 1947–53*

Dmitry Lebedev	*St Vincent, 2011–*
Oscar Lee	*Hawke, 2010–*
Peter HF Lee (Boris)	*Hawke, 1947–51*
Keir Leeson	*Raleigh, 2011–*
Jack Leggett	*St Vincent, 2009–*
Oliver Leggett	*Drake, 2011–*
Cheng San Lei	*Hood, 2012–*
Cheng Wai Winnie Lei	*Howe, 2011–*
Saul Creasey-Levine	*Collingwood, 2007–12*
Wai To Allen Lin	*St Vincent, 2011–*
Commander Peter Lindstead-Smith OBE RN	
	Greenwich Hospital
Chun Wing Lo	*Anson, 2012–*
Lok Him Lo	*Hawke, 2007–*
James Lockwood	*Headmaster, 2012–*
Oliver Lockwood	*Raleigh, 2010–12*
Ned Long	*Teaching Staff, 1957–96*
Jim Loveday	*Cornwallis, 1959–64*
Oliver Lovejoy	*Raleigh, 2009–*
Andrew Loveland	*Teaching Staff, 1984–*
Edward Lowther	*St Vincent, 2009–*
Sebastian Lucas	*St Vincent, 2009–*
Constantin Mackel	*Anson, 2012–*
Lt Cdr Howard MacKenzie-Wilson RNR (Retd)	
	Anson, 1954–60
Yin Mak	*Cornwallis, 2009–*
Ruth Mallett	*Hood, 2008–*
Baillie Malyon	*Drake, 2011–*
Charlie Mann	*RHS Community*
Nicola Mann	*Teaching Staff, 1998–*
Oliver Mann	*RHS Community*
Rob Mann	*Teaching Staff, 2000–*
William Mann	*RHS Community*
Alexander Mannion	*Hawke, 2007–12*
Sarah Mannion	*Hood, 2010–12*
David Marsh	*Hood, 1968–75*
Calder Trewin Marshall	*St Vincent, 2007–*
Jessica Marshall	*Howe, 2011–*
Rosslyn Trewin Marshall	*Howe, 2011–*
Elsie Mason	*Hood, 2011–*
Leslie Mason	*St Vincent, 2010–*
Sebastien Charles Piers Mathewson	*Collingwood, 2007–*
Achala Matthews	*Cornwallis, 2011–*
Andy Matthews	*Blake, 1963–70*
Annaleise Matthews	*Howe, 2005–12*
Edward Matthews	*Drake, 2011–*
Michael J Matthews	*Cornwallis, 1946–50*
William Matthews	*Collingwood, 2009–*
Bertram Maunder	*Drake, 2011–*
Phoebe Maunder	*Raleigh, 2009–*
Charles Mayes	*Holbrook Music Society*
Elaine McConnell	*Teaching Staff, 2012–*
Revd Philip McConnell	*Chaplain, 2010–*
Ross McConnell	*Collingwood, 2010–*
Adam McGlynn	*Collingwood, 2005–12*
Peter McKenzie	*Hawke, 1958–66*
Brian McMunn	*Howe, 1983–90*
Thomas McNally	*Drake, 2011–*
Colin J McPhee	*Hood, 1973–80*
Barbara J McRink	
Daniel J McRink	*Raleigh, 2001–08*

Joshua Mellors	*Hawke, 2009–*
Nathan Mellors	*Drake, 2011–*
David Merrey	*St Vincent, 1955–58*
Andrew Miles	*St Vincent, 2007–12*
Charlie Miles	*Drake, 2011–*
Rachael Miles	*Cornwallis, 2010–*
Andy Miller	*Blake, 1971–76*
Thomas Miller	*Raleigh, 2008–*
Patricia Milnes	*Holbrook Music Society*
William Milsom	*Raleigh, 2010–*
Carla Mini	*Blake, 2012–*
Andrew Mitchell	*Anson, 2006–*
Charlotte Monk-Chipman	*Blake, 2003–09*
Simon Monk-Chipman	*Collingwood, 2005–12*
Stephen Monk-Chipman	*Collingwood, 2003–07*
Connor Moonan	*Collingwood, 2006–*
Hope Moonan	*Howe, 2010–*
Benjamin Moore	*Collingwood, 2006–*
Georgia Moore	*Hood, 2008–*
Oliver Moore	*Drake, 2011–*
Ophelia Moore	*Hood, 2008–*
Francesca Morelli	*Howe, 2010–*
Jack Morelli	*Hawke, 2009–*
Colin and Barbara Morgan	*Teaching Staff, 1973–*
RS Morgan	*Howe, 1944–48*
Robert Moritz	*Raleigh, 2007–12*
Zofia Moritz	*Hood, 2012–*
Desmond Morris	*Staff, 1958–91*
Keith Morris	*Hawke, 1964–71*
Benjamin Morrison	*Anson, 2006–*
John Morrow	*Collingwood, 1962–69*
Peter Morrow	*Collingwood, 1962–69*
Graham Moxey	*Howe, 1967–74*
Kate Moxey	*Cornwallis, 1998–2005*
Michael Moxey	*Howe, 1964–71*
Patricia Moxey	*Cornwallis, 1996–2001*
Peter Moxey	*Raleigh, 1995–2000*
Annabel Murrison	*Blake, 2004–11*
Arabella Murrison	*Hood, 2008–*
Harriet Murrison	*Blake, 2006–*
Henrietta Murrison	*Blake, 2011–*
Katherine Murrison	*Blake, 2003–10*
Philippa Murrison	*Hood, 2009–*
Robert Murrison	*Howe, 1971–78*
Sarah Murrison	*Hood, 2009–*
Sophia Murrison	*Cornwallis, 2008–*
Simon Murton	*Cornwallis, 1967–73*
Johannes Musger	*Anson, 2011–12*
Peter William Eric Musselwhite	*Drake, 1947–51*
Chris Myatt	*Collingwood, 2004–11*
Huw Myatt	*Collingwood, 2001–08*
Jennifer Myatt	*Hood, 2006–*
Phillip Mytom-Hart	*Hawke, 1963–68*
Richard Napier	*Hawke, 1963–71*
Kevin Neave	*Hawke, 1977–82*
Robin Neave	*Hawke, 1949–52*
Pedro (Alex) Nelson	*Collingwood, 2006–09*
Serena Nelson	*Hood, 2011–*
Douglas Neville	*Anson, 2005–12*
Eleanor Neville	*Howe, 2000–07*
James Neville	*Anson, 2002–09*

Robert Neville	*Anson, 1959–64*	George Petrides	*St Vincent, 2007–*	Sally Rodway	*RHS Community*
Michael Newland	*Howe, 1954–59*	Henry Petrides	*Drake, 2002–09*	Daryl Roper	*Drake, 1998–2004*
Hin Lam Allan Ng	*Anson, 2008–12*	Graham Phillips	*Drake, 1956–60*	Francois Rossouw	*Hawke, 2010–*
Chi Nguyen	*Hood, 2006–12*	Leonor Pineira	*Hood, 2011–12*	Simone Rossouw	*Hawke, 2009–*
Georgina Nicholls	*Blake, 2012–*	Daniel Pittock	*Drake, 2012–*	Nicola Rouse	*Teaching Staff, 2010–*
Henry Nicholls	*St Vincent, 2010–*	Linda Pollard	*Staff, 1996–12*	Oscar Rowe	*Collingwood, 2009–*
Joel Nixson-Evans	*St Vincent, 2008–*	Rebecca Pollitt	*Hood, 2008–*	Oliver Royle	*Drake, 2012–*
Simon (Bod) John Norris	*Collingwood, 1976–81*	Benjamin Pooley	*Collingwood, 2011–*	Ivan William Rudrum	*Anson, 1947–51*
Isabelle North	*Hood, 2011–*	Lucy Pooley	*Hood, 2007–12*	Michael Vivian Arthur Rudrum	*Anson, 1947–50*
Dominic Nute	*Cornwallis, 1970–77*	Richard Pooley	*Collingwood, 2005–12*	Abigail Ruffles	*Howe, 2004–07*
Steve O'Connell	*St Vincent, 1970–74*	Harriet Pope	*Hood, 2006–*	Toby Ruffles	*Drake, 2012–*
Michael O'Neill	*Cornwallis, 1947–50*	Rupert Powell	*Hawke, 2006–*	Ellie Rump	*Blake, 1998–2005*
Summer Oliver	*Cornwallis, 2006–*	Tristan Powell	*Collingwood, 2009–*	Sam Rump	*Hawke, 2004–11*
Toby Oliver	*Collingwood, 2010–*	Rodney Pratt	*Blake, 1960–68*	Tom Rump	*Hawke, 2000–07*
Alexander Olkhovskiy	*St Vincent, 2010–*	Thomas Precious	*Collingwood, 2006–*	Laurence Russell	*St Vincent, 2005–12*
Friedrich Opatz	*Hawke, 2011–12*	David Presley	*Hawke, 1961–65*	William Russell	*St Vincent, 2007–12*
Jack Orr	*Hawke, 2009–*	Benjamin Price	*Hawke, 2010–*	Ben Rutledge	*Collingwood, 2009–11*
Max Orr	*Drake, 2012–*	Christian Proctor	*Collingwood, 2005–12*	James Rutledge	*Collingwood, 2009–*
Millicent Orr	*Howe, 2010–*	Abigail Provan	*Blake, 2011–*	Nastasya Ryapisova	*Howe, 2011–*
Ben Osbourne	*St Vincent, 2007–*	Charlie Provan	*Hawke, 2009–*	Shila Sadeghi Kaji	*Hood, 2011–*
Bogdan Padalko	*Anson, 2011–*	Zachary Puckey	*Drake, 2011–*	Hugo Sadler	*Raleigh, 2010–*
The Paddon Family	*2011–*	Si Man Natalie Pun	*Hood, 2011–*	Emilia Salter	*Blake, 2012–*
Tabitha Palmer	*Howe, 2008–*	Geoff Quade	*Cornwallis, 1967–71*	Harry Salter	*Raleigh, 2009–*
Mike Pamment	*Hood, 1985–90*	Piers Quinn	*Collingwood, 2010–*	Elena Sanchis Andres	*Blake, 2011–12*
Simon Pape	*Hawke, 2006–*	Thomas Ralph	*Drake, 2012–*	Rocio Sanchis Andres	*Howe, 2010–*
Hannah Parker	*Hood, 2009–12*	Arush Rana	*Anson, 2009–*	Peter Sargeant	*St Vincent, 1942–44*
James Parker	*Collingwood, 2008–*	Sangya Rana	*Cornwallis, 2011–*	Oliver Saunders	*Hawke, 2007–12*
Matthew Parker	*Raleigh, 2008–*	Andrew Ranson	*Nelson, 1962–67*	Tabitha Saunders	*Blake, 2011–*
Peter Arnold Parker	*Collingwood, 1956–60*	Garry Ravenhall	*Teaching Staff, 1994–*	Thomas Saunders	*Drake, 2011–*
Robert Parkin	*St Vincent, 1969–76*	Alex Rayment	*St Vincent, 2009–*	William Saunders	*Raleigh, 2012–*
Simon Parkin	*Blake, 1987–92*	Elliot Rayment	*Drake, 2011–*	Charles Robert William Savage	*Blake, 1952–58*
William Parmenter-Stratta	*St Vincent, 2012–*	Robert Read	*Collingwood, 1986–92*	Matthew Saxby	*St Vincent, 2010–*
Eleanor Partington	*Hood, 2008–11*	Simon Read	*Collingwood, 1987–94*	Bob Scantlebury	*Raleigh, 1945–48*
Jatin Patel	*Anson, 2008–12*	Tim Redmond	*Drake, 1964–72*	Jordan Scott	*Howe, 2011–*
Nandish Patel	*Hawke, 2007–12*	Joseph Reid MBE RD	*Hood, 1946–48*	Natasha Scott	*Howe, 2011–*
Daniel Patten	*Drake, 2011–*	George Rennison	*Raleigh, 2008–*	Toby Seabright	*Collingwood, 2005–12*
Conrad Pattenden	*Anson, 2005–12*	Jack Rennison	*Collingwood, 2006–*	Philip Self	*Staff, 1979–*
John Pattenden	*Hawke, 2008–*	Sophie Rennison	*Raleigh, 2010–*	Harvey Sellers	*Collingwood, 2009–*
Christopher Pattinson	*Collingwood, 1953–57*	Olivia Renny	*Raleigh, 2010–*	Oliver Sellers	*Collingwood, 2008–*
Kenneth Pattinson	*Collingwood, 1955–59*	Henry Restell	*Collingwood, 1994–2004*	Rory Sellers	*Collingwood, 2010–*
Jeremy Paul	*Collingwood, 2003–06*	Thomas Restell	*RHS Community*	Peter Sewell	*Howe, 1979–86*
Nathanael Paul	*Collingwood, 2003–08*	Cillian Rew	*Drake, 2012–*	Beth Sharpe	*Cornwallis, 2011–*
Cassia Peacock	*Howe, 2012–*	David Keith Richards	*Drake, 1965–71*	Harrison Sharpe	*Blake, 2003–07*
Elspeth Peacock	*Howe, 2008–12*	Beth Richardson	*Howe, 2009–*	Charlotte Shelley	*Howe, 2008–*
Flora Peacock	*Howe, 2009–*	Jessica Richardson	*Howe, 2008–*	David Sheppard	*Drake, 1945–50*
Olivia Peacock	*Raleigh, 2008–*	Freya Richmond	*Howe, 2007–12*	Cheuk Wing Victor Shing	*St Vincent, 2010–*
Keith Pearce	*Howe, 1952–56*	Jack Rickards	*Raleigh, 2010–*	Molly Shoesmith	*Cornwallis, 2008–*
Ryan Pedley	*St Vincent, 2006–11*	Jade Ridge	*Howe, 2012–*	Brittany Shrestha	*Raleigh, 2010–*
Sebastian Pedley	*St Vincent, 2005–12*	Elizabeth Rigby	*Cornwallis, 2011–*	Michael B Silcox	*1947–64*
The Pembroke Family	*Drake, 2012–*	Allan Ritchie	*Raleigh, 1984–89*	Michael Simmonds	*RHS Community*
Mr and Mrs Jeremy Pembroke		Jemima Roberts	*Raleigh, 2010–*	Yevheniya Jane Siryk	*Hood, 2010–*
James Pendle	*Raleigh, 2008–*	N Roberts	*Drake, 1954–58*	Barrie Slade	*Hawke, 1945–49*
Richard Andrew Pennifold	*St Vincent, 1977–82*	Peter Roberts	*RHS Community*	Alexander Slatter	*Hawke, 2009–*
Carolin Peper	*Cornwallis, 2010–12*	Craig Alexander Robertson	*Nelson, 1976–80*	Felicity Slatter	*Howe, 2009–*
Elizabeth Perrott-Griffiths	*Cornwallis, 2010–*	Michael Robertson	*Staff, 2010–*	Hannah Small	*Howe, 2010–12*
Adam Peters	*Drake, 2002–07*	Nicholas John Robertson	*Nelson, 1971–77*	Daniel Smith	*St Vincent, 2011–*
Thomas Peters	*St Vincent, 2006–12*	Sean Naughton Robertson	*Nelson, 1975–80*	Jack Smith	*Anson, 2009–*
Alexander Jorge Peterson	*Anson, 2010–*	Esmé Robson	*Blake, 2012–*	Kimberley Smith	*Howe, 2006–*
Imogen Frances Peterson	*Blake, 2012–*	Sacha Robson	*Hood, 2011–*	Stephen G Smith	*Hood, 1952–57*
Anna Petrides	*Cornwallis, 2004–11*	Ian Rockett	*Hawke, 1968–74*	Allan Solley	*Hawke, 1972–78*
Eleanor Petrides	*Cornwallis, 2002–07*	Jeremy Rockett	*Hawke, 1977–84*	Hannah Southerton	*Howe, 2010–*

Nathan Southerton — *Collingwood, 2009–*
Olufusibi Sowemimo — *Anson, 2008–*
Trev Spencer — *Howe, 1940–43*
Ruby Spendlove — *Cornwallis, 2009–*
William Spurr — *Collingwood, 2009–12*
James Stacey — *Raleigh, 2010–*
Simon Stanford — *Anson, 1969–74*
Sebastian Starling — *Collingwood, 2007–*
Alexander Steeds — *Hawke, 2008–*
Conor Steeds — *Hawke, 2007–*
Amber Stephenson — *Hood, 2008–*
Lauren Stephenson — *Blake, 2011–*
Charlie Steptoe — *Collingwood, 2009–*
Oliver Steptoe — *Collingwood, 2007–*
Bethany Stimpson — *Cornwallis, 2010–*
Caitlin Stimpson — *Blake, 2011–*
Catriona Stirton Smith — *Howe, 1993–98*
Paul Stoddart — *Raleigh, 2008–*
Alistair Stokes — *St Vincent, 2004–11*
Michael Stokes — *St Vincent, 2006–*
Elizabeth Street — *Blake, 2011–*
Robert Street — *Raleigh, 2009–*
Emma Stuart-Thompson — *Drake, 2011–*
Bonnie Stuart — *Howe, 2002–09*
Charlie Stuart — *Collingwood, 2005–12*
Freddie Stuart — *Collingwood, 2002–09*
Molly Stuart — *Howe, 2011–*
Koseli Sunuwar — *Howe, 2009–*
Tapashya Sunuwar — *Howe, 2009–*
Arieanto P Sutrisno — *Anson, 2002–04*
Angus Suttle — *Raleigh, 2008–*
Abigail Sweeney — *Howe, 2007–*
Annabelle Sweeney — *Howe, 2009–*
Emily Sweeney — *Howe, 2006–*
Albert Symons — *Raleigh, 2008–*
Auriol Symons — *Blake, 2011–*
Matilda Tabor — *Blake, 2011–*
Zachary Tabor — *Collingwood, 2010–*
Bradley Tai — *Raleigh, 2012–*
Brendan Tait — *St Vincent, 2011–*
Charlene Tait — *Howe, 2012–*
Cameron Talbott — *Anson, 2005–12*
Rory Talbott — *St Vincent, 2007–*
Lok Man Thomas Tam — *Anson, 2010–*
Lok Yung Tam — *Cornwallis, 2012–*
Joey Tang — *Hawke, 2009–*
Ro Kevueli Tavainavesi — *Drake, 2011–*
Ro Mereani Tavainavesi — *Blake, 2012–*
Austin G Taylor (Aggie) — *Raleigh, 1960–67*
Katherine Taylor — *Hood, 2007–*
Scott Taylor — *Drake, 2011–*
Charlie Tedora — *Collingwood, 2009–*
John (JT) Temple — *Anson, 1976–83*
Jonathan Terry — *Hawke, 2006–*
William Terry — *Hawke, 2007–*
Anish Thapa — *Anson, 2011–*
Julia Theilmann — *Cornwallis, 2011–12*
Zoe Thesigner — *Blake, 2001–06*
Nutchanon Thipvilai — *Hawke, 2011–*
Neil Thomas — *St Vincent, 1989–94*
Paul Thomas — *Hawke, 1981–88*

Les Thompson — *Teaching Staff, 1977–*
Jorgyella Thorpe — *Blake, 2011–*
Lyam Thorpe — *Anson, 2011–*
Colin J Tibble — *Hood, 1965–70*
Katherine Tilney-Bassett — *Hood, 2009–*
William Timmis — *St Vincent, 2011–*
Anna Tindale — *Cornwallis, 2010–*
Grace Tindale — *Cornwallis, 2010–*
Georgia Tindale — *Cornwallis, 2008–*
Maria Tkachenko — *Cornwallis, 2012–*
Ilya Tkhoruk — *Anson, 2011–*
Amelia Todd — *Blake, 2011–*
Carys Todd — *Cornwallis, 2006–*
Imogen Todd — *Hood, 2009–*
Kate Todd — *Blake, 1999–2006*
Mattea Todd — *Howe, 2005–12*
Nicholas Todd — *Drake, 1973–79*
Oliver Todd — *Collingwood, 2007–12*
Rupert Todd
Samuel Todd — *Drake, 1997–2004*
Peter Tomkins — *St Vincent, 1984–92*
Dominic Torrington — *St Vincent, 2010–*
Martha Torrington — *Hood, 2012–*
Aana Tortajada — *Cornwallis, 2012–*
David Traynor — *Blake, 1965–72*
John Traynor — *Blake, 1962–66*
Peter Traynor — *Blake, 1969–74*
Stephen Traynor — *Blake, 1968–75*
Chloe Tribe — *Raleigh, 2008–*
Fergus Tribe — *Raleigh, 2010–*
Anna Tyurina — *Howe, 2011–12*
Richard Vallance — *Hawke, 2010–*
Peter van Os — *Hawke, 2011–*
Olivia Vanner Thompson — *Blake, 2012–*
Nicholas Vanner — *Collingwood, 1980–86*
Charles Venables — *Collingwood, 2007–*
George Venables — *Collingwood, 2008–*
Pietro Vendittelli — *Drake, 2011–*
Alice Vickers — *Hood, 2009–*
Patrick Vickers — *Drake, 2012–*
Jacob Vincent-Wright — *Raleigh, 2010–*
Derek 'Dibble' Vingoe — *Teaching Staff, 1962–95*
Flora Vivian — *Howe, 2009–*
Jessie Vogel — *Hawke, 2009–*
Jessica Walker — *Howe, 2012–*
Stephanie Walker — *Howe, 2010–12*
William A Walkington — *Drake, 2012–*
Allan Ward — *Howe, 1961–67*
Adam Warren — *Drake, 2012–*
Jamie Warren — *Hawke, 2009–*
Ron Wash — *Drake, 1935–39*
Daniel Waterman — *Drake, 2011–*
Richard Waters — *Raleigh, 1945–50*
Elizabeth Watson — *Cornwallis, 2009–*
Jessica Watson — *Cornwallis, 2009–*
Lucy Watson — *Hood, 2010–*
Paige Watson — *Cornwallis, 2010–*
Sally Watson — *Hood, 2010–*
Claire Diana Waugh — *Cornwallis, 1993–99*
Jack Weaver — *Anson, 2009–12*
George Wedd — *Hawke, 2009–11*

Amelie Weinstock — *Cornwallis, 2010–12*
Christine Welham — *Staff, 1972–2008*
James Andrew Wheatland — *Hawke, 1996–2003*
Bethany White — *Howe, 2011–*
Harry White — *Hawke, 2009–12*
Suzanne Whiting — *Staff, 1985–*
Graham Wicks — *Howe, 1953–57*
Jeanne Wilby — *Teaching Staff, 1997–*
Rory Wild — *Anson, 2008–*
Eunice Anne Williams
Isabelle Williams — *Hood, 2009–*
Jamal Williams — *Anson, 2010–*
Jonathan Williams — *Raleigh, 1965–71*
Joseph Williams — *St Vincent, 2010–12*
Oliver Williams — *Raleigh, 2010–*
Paul Williams — *Raleigh, 1975–80*
Victoria Williams — *Blake, 2012–*
Benjamin Willis — *Drake, 2011–*
Terry Willis — *Blake, 1953–57*
Giles Wilson — *Drake, 2011–*
Kin Tai Ken Wong — *Collingwood, 2011–*
Kwun Kit Jason Wong — *Anson, 2008–12*
Tsun Yin Eason Wong — *Anson, 2008–*
Wai To Jacky Wong — *Anson, 2010–12*
Alan Wood — *Blake, 1961–69*
Nicholas Wood — *Howe, 1987–94*
Ned Woodcraft — *St Vincent, 2010–12*
Paddy Woodcraft — *St Vincent, 2010–*
Christopher Worcester — *Collingwood, 1965–69*
Paul Worcester — *Collingwood, 1961–65*
Jeven Wright — *St Vincent, 2007–*
Charles Wuidart Gray — *Collingwood, 2008–*
Andrew Wynn — *Teaching Staff, 2007–*
Anna Wynn — *Cornwallis, 2007–*
James Yarde — *St Vincent, 2005–12*
Kwan-Ching Robin Yeung — *Collingwood, 2008–*
TE Youldon
Andrew Young — *Drake, 1967–72*
Wei Yu — *Nelson, 2011–*
Ho Tin Peter Yuen — *St Vincent, 2010–*
Olga Zadvorna — *Cornwallis, 2010–12*
Anatolii Zadvornyi — *Hawke, 2010–12*

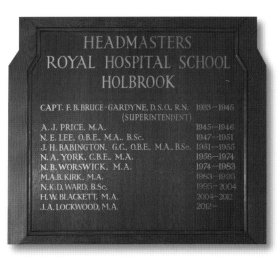

HEADMASTERS
ROYAL HOSPITAL SCHOOL
HOLBROOK

CAPT. F. B. BRUCE-GARDYNE, D.S.O. R.N. 1933–1945
(SUPERINTENDENT)
A. J. PRICE. M.A. 1945–1946
N. E. LEE, O.B.E., M.A., B.Sc. 1947–1951
J. H. BABINGTON, G.C., O.B.E., M.A., B.Sc. 1951–1955
N. A. YORK, C.B.E., M.A. 1956–1974
N. B. WORSWICK, M.A. 1974–1983
M. A. B. KIRK, M.A. 1983–1995
N. K. D. WARD, B.Sc. 1995–2004
H. W. BLACKETT, M.A. 2004–2012
J. A. LOCKWOOD, M.A. 2012–

Index

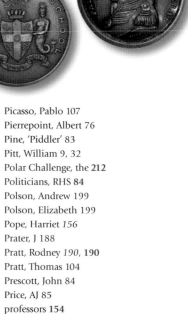

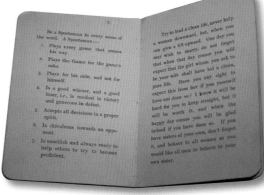

Acknowledgements, Bibliography and Picture Credits

Acknowledgements

The authors and the School would like to thank everyone associated with this publication. There have been many contributors who have helped bring this book to the Royal Hospital School readership and wider public. Of course the former Headmaster, Howard Blackett, should be thanked for initiating this process and the current Headmaster, James Lockwood, for continuing support. Particular acknowledgement should go to all those who so generously agreed to have their oral histories recorded (over 50) and also to the many individuals who provided photographs, ephemera, artefacts, stories and reminiscences for this book. We are so pleased to have these memories preserved for posterity and we hope this process will continue.

Our parent charity, Greenwich Hospital, should also be thanked for their support and in particular John Gamp, Sara Kortenray and Peter Linstead Smith who all helped check the document. Similarly the National Maritime Museum provided valuable support and we thank Geraldine Charles and in particular Pieter van der Merwe for his tremendous efforts with proofing and sense checking. This process was further enhanced by the efforts of Sophie Braybrooke and Matthew Christmas who again thoroughly reviewed the document. A big thank you to Lucy Pembroke for administering the advanced sales that helped fund this publication and for ensuring all subscribers' names were included in the book. It is still possible that an occasional mistake may have been made and we would like to apologise for any errors in dates or name spellings or indeed factual error. A huge special thanks should go to Dan Turner, Philip Newell and Paul Waldie for their books which have been invaluable sources of information and also to the RHSA, who over the years have helped establish a detailed record of events, memories, reminiscences and stories relating to the School and its history.

Finally and importantly our grateful thanks go to the publisher Third Millennium Information; to all their staff for their professional guidance, hard work and encouragement and in particular Joel Burden for overseeing the project, Michael Jackson (marketing materials), Sarah Yeatman (subscribers list), Bonnie Murray (production) and Neil Burkey for his efforts with picture research. Particular mention should be made of the contribution of Matthew Wilson; for his great patience and unstinting commitment throughout the design phase and beyond.

Bibliography

- Desmond, Morris, *The Royal Hospital School Holbrook 1933–1993*, United Kingdom
- Kaye Wilson, Mrs A, *The Life of Gifford Sherman Reade*
- Lloyd, Prof. Christopher, *A History of the Royal Hospital School*, 1962
- Merwe, Pieter van der, *A Refuge for All: A short History of the Greenwich Hospital*, Greenwich Hospital (2010, originally 1994)
- Newell, Philip, *Greenwich Hospital: A Royal Foundation 1692–1983*, United Kingdom
- Turner, HDT, *The Cradle of the Navy: The Story of the Royal Hospital School at Greenwich and at Holbrook, 1694–1988*, William Sessions Limited of York, United Kingdom, 1990
- Turner HDT, *The Royal Hospital School, Greenwich*, Phillimore & Co Ltd, London and Chichester, United Kingdom, 1980
- Waldie, Paul, *Ghosts and Kippers: Schoolboy Memories, from the Royal Hospital School, Greenwich*, United Kingdom
- *The Royal Hospital School: Built for The Lords Commissioners of the Admiralty*, J Gerrad & Sons, 1933
- *Souvenir Album of the Royal Hospital School*, Greenwich, Gale and Polden, c1909
- *The School Log Book*, 1st April 1905 to 13th July 1981
- *The Royal Hospital School Magazine*, 1907 to present (plus other marketing publications)
- *The RHSA Gazette*, other RHSA publications and associated resources (all since formation in 1925)

Picture Credits

T = Timeline (dates) p = Page no (p or pp) a = all t = top b = bottom c = centre l = left r = right i = inset m = main x = except

Most of the pictures and images came from the Royal Hospital School archive which contains a wealth of materials sent in to the School over the years. In particular thanks should go to all the editors of and contributors to the School magazine since 1907. We have used these resources to borrow anecdotes, images and sections of text and we thank all those who may have helped develop this resource. The National Maritime Museum has provided a tremendous bank of images relating to the School and we thank their picture library staff, Doug McCarthy and Julie Cochrane for their assistance. Many photographs have been supplied by staff (eg David Goodwin) and former pupils (eg George Franks) – thank you one and all. The main contemporary photographic content was supplied by Julian Andrews and we extend our thanks to him for his professional approach, long hours and splendid images.

The School and publishers would also like to thank the following people and organisations for allowing us to reproduce images:
Alexander Turnbull Library: p56; **Amberley Publishing:** p78b; **Bob Anderson Family:** p182; **Charlotte Anderson:** p99b; **Julian Andrews:** c Front, p4 (x2), Rear (x4), p8T (1694, 1715), p13T (1958t), p14T (1971), p15T (1998), pp66–7, p71a, p77both, p88l, p97t, p109, p110t+b, pp112–3, p116t, p118, p125a, p126t+b, p128l, p130, p131b both, pp136–7, p149, p153t, p155c, p156b, p157t, p157b, pp158–9a, pp160–1a, p163b, p164, p165r, pp167–8+i, p168tr+cl, p17r, p174t, p178, p179br, p180t, p183b, p184t+c, p185t+br, pp192–3, p193bl, pp194–5, p195bl, p196m, p197br, pp200–1, p202cl, pp202–3, p203, p204t+cl, p210, p213b; **Alex Baker:** p172tr; **BBC** *Antiques Roadshow:* p141r; **Bentley Photographic:** helping with c p61b, p139b; **Boston University Photography:** p190tl; **Sophie Braybrooke:** p213t; **Bridgeman Library:** p40; **British Library:** p36; **Trevor Brown:** p72, p156t; **Courtesy Dave Cash:** p172l; **Matthew Christmas:** p204b; **Courtesy of Churchill College, Cambridge:** p58t; **Colorsport/Stewart Fraser:** p188b; **Bernard de Neumann Collection** (former pupil): c front boards, p19, p45 medal, pp52–3b, p59t, p154b; **Courtesy Rory Dobner:** p177l; **The Drapers' Company:** p51t; **EADT:** c p14T (1994i), p15 (2005t), p38b, p94t; **Russell Edwards:** p123 (many more in RHS archive – thank you); **Field Museum, Chicago:** p153b; **George Franks** (former pupil): c p10 (1821t), p32 drum, p34l, p51 (a x portrait), p59b, p61ti, p65 key stone trowel, p81 stone, p87 medals, p92 cushion, p139b, p142, p148b; **Chris Gaine:** p154t; **Getty Images:** p105b; **David Goodwin** (staff): c p33 swords, p 140 dirk, p163t; **Matt Hall:** p199t; **Alice Hawkins:** p177; **Courtesy Philip Henderson:** p172r; **Courtesy Jeremy Hinton:** p212l; **Imperial War Museum:** p80b; **In memory** of Moore, French, Lewington and Cooper and all those lost with HMS *Hood:* p81t; **Sara Kortenray:** p224; **Library and Archives Canada:** p84l; **Rob Mann** (staff): c pp2–3, p10T (1831), p12T (1989i), p15T (2005b), p61b, p62t, 81 penknife, p81 trophy, p88 RHS Awards, p93i, p139 shield & plaque, p140 relics (not dirk), p142t, p143br, p168 lunette, p174ci, p191 bat, pp221–3, p224tr; **David Marsh:** p183t; **Graham Morris** (www.cricketpix.com): p191b; **John Morrow:** p154t; **National Archive:** p89bl; **National Library of Australia:** p25r, p27t; © **National Maritime Museum, Greenwich, London** (*with © Greenwich Hospital Collection images shown in bold italics*): p8T (*1703*, 1730s/40s, 1758, 1765, *1768*), p9T (6 images, a x cannon), p10T (1821b, 1843, 1845, 1872, 1874t), p11T(1892, 1922i, 1933), *p18l*, p18r, p19, *pp20–1* (a x coin), p21, *p22t*, p22b, p23t, p25bl, p26, p28, pp30–1, p32t, *p37*, p38t, p39, pp40–1, p42, p43, p44 (bl2), p46, 47 (a x portrait), p48, 49l, p50r, p57br (© Caird Fund), p59 model boat, p79t, p81, p93b, p101t, p108, p115, p116b3, p119, p129t, p132t, p133i, p140, p145t, p144t, p146t; **National Portrait Gallery:** 24l, p35; **Lucy Pembroke:** p139t; **Ray Quick family album:** p78; **RHS Archive:** c Rear (x3), Rear boards, p9T (cannon i), p10T (1873, 1874b), p11T (1886, 1894, 1909, 1922m, 1925), p12a, p13T (a x 1958t), p14T (1978, 1983, 1989, 1994,1991, 1994), p24r, p27b, p33l, p34 (r2), p45tl, p45b, p50l, p53 invitation, pp54–5a, p58b2, p59ri, p61tl, pp62–3, p63a, p64, pp64–5, p65i+l, pp68–9a, p70, p72b, p73, pp74–5a, p76b2, p81 two boys, pp82–3, p85l+r, p87t+l, p88 swim, p90, p91, p92 a x cushion, p93l, p94b2, p95, p96, p100, p101b, pp102–3a, p106, p110c3, p111, p114t, p117t, pp120–1a, p122, p128 nurses, p129b, p131t, p132b, p134, p138, pp144–5, pp146–7, p148, p152a, p153c, p162, p170, p173 Volskys, pp180–1, p181, p184 b, pp186–7 teams, p188t, p201br, p206, p224; **RHS Development:** p143 leaflet; **RHS Marketing:** c Rear (x8), Flaps (x2), p14T (1978), p15T (1995, 1998i, 2006, 2008, 2009), p88r, p97b, p98, p104, pp104–5, p107, p117b, p123t, p124, p126c, p127, p135m, p145bl, p132lc, p133, p149, pp150–51, p157c, p165t, p166b, p171, p173cl+br, p174bl, p175, p176t, p179 a x br, p180b, p182t, p185bl, p189, p190cl, p190, p190bl, p191 rugby, p190tr, p192, p193tr+r, p194tr, p195tr+br, p197bl+cl, p198, p200, p201t, p205, p207, p208, p209, p211, p212t; **RHSA:** c p114l (and a big thank you to Dan Turner); **Royal Geographical Society:** p57tl; **Science & Society PL:** p145i; **Science Photo Library:** p47l; **Skandia Team GBR:** p148l; **Suffolk Journal:** p212l; **John Thompson:** p15T (2012); **Richard and Lissie Todd:** p155b; **Don Topley:** pp190–1, p193c; **Paul Waldie:** p114r (a big thank you); **Claire Westerman:** p199b; **Courtesy John Wonnacott:** p154b; **Thomas Wood:** p99t